Reactions to *North Pole Tenderfoot* from four who were on the expedition

Thrills and spills abound on each of the dogsled treks I've guided to the North Pole. But the one recounted here resulted in something extraordinary—Doug Hall's maverick perspective that sparkles fresh as sea ice on why a regular guy would pit himself against one of the world's most extreme challenges and, more importantly, how Doug has employed that experience to expand horizons for both himself and others. You'll want to don a sweater and warm socks for this lively read (and maybe a life jacket for that upcoming plunge in the drink). Be prepared to journey with Doug beyond the North Pole—to the realm of what's possible when you put your mind to something big.

> —Paul Schurke, Aspirations Expedition Leader

Doug Hall, one of America's most creative business minds, "freezes" his way to enlightenment. Laughing at 62 below? Why not, tears would only freeze that panicked look on your face. Doug illustrates why adventurers have extremely short memories. He is always looking ahead.

> —Bill Martin, Aspirations Expedition Co-Leader

So I'm sitting around one day when Doug Hall says, "Hey Craig, let's go to the North Pole!" "Sure, Doug, I'll go." Ten months later we're standing at thirty-something below zero! *North Pole Tenderfoot* is not your average adventure story of an executive schlepping his way to the North Pole just to impress his friends. Rather, it's a story of honest failures and flubs mixed with a healthy dash of fun and inspiration. The story is so real you'll get frostbite just reading it! And I know something about frostbite.

> —Craig Kurz, CEO The HoneyBaked Ham Company
> and Fellow North Pole Tenderfoot

Just finished reading your draft of our Arctic adventure. I am sincerely amazed at the accuracy of miscellaneous comments. My reaction is that it's a great chronicle. It should be of interest to anyone dreaming of an extended bike trip, a mountain climb, or any other physical exertion—where turning back is not an option.

> —Corky Peterson, A

A Rookie's Adventures and Misadventures
Walking in Admiral Peary's Footsteps

Published by Clerisy Press
Printed in the United States of America
Distributed by Publishers Group West
First edition, first printing

For further information, contact the publisher at:

Clerisy Press
1700 Madison Road
Cincinnati, OH 45206
CLERISY PRESS www.clerisypress.com

Library of Congress Cataloging-in-Publication Data
Hall, Doug, 1959–
    North Pole tenderfoot : 18 dogs, 62 below, 200 miles :
a rookie's adventures and misadventures traveling in
Admiral Peary's footsteps to the North Pole / by Doug
Hall. — 1st ed.
        p. cm.
    ISBN-13: 978-1-57860-328-2
    ISBN-10: 1-57860-328-5
    1. Hall, Doug, 1959– 2. Explorers—United States—
Biography. 3. Peary, Robert E. (Robert Edwin), 1856–
1920. 4. North Pole--Discovery and exploration. I. Title.
II. Title: Rookie's adventures and misadventures travel-
ing in Admiral Peary's footsteps to the North Pole.
    G635.H22A3 2009
    910.911'3—dc22
                                        2009015590

Cover designed by Stephen Sullivan
Interior designed by Donna Collingwood

Dedication

*T*HIS BOOK IS DEDICATED IN MEMORY OF MY MOM, JEAN HALL.
In her memory, 100 percent of my net profits from this book will be donated to programs that encourage the four Great Aspirations! principles.

Doug Hall
Springbrook
Prince Edward Island, Canada
December 28, 2008

Thank You!

Special thanks to the following incredible people who made the expedition, this book, and the theatrical play of the same name possible.

Paul Schurke – Leader of the expedition and Arctic explorer extraordinaire.

Craig Kurz – Friend and fellow "tenderfoot" on the expedition.

David Wecker – Expedition base camp commander and friend whose humor, encouragement, and writing wisdom helped this book come to life.

The rest of the Aspirations Expedition Team: David Golibersuch, Alan Humphries, Bill Martin, Celia Martin, Corky Peterson, Paul Phau, Randy Swanson, Mike Warren.

Thank you to my family for all of their love and support: **Debbie, Kristyn, Tori, Brad;** my siblings **Pam and Bruce;** and my mom and dad, **Buzz and Jean Hall.**

Erskine and Pat Smith – Victoria Playhouse creative director and general manager who shared their stage and wisdom with me.

Richard Hunt and Jack Heffron – The world's best book publisher and editor.

Ziggy, Fuzz, and Tom Wilson – Thanks to Ziggy and Fuzz for making the trip so much fun, and for Tom's never-ending support of helping inspire children's aspirations.

Special Thanks to the Great Aspirations! Charity Sponsors: American Express, Bicycle Playing Cards, Curel, Eureka! Ranch, HoneyBaked Ham Company, Johnson & Johnson, M&M's, Mercy Health Plex, Pringles, Nestle's Quik, Qwest, University of Maine, Valassis Communications, Viking Ranges, WBK Design, Wintergreen Lodge, Ziggy.

Expedition, Book, and Play Support Team: Kevin McNamara, Kari McNamara, Sarah Hawkins, Corie Roudebush Spialek, Judith Hokanson, Tom Ackerman, Chris Stormann, Sean McCosh, Mike Salvi, Kara Gibson, Maggie Nichols, Scott Dunkle, Jeff Stamp, Bruce Forsee, Margaret Henson, Teresa Cosby, Leah Hunter, David Nicholson, Ron Quesnel, and Dick Steurweld.

Writing Base Camps: This book was primarily written at four spectacular locations.

- Anthony's Key Resort, Roatan Honduras
  www.anthonyskey.com

- Hotel Hana-Maui, Hana, Hawaii
  www.hotelhanamaui.com

- Canyon Ranch, Lenox, Massachusetts
  www.canyonranch.com

- Springbrook, Prince Edward Island, Canada

Multi-Media Bonus

www.Aspirations.com features audio from the nightly phone calls from the Arctic, plus video and color photos from the Arctic.

One Hundredth Anniversary Celebration of One of America's Greatest Explorers

*T*he one hundredth anniversary of Admiral Peary's historic expedition that reached the North Pole with his American assistant Matthew Henson and Inuit assistants Ootah, Egigingwah, Seegloo, and Ooqueah is 2009.

In honor of the admiral's achievement, the North Pole Tenderfoot logo features the globe and star from his memorial at Arlington National Cemetery.

Table of Contents

Prologue

JULY 19, 2005, 7:58 P.M.

Victoria Playhouse

I STOOD IN THE WINGS OF THE nearly one-hundred-year-old Victoria Hall, home of the Victoria Playhouse in Victoria by the Sea in Prince Edward Island, Canada. It's a big name for a very small village, which not long ago was listed as one of the fastest-shrinking municipalities in Canada as a result of the conversion from year-round to seasonal residents.

I was preparing to perform *North Pole Tenderfoot*, a one-man play based on my rookie experience as an Arctic explorer. I had

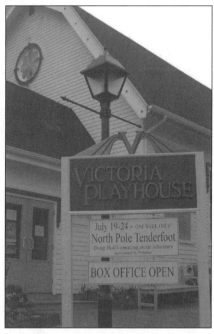

The historic Victoria Playhouse was where the story of *North Pole Tenderfoot* was first told.

always dreamed of performing a play of my own, but as I stood in the wings I wondered if I was about to fulfill a dream or live out a nightmare. The next hour and a half could be the worst ninety minutes of my life.

The house was full, for reasons I still don't understand.

In the second or third row in the center sat Charles Mandel, the theater critic from the *Guardian*, the largest newspaper on Prince Edward Island. He'd written some caustic reviews that summer, even firing shots at the College of Piping and Celtic Performing Arts' performance of *Highland Storm*—performed by island youth.

I worried that he would take my play to task (or to the woodshed). And as the playwright and sole actor, I'd have no one else to blame.

Though I'd delivered over a thousand talks to business groups and co-hosted national radio and television shows for millions, this felt different. This was ninety minutes, plus intermission, with just the audience and me—performing in my first play since a high school appearance in *The Pajama Game*, performing the first play I'd ever written.

The stage featured the actual sled from the expedition and a replica of Peary's sled. A rear projection screen displayed trip images and video.

On the stage was the actual dogsled we'd taken to the North Pole, along with a near perfect replica of one of Admiral Peary's sleds, designed from photographs taken at the Berkshire Museum in western Massachusetts.

To bring the full theater experience alive we had Styrofoam blocks cut to look like ice and a team of four Inuit dogs—well, actually they were children's stuffed animals. At the back of the set stood a monstrous rear projection screen, on which we'd project the images, video, and audio of my adventure.

I'd chosen to create and perform this one-man play to fulfill a dream as well as to improve the chances of success for this book. Of my four previous books, the two that had been best sellers—*Jump Start Your Brain* and *Jump Start Your Business Brain*—had been performed as lectures before they were written. The two that sold poorly, *Maverick Mindset* and *Meaningful Marketing*, had been written without being performed.

From this sales history, I could reach three possible conclusions: I should only write books titled *Jump Start Your Brain*; I should never write a book with a two-word title with each word beginning with *M*; I should perform all books before writing them to improve the storytelling.

Truthfully, I'd never intended to become an author. In fact, I studied chemical engineering at the University of Maine, in part, because it required mostly math and science courses and virtually no English classes.

However, in the early 1990s, a story about my Eureka! Ranch in the *Wall Street Journal* caught the eye of three book

I filled a half dozen journals with notes—my primary focus was on what it "felt" like to be in the high Arctic.

editors, and following a spirited bidding process I landed a hefty advance and a contract to write a book. Frightened of writing, I followed my instincts and assembled a lecture, telling the story of what would become the book. I performed it for audiences around the world. After refining the story based on the performances, I wrote the book quickly.

But books about business creativity are far different from an adventure memoir. In the world of corporate innovation, my Eureka! Ranch team and I have had the honor of helping some of the world's greatest companies grow their business—from Nike to Walt Disney to American Express. We've invented cat foods, candy bars, chips, colas, and caskets. In those books, I knew what I was doing. This time I was, to use an appropriate cliché, standing on thin ice. Still, as I paced in the wings, waiting for the curtain to rise and to meet all those eager faces in the audience, I knew I had stood on even thinner ice—at the North Pole.

A middle-aged guy with "no business" going on a North Pole expedition

On that expedition, I was a "tenderfoot," as Admiral Peary called George Borup, George MacMillian, and Dr. John Goodsell, the Arctic rookies on his 1909 expedition. I was a first timer who, frankly, had no business going to the North Pole. I was forty pounds overweight and out of shape. If there were such a thing as an obese-o-meter, I would have registered somewhere beyond plump. Sure, I knew a textbook ton about exercise, but there is a vast difference between knowing about fitness and actually being fit. I was a forty-year-old man in a fifty-year-old body.

With the play, and with this book, I find myself in a similar role—the tenderfoot. My literary inspirations include George Plimpton's classic *Paper Lion* and Bill Bryson's *A Walk In the Woods*. Their adventures and misadventures inspired me to not let inexperience get in the way of participating in great adventures.

I do not presume that this book matches their literary genius. My goal simply is to show what it's like for an ordinary, middle-aged, overweight guy to travel to the North Pole as Admiral Peary did. This is my story of the Aspirations! Expedition as I remember it. It's filled with my perceptions, misconceptions, and delusions. I am sure that my expedition teammates have their own perceptions, misperceptions, and delusions.

Still pacing in the wings, I heard Erskin Smith, the artistic director of the Playhouse and the director of *North Pole Tenderfoot*, explain to the audience that there would be one intermission. He mentioned the Playhouse's upcoming schedule, announcing that in a few weeks, they could see the world premiere of *Anne and Gilbert*, based on the writings of islander Lucy Maud Montgomery. It would be a professional musical that tells the story of Anne Shirley's life after the events made famous in *Anne of Green Gables*.

He ended with my cue, "But first we travel to the top of the earth. Ladies and gentlemen, the Victoria Playhouse is proud to present the world premiere of *North Pole Tenderfoot*."

I heard the opening strains of "I'm Looking Over a Four Leaf Clover," as performed by my father's Dixieland band, The Presumpscott River Bottom Boys. I'd selected it because it was a personal favorite and I figured four-leaf clovers were lucky.

The rookie took to the stage.

As the song came to an end, the lights came up and I sprang onto the stage reciting as Erskine had directed.

Tonight we're going on an adventure to the North Pole—to the top of the earth, to the spot around which the whole earth spins. Leading our expedition will be Paul Schurke of Ely, Minnesota, a genuine adventure hero. My name is Doug Hall. By day I help the world's leading companies invent big and bold innovations. On this trip I'm a rookie, a raw beginner, a tenderfoot, as Admiral Peary called rookies.

The purpose of our expedition is to recreate Admiral Peary's last dash for the pole.

Tonight's performance is like those performed in halls like this at the beginning of the century before last. It's an adventure story told with slides and audio as Admiral Peary, Shakelton, Admunsen, and Nansen would have done to raise funds for their next adventure.

I'm not here to raise funds. I'm here to raise awareness for the need for parents and grandparents to help inspire children's aspirations. To that end, as you entered the theater you received a free audio CD with a program designed to help you inspire your children.

As a special bonus, tonight on this stage I will reveal the answers to the three great mysteries of Robert Peary's 1909 North Pole Expedition. Tonight you will learn the answers to three questions:

1. **Why was Peary so silent upon his return to the ship?**

2. **Why did he take Henson instead of Bartlett to the pole?**

3. **Did he actually make it to the pole?**

And that was how the story that became this book began…

ROBERT PEARY

Giving lectures was one of Peary's primary sources of funding for his expeditions.

Chapter 1
Why Are You Going to the North Pole?

"WHY ARE YOU GOING TO THE NORTH POLE?"

It was the most common question from family and friends when I announced my plans to join a dogsled expedition to the North Pole.

It was a fair question, as the North and South poles are some of the most inaccessible and unpleasant places on the planet.

Apsley Cherry-Garrad, in his book *The Worst Journey in the World*, detailing the Scott expedition to the South Pole, described polar trips this way:

> Polar exploration is at once the cleanest and most isolated way of having a bad time that has yet been devised.

The plan involved traveling about two hundred miles to recreate Admiral Robert E. Peary's "last dash" to the pole, from 88 degrees to 90 North.

The temperatures, with wind chill, ranged from minus 15 to minus 62 degrees Fahrenheit despite the endless sunlight of spring in the Arctic.

People thought I was crazy. Traveling to the North Pole is not an endeavor a person with complete possession of his marbles would undertake.

To risk understatement: It's not a popular trip. At the time of our adventure in 1999, only thirty-four people had made the journey by dogsled, as Admiral Peary did. Contrast this with Mount Everest, where more than two thousand people have reached the summit.

Admiral Robert Peary, the North Pole iron man.

If there were a travel brochure for the trip, it would read like this:

On This Trip You'll Enjoy: Minus 60 Degree Cold,
Blinding Whiteouts, Bouts of Diarrhea.
Frostbite Is a Certainty,
Loss of Fingers and Toes a Real Possibility.

Sounds grim. But at least it's more optimistic than the ad Ernest Shackleton supposedly ran in London to find crew members for his South Pole expedition:

Men wanted for hazardous journey. Small wages.
Bitter cold. Long months of complete darkness.
Constant danger. Safe return doubtful.
Honour and recognition in case of success.

The question of why are you going to the North Pole can be asked in two ways:

Why are you going
to the **NORTH POLE?**

In this case the emphasis was placed on why the *North Pole*. The place itself. However, it was most often asked with emphasis placed on the front of the question, with the emphasis on *me*:

Why are **YOU** going
to the North Pole?

For some reason, my family and friends didn't see me as a great explorer.

Maybe it was my robust profile.

Maybe it was my passion for gourmet cooking.

Maybe it was my habit of exercising my mouth more than my body.

When asked why, my first answer was that I was going to use the expedition to raise money and awareness for my Great Aspirations! charity. Great Aspirations! provides ideas to help parents inspire their children. I'd created the charity based on the work of Dr. Russ Quaglia, director of the National Center for Student Aspirations, located at my alma mater, the University of Maine.

My idea was to use the trip as a publicity tool for raising money from corporate sponsors and to provide a media event to connect parents and children to the Web site, where they could get free educational materials. The www.Aspirations .com Web site provides a free one-hour audio workshop as well as eighty newspaper columns filled with ideas for helping parents inspire their children's aspirations.

Helping the charity was not a very effective answer to the question. Friends would respond, "Aren't there less extreme ways to raise money and awareness for the charity?"

For a month or so I brushed off the question with the common answer "Because it's there."

Then I did a little research and found the source of that statement. It was first said by British mountaineer George Leigh Mallory in a March 1923 interview in the *New York Times* when asked why he wanted to climb Mount Everest. I stopped saying it when I learned that the primary reason the quote is so famous is because Mallory was lost on Everest the following year. He died! Not the sort of inspiration I needed.

In 1999, the same year I went to the pole, Mallory's body was found on Everest with his fellow climber, Andrew Irvine. The media debated if Mallory was "going down" or "up" at the time of his death. If he were "going down" then that would mean that he achieved the summit twenty-nine years before Edmund Hillary. Mallory's son John didn't see it as a debate. As he said, "To me the only way you achieve a summit is to come back alive. The job is half done if you don't get down again."

I'm with John Mallory—coming back alive is key to a truly successful adventure.

When pushed deeper on "why," I had plenty of flip responses but few honest answers.

If the discussion was taking place over a nip or two of the only alcohol to be named after a country (Scotch whisky), I would wax philosophically about the neglected spirit of adventure in today's high-tech souls. I would invoke the cosmic karmic nature of the pole—the place where all time zones and all people blend into one. I might even blab eloquently about the spiritual symbolism of standing on top of the world.

These responses rarely worked to answer the question.

Sometimes I would talk of how this trip would allow me to recapture my neglected physical nature. As a youth I earned the rank of Eagle Scout, participated in winter survival training, and spent summers leading canoe trips at Camp Carpenter Boy Scout Camp.

Then, as a teenager, I broke my hip in a pickup football game. It was a freak accident. The doctors at Boston Children's Medical Hospital gave me a 5 percent chance of walking again.

The skill of my physician, Dr. Trott, some prayers, and some luck, had me walking and running again two years later. In the process my focus moved from the great outdoors to entrepreneurship.

I developed a passion for magic and juggling and created my own show. The excitement of creating, selling, and performing set off a chain reaction of entrepreneurial adventures. I soon had a line of learn-to-juggle kits and magic tricks.

My entrepreneurial ventures helped me land a marketing job in the brand management department of Procter & Gamble in Cincinnati, Ohio. After ten years I retired from P&G to fulfill my entrepreneurial destiny. With my basement as my office and two

I took to the stage as Merwyn the Magician.

rounds of venture financing from some of the biggest names in new business investment (Visa and MasterCard), I connected with some great people to build the Eureka! Ranch, an innovation research and development company.

The North Pole expedition would give me the ability to recapture my lost interest in the great outdoors. At midlife I had the luxury of going back for a moment and exploring the path of high-adventure expeditions. I could restore my sense of sport and adventure, and I could challenge my physical self.

Friends had sympathy for my story, but it didn't convince them of why I was going to such extremes. More often than not, they would nod in agreement and secretly think I was bonkers.

My wife, Debbie, had a simpler answer to the question. "He's turning forty," she would say, triggering expressions of sympathy, as if to say, "Oh, I see."

I protested. It's a mere coincidence that I was born in 1959 and that this trip happened to be in 1999 (and that this book is coming out in 2009!).

I mean, come on, I wasn't in denial of my aging—or at least not in more denial than every other baby boomer. At least I hadn't done any of the "hair things." I didn't color the gray or comb it over to make it look like I had more. I hadn't done hair implants or bought a "rug," or had my chest hair lasered or stripped off. "I am what I am," as Popeye said.

In 1909 Admiral Peary succeeded where 578 other expeditions failed.

Frankly, a big part of my inspiration for going to the North Pole was a six-foot Naval Officer from the Great State of Maine—Admiral Robert E. Peary.

Unlike the instant heroes of pop culture, Admiral Peary is the real thing. For twenty-three years, he dedicated himself to a single goal: standing on the top of the world. When he was not on an expedition he spent most of his time raising money and preparing for the next journey.

His wife called his compulsion "Arctic Fever."

He succeeded where some 578 expeditions before him had failed. His success was driven by persistence and a dedication that is especially inspiring when compared to today's need for instant gratification, with short-term business success, and our general lack of sustained dedication to grand and great causes.

I believe the admiral ranks as the greatest all-around explorer in American history. Apologies to Lewis and Clark, but they didn't travel in conditions that were nearly so extreme. Apologies, too, to John Glenn, Neil Armstrong, and all the other great astronauts who had the brilliant support of the National Aeronautics and Space Administration.

Peary did it all. He raised the money, designed the equipment, selected the team, and led the expedition. He was a one-man NASA complex.

My focus on Peary is based on my respect and emotional awe of the man. Plus, I just plain like the guy.

I'm not saying he was perfect. He had his faults like all of us.

However, when I add up the balance sheet of his assets and liabilities I come out on his side. I believe he's a rich source of wisdom and inspiration that deserves a deeper look and understanding than he has received up till now.

When it came to inspiration, there may be no grander figure than Admiral Robert E. Peary. The admiral "rocked" when it came to **THINKING BIG!** In a commencement address at Rensselaer Polytechnic on June 14, 1911, he described his dreams this way:

> I have dreamed my dream; and working incessantly with all my strength, have done what it is given to few men to accomplish fully. The determination to reach the pole has been so much a part of my being that, paradoxical as it may seem, I have long ago ceased to think of myself save as an instrument for the attainment of that object. An inventor can understand this, or an artist, or anyone else who works for an idea.

Sadly, five days before Admiral Peary announced his achievement of the pole, his former assistant, Fredrick Cook, announced that he had been to the North Pole the year before. The result was a frenzy of questions and scrutiny that continues to this day. Who was first? Who lied? Who told the truth?

The explorers were supported by competing newspapers, the *New York Times* (Peary) and the *New York Herald* (Cook), which fanned the flame of controversy.

Having been to the pole by dogsled, I can't see how Cook

could have traveled the distance he claimed with the supplies he claimed to have taken. Most Arctic enthusiasts have reached the same conclusion.

Admiral Peary's place in history is still not certain. Three mysteries hang over Peary's expedition, and part of my goal in recreating his "last dash" was to find answers to those questions.

Some feel that Peary chose to take Matthew Henson (above) with him to the pole instead of Captain Bob Bartlett because he had something to hide.

1. Why was he so silent upon his return to the ship? After returning to the ship, he was very quiet and did not talk to anyone about what happened on the "last dash" from 88 degrees to the pole. It's been speculated that he had something to hide.

2. Why did he take Henson instead of Bartlett to the pole? The decision to take Henson, a black man, instead of Bartlett, a white man, sparked great controversy in the racist world of the time. Matthew Henson was Peary's most experienced expedition aide. Bartlett was his most trusted friend and confidant on the expedition. Peary naysayers feel that his decision proves Peary had something to hide.

3. Did he actually make it to the pole in 1909? The fundamental question: Is there evidence "beyond a reasonable doubt" that Admiral Peary, Matthew Henson, Ootah, Egigingwah, Seegloo, and Ooqueah actually reached the North Pole on April 6, 1909?

Responses to other Peary controversies, such as his sled speeds from 88 degrees to the pole and his method of navigation, have been addressed by others in the hundred years since Peary's expedition.

Finding answers to these questions about my hero made up a big part of the answer to the question people asked about why I was going to the pole. And, okay, turning forty may have played a role in it too. But even before I left I knew at some level that I didn't really know the answer to the question. Though all my answers were true, they didn't quite add up to the full answer. Before I could truly understand why I was going to the North Pole, I would have to go.

Chapter 2
The Adventure Begins
DECEMBER 1998

AS AN EXPLORATION ROOKIE, my first challenge was to prove that I had the "right stuff" at an Arctic try out at Paul and Sue Schurke's Wintergreen Dogsled Lodge in Ely, Minnesota. It involved a week of training, spiced with a handful of oddball challenges created by our expedition leader, the world's leading authority on high-Arctic travel, Paul Schurke.

Craig Kurz, fellow tenderfoot on the expedition

The purpose of our week in training was to see if the candidates—one woman and eight men, including myself—would "make the cut" for the expedition, although the real test would be whether we each could write a $20,000 check to pay for the privilege of freezing our fingers, toes, and noses. It was here that I would meet the other candidates. It was here, too, that we would bond as a team and determine our roles.

My friend Craig Kurz agreed to join me. Craig, who was thirty-seven, was the perfect companion for a wilderness expedition—a dynamo with unlimited energy. A natural leader, a go-to kind of guy, Craig has never known a favor he can't do for another. He is the CEO of The HoneyBaked Ham Company in northern Kentucky, a five-time world champion equestrian, a runner, scuba diver, white-water rafter, and a cross-country and downhill skier.

On the pole trip, Craig was a rookie like me. He'd done a few trips at Paul's lodge but nothing to compare to the high adventure of a real Arctic expedition.

We agreed to provide each other with the inspiration or motivation necessary to make the trip a success.

"We might need to give each other a kick in the butt sometimes," Craig said. "There won't be time for feeling hurt or letting personal feelings get in the way."

As we traveled to Minnesota, we also agreed that we felt privileged to be part of a trip of this magnitude. From what we'd read about our teammates in the e-mails prior to this "try out" trip, we were in over our heads. We would be stepping into a brave new world.

Our plane landed in Hibbing, Minnesota, the birthplace of the bus industry in the United States. It started in 1914 when miners were transported to and from the Iron Range towns and developed into the Greyhound bus company, a story told through exhibits and memorabilia at the Greyhound Museum. Sadly, our timing didn't allow a visit to this local landmark.

For a small town, Hibbing has a healthy share of famous sons, from folk singer Bob Dylan to sports stars Roger Marris and Kevin McCale to Vincent Bugliosi, the prosecutor in the Charles Manson case who later became an acclaimed author. More relevant to my taste buds, it's also the home of food entrepreneur Jeno Paulucci, creator of over eighty food brands, including Jeno's Pizza Rolls, Chun King, and RJR foods.

From Hibbing we pointed our rental car north to Ely, population 3,968. Ely is literally the end of the road. Its primary fame is as the leaping off point for summer canoe camping trips into the Boundary Waters Canoe Area Wilderness, which has over a million acres of wilderness and waterways. It's famous for spectacular views and black flies. Fortunately, we visited during the off season so there was no need for bug spray.

Not to be outdone by Hibbing, Ely has its own famous sites, including the Native American Heritage Center, which celebrates the life and ways of the Bois Forte Band of Ojibwe. Visitors also can see the International Wolf Center, a multimillion-dollar complex dedicated to wolves. The independent spirit of Ely also comes to life at the Dorothy Molter Museum. Known as the Root Beer Lady, Dorothy's cabins were a famous stop-

Wintergreen DOGSLED LODGE

over point for canoeists who would come for a sip of her home-made root beer. Dorothy was the last resident of the Boundary Waters. After she died in 1986, her two cabins were transported out of the Boundary Waters and made into a museum.

Foregoing all of these points of interest, we headed to Paul Schurke's lodge, where we parked the car with the windshield wipers flipped up to keep them from freezing to the windshield. The winter sun cast dim rays over White Iron Lake as we walked the gravel road from the parking lot to the lodge. Along the way, I thought about my first visit here a few years earlier. I'd Paul Schurke signed up for a lodge-to-lodge "comfort class" trip, with dogsledding during the day followed by a hot shower, a gourmet meal, and a warm bed. At night in the comfort of the lodges, Paul showed video from his Arctic trips. On one of those nights I caught Arctic Fever, burning up with the idea that I could and should be part of one of those trips.

Paul Schurke was a large part of the reason my wife, Debbie, was confident I would return safely from my polar adventure. In a world of ten-minute heroes, Paul is the genuine article. He's been featured in cover stories in *National Geographic* magazine and various television specials. *Outside* magazine has named him "person of the year" and *Backpacker* magazine named him the king of cool for his passion for winter camping.

He's led four dogsled adventures to the North Pole—three of which were successful. His landmark 1986 journey, which included adventurer Will Steger, was the first surface trek to the pole without resupply since Admiral Peary in 1909.

In 1989 he led the Bering Bridge expedition, a twelve-hundred-mile dogsled and ski trek with a twelve-member Soviet-American team, from Siberia to Alaska via the Bering Strait to reestablish cultural connections among Arctic natives long separated by the Cold War.

Paul's excursions depart from most so-called adventure trips, where clients fork over big bucks to have Sherpas schlep their gear up mountaintops and provide whatever is needed. With Paul, I paid handsomely to be a grunt bearing the brunt of the load. I figured that after I got over the pain, the trip would provide massive bragging rights in the world of macho exploration.

If the North Pole has a PR man, Paul is it. In an interview for our Expedition Web site, Paul was clear about his preferences for the North Pole versus the other two major adventures—Antarctica and Everest.

"Trekking to the top of the world represents one of the world's greatest geographic challenges," he said. "Of course, the bigger the challenge, the bigger the rewards, and I've always considered my polar successes to be a marvelous gift. They're a resource I draw on each time I tackle other personal or business goals. The North Pole puts all other challenges in perspective and, for me, has made many other dreams achievable.

"A South Pole trek is obscenely expensive—upwards of one hundred thousand dollars per person. It's also boring. The South Pole sits amid an absolutely featureless expanse of ice. And it's anticlimactic. You arrive there to find a research station staffed by hundreds.

"An Everest climb is nearly as expensive and insanely dangerous. One of eight climbers is injured or killed. Besides, climbing Everest has been accomplished by a whole lot more people than the North Pole."

As we entered the lodge, I felt confident about my abilities. Over the previous few months, I'd exercised like crazy, working overtime to make myself as fit as possible for the expedition. I had also read numerous books about the world of Arctic explorers with particular emphasis on the admiral.

But over the course of the next few hours, as I met my fellow North Pole adventurers, my confidence melted away.

The first prospective teammate I met was David Golibersuch, Ph.D. He said he was a Hivernaut.

David Golibersuch

"A what?" I asked.

"Hivernaut," David said, pronouncing it *EE-ver-not*. "Paul coined it. 'Hiver' is French for 'winter' and 'naut' is Greek for 'explorer.'"

I nodded, peering at him to determine if he was joking. He wasn't. He was serious.

David was fifty-six, a native of Buffalo, New York, unmarried with two daughters. Since 1970 he'd worked in corporate research and development for General Electric in Schenectady, New York. An experienced cross-country skier, he made his first journey to the high Arctic in the spring of 1998, on a Schurke-led excursion to Ellesmere Island.

Mike Warren

Next, I met Mike Warren, fifty-one, a real estate developer in Gainesville, Florida. He had climbed Mt. Rainier and trekked to Kala Patar in Nepal. He told stories of climbing the Rainier, becoming intimate with the sight of the heel of the person in front of him so he could step in his footstep.

I asked him what he expected from the trip to the pole.

"I do not—repeat, do *not*—expect it to be fun," he replied. "You do trips like this for the physical, mental, and spiritual challenge. It's absolutely grueling, but there's tremendous satisfaction when you complete the journey. And there's great camaraderie when a group of people come together and combine their talents to achieve a goal."

On and on it went. Each team member was more macho than the last. Each was a veteran of pain and punishment. I was a veteran of meetings and memos.

I introduced myself to Bill Martin, the co-leader of the trip, a lanky guy of forty-nine with a big smile. A resident of Gainesville, Florida, he had led climbing expeditions in North and South America, Russia, the Himalayas, and Antarctica.

Bill wondered if I was related to Rob Hall, who had been a good friend of his.

"Had been?" I asked.

Bill explained that Rob was the guide whose death on Everest was made famous by Jon Krakauer's book *Into Thin Air*. "Rob was a major dreamer who lived the dreams that others merely dream," Bill said.

Thinking I might find an answer to the eternal question, I asked, "Why do you do it?"

"Because I'm brain damaged," Bill explained with a proud smile. "I spend six weeks a year on adventures. I'm an orthodontist. I arrange my practice so that I can train and make trips like this."

"So what's it really like on a trip like this?" I asked, a thinly veiled attempt to understand what I had gotten myself into.

Bill quickly became analytical: "When I climbed in Antarctica I learned that first you're freezing—colder than you've ever been before. Then, as time goes on, you acclimate, your body adapts—assuming, of course, you're in good enough shape to handle the trip."

Good enough shape?

I wondered what was good enough shape. Again, I consult this Jedi Master: "What's good enough shape?"

"I run up and down the stairs of the local university's football stadium," Bill said, "wearing a full pack."

He paused to let me explain my training regimen. Figuring that my daily two-mile run wasn't macho enough, I did the only thing I could think of—I took a long slug of Scotch.

Gulp!

I was in trouble. What had I been thinking?

Sensing my anxiety, Bill suddenly shifted from macho mountain man to mentor. He assured me I would be okay. "Listen close and train hard, harder than you can imagine, and you'll be fine."

I took a deep breath, and made a mental note to keep close to Bill during this Hell week. He could be my guide to the world of high adventure.

The rest of the expedition team included:

• Celia Martin, Bill's forty-five-year-old sister, also from Gainesville, also an orthodontist. Our teeth would be straight for this trip. An alumnus of Outward Bound wilderness courses, Celia was an avid hiker. I would learn that she's quick to speak her mind. When I messed up, she was blunt about saying so, but she conveyed the message with a gentleness that made me feel okay about my incompetence.

Celia Martin

• Alan Humphries, thirty-six, from County Down in Northern Ireland, near Belfast. Alan was an entrepreneur with a chain of small casinos in and around Northern Ireland. Next to Paul, Alan was our most experienced musher, having dogsledded

Alan Humphries

across Hudson Bay in 1996 and piloted an eight-day team in the 1997 World Dogsledding Championships, a time-trial sprint race covering twenty-five kilometers a day over three days in Finland.

He said he had dreamed of going to the North Pole since childhood. "I remember getting a gift as a child, a little guy known as Action Man who came with a polar exploring expedition kit, complete with dogs and sleds and the whole works. I've had the bug since then."

• Randy Swanson, forty-two, was from Grandville, Michigan, where he owned an auto repair business. He had climbed Africa's Mt. Cameroon and Mt. Bartle-Frere in Australia. Like Alan, he was also an alumnus of one of Paul's Arctic trips.

Randy Swanson

I asked Randy what drew him to this kind of trip.

"I love the physical rigors," he said. "I like it when the going gets tough. That's when I shine."

Gulp. Who were these people?

An accomplished guitarist with tastes ranging from classical to alternative, Randy said he found it difficult to explain to friends why he wanted to go to the North Pole.

"Nobody understands," he said. "They all think I'm going to Alaska. Or they wonder if I'm going to stay overnight in lodges. Or they want to know if there's a certain path I'll be following. Most people don't have any idea what this trip will be like."

• Corky Peterson was from Minneapolis, where he had been the Hennepin County data processing director until his retirement. On the trip up to Wintergreen, Craig and I were most impressed (or intimidated) by Corky's bio. We wondered what kind of guy at sixty-nine would sign on for a trip like this.

He clearly was no ordinary person. He had an intensity of

focus and sense of priority unlike any of the rest of us.

"I went on a wilderness trip to Ellesmere Island last year and thought everyone would be about my age," he said. "I was shocked to find they were mostly twenty years younger. People thought, 'Oh, how wonderful it was that someone my age would undertake such an endeavor.' I thought, 'Hey, what's the problem?'"

Corky Peterson

On our trip, Corky stood to become the oldest person to ever reach the North Pole by foot.

"But I hope I can do something worthwhile with the Aspirations! Expedition for people my age," he said. "Maybe within my church and with others in my age group, maybe I can be an encouragement for us to get off our duffs, to stop letting people tell us we can't do this or that."

Like Alan, Corky has dreamed of going to the North Pole since he was a boy.

"I used to stare at the globe in school and wonder what was underneath that spindle at both ends. I want to be where time has no meaning, where all the longitudes come together. The pole is within reach, and now I have the time to do this," he said.

"What do you think of the risk?" I asked. "What scares you?"

"I've read a lot about previous polar teams. Falling through the ice is a challenge, keeping up physically is a challenge. But I haven't read anything that seems too difficult. Whatever happens, I'll handle it."

I knew I was in big trouble. Even Grandpa Corky had more of the "right stuff" than I had.

He was calm and ready. I was nervous and uncertain.

• Paul Pfau, Los Angeles County Assistant Attorney. Paul was the last to join the expedition. He'd helped run base camps on Mount Everest for numerous expeditions. He was very calm and focused. I took the calm as the sign of a real expert.

Paul Pfau

That night, Paul Schurke called us together to talk about the week ahead and about the trip to the North Pole. "You'll be training at the lodge for a day or two, then we'll head out on a camping trip with dogs, sleds, and skis. At the end of the week Bill and I will meet with each of you to discuss your suitability for the expedition, your role on the trip, and what you have to do to be more prepared."

Then he asked for our questions. Craig, never timid about plunging forward, broke the ice with the most obvious one.

How cold will it be in the Arctic?
"Hopefully, very cold," Paul said. "I'm hoping for minus 30, which will keep the ice fairly firm. As conditions warm, the ice breaks up and makes it a lot tougher to reach the pole. During my '95 trip, we had to make a dash to the pole because the ice was breaking up. And on my last trip in '97, we didn't make it because of open water."

I suddenly realized that reaching the pole was not a given. Even if I overcame my lack of physical fitness, even if I overcame my fear, circumstances beyond our control could prevent me from standing on top of the earth. It was not a happy moment.

More questions followed rapid fire. Paul's answers were direct and honest. He should never run for public office.

How far will we be going?
"We'll start about 130 miles from the pole as the crow flies. But since we can't fly like a crow, we'll end up walking two hundred miles when you add 25 percent for detours and three to four miles a day for the southerly ice drift. Remember, we'll be traveling on a sheet of ice that historically floats south as we travel north."

This is the portion of Peary's trip known as the "last dash." It was here that Peary decided to send back Captain Bob Bartlett, a white man, and to take Matthew Henson, a black man, with him to the pole. In 1909 a black man was not considered a reliable witness. Peary's choice of Henson was made for many reasons, as I'll explain later. However, to many who still harbored deep prejudices it was clear evidence that Peary had something to hide.

How dangerous is it?
"Safety will be our paramount consideration. But I do not consider a North Pole expedition to be a life-threatening or even a significantly dangerous endeavor. To my knowledge, only one casualty has resulted from North Pole expeditions in this century and that was a member of Peary's support team who was allegedly bumped off by a couple of severely disgruntled teammates. None of our treks from 88 to the pole have resulted in injuries. The only significant situations we've had to deal with were a few unexpected dips in the drink. In each case, team members were dried off, warmed up, and back on track within an hour or two."

How many dogs will we take?
"I'm guessing eighteen—two teams of nine each."

How many people will we have on the team?
Looking around the room he said, "This is it. It looks like we'll have eleven."

As Paul talked I did some quick math. Although this trip is extreme, it is nothing compared to the admiral's 1909 trip. We will be traveling from 88 degrees. He started from land, which is at 83.7 degrees, traveling over three times farther. We will be flown up to 88 degrees, then travel on foot to the pole where planes pick us up.

What if someone gets hurt?

"We'll have to handle it on the ice. We'll be sixteen-hundred miles north of Alaska. It can take as long as a week before a plane can get to us."

A week? Jeez.

How do we get there?

"We'll meet in Edmonton, Canada, then fly to Resolute, a small Inuit town well inside the Arctic Circle. From there, we'll take Twin Otter planes to 88 degrees. We'll stop along the way at the Eureka weather station and possibly at a fuel cache that's been set up on the ice. If all goes well, we'll be flown back from the pole a couple weeks later."

What's the biggest danger?

"Water. Not enough and too much. You can easily get dehydrated because the air in the Arctic is very dry and we'll be sweating a lot. We'll make water by melting snow. But while we need to stay hydrated, it's important to get the water out of our systems. As you sweat, the water needs to be wicked away from your body. If it seals in, you'll freeze when you stop moving. Water transfers your body heat twenty-five times faster than air."

What about polar bears?

"Polar bears are known to travel the polar realm, but none have been sighted on our North Pole treks and the few I've seen elsewhere in the Arctic are always in a hasty retreat. They're notoriously shy of dog teams. Of course there's not much risk, as long as you're not the slowest runner."

As Paul chuckled at his little joke, I looked at the folks around me and sized up their running skills. I decided I would in no way be fastest, but I'd probably be two up from the slowest.

"There's actually little risk," Paul continued. "The dogs' barking tends to keep bears away. On the ice, only eighteen deaths from polar bears have ever been reported."

At first I felt comforted by such a low number, but then considered the ridiculously low number of humans who ever go on the polar ice. The probability of dying from a bear attack was considerably higher than dying in a traffic accident less than ten miles from your home. As Paul talked for a few minutes about bears, I imagined trying to fight off two of them—an eight-hundred-pound female and an eleven-hundred-pound male. Then I imagined myself being eaten.

What about falling into the ocean?

David Golibersuch was quick with an answer based on his statistical analysis of past Arctic treks: "Roughly one in four people who travel to the far north go for a swim."

A shiver shimmied up my spine. Craig's face showed the same fear. I did the math: eleven people on the trip meant that Craig and I would probably both go for a swim. Or, I'd go swimming two or three times.

Paul sensed our apprehension. He said, "Don't worry. At the end of this week we'll all go for an icy swim. You'll learn what it's like and how to get out."

I looked for a sign that he was kidding. He offered none. I asked if he'd ever fallen in.

"Nope," he said with a big, unabashed grin.

So how would he know what it's like to fall in at 30 below with no lodge nearby offering warmth and dry clothes?

The topic chilled the conversation. Bill jumped in with a positive spin, talking about why this trip excited him. He said it was the first expedition he'd been on with a mission that went beyond personal achievement. He talked about how this level of expedition was about man against nature; about how all the great challenges had been faced; about how the only option was to add another level of craziness—to be the first to climb a mountain without a jacket, without oxygen, aboard a pogo stick, or on a unicycle.

Paul then asked me to discuss the Great Aspirations! charity. He had told me previously, that in order to use the trip as a publicity tool for my charity, I'd need to get the approval of the team. I explained to the group that during the fall of 1997, I came across an article about Dr. Russ Quaglia, Director of the National Center for Student Aspirations at the University of Maine, my alma mater. After fifteen years of research, Dr. Quaglia had developed a set of principles on how to build student aspirations. Russ's primary work was with schools.

After meeting him I proposed the creation of a charity that would translate and publish his work to parents. The result was a nonprofit charity called Great Aspirations! The charity's purpose was to create and publish ideas that could help parents help their kids. We accomplished this through a national newspaper column distributed by Universal Press Syndicate and through the free distribution of audiotapes and CDs to parents.

I explained that the program came from a no-whining-allowed perspective. It was based on a commonsense approach and principles that really work. I went on to explain some of the data behind the program:

- Working with at-risk fourth and fifth graders, kids whose previous academic performances were far below average, we were able to affect an overall increase in these kids' grades by some 50 percent and an increase of 80 percent of their grades by a full letter grade. On average, their national test scores increased some 150 percent. Discipline problems virtually disappeared, and all said they were actually excited about learning.

- A separate field study with a group of Cincinnati third graders found that discipline problems declined 72 percent, absentees declined 25 percent, and tardiness declined 54 percent. Moreover, report card evaluations showed an increase in all the standard measures of "good student citizenship." Once the Aspiration principles were put into place, our test group demonstrated better self-control, more cooperation with others, respect and consideration for others, and the ability to follow directions. At the same time, their ability to focus on tasks doubled. And some 81 percent of these students get strong ratings in terms of completing all their assignments.

By this point in my presentation I seemed to be getting interest, but I wasn't sure. So I went for the jugular. I reviewed research my team had conducted with Johnson & Johnson that found a near one-to-one relationship between a child's self-image and that of his parents. That means that, for every parent with a low self-image, there's at least one child with an equally low self-image. If they even try, are they as likely to try their best? Or are they going to be conditioned to failing? Will they see opportunity as something to seize or shy away from? It's a bleak picture.

And there's more. While reviewing research about childhood growth, we made another discovery. There's a high correlation between a child's grades in the third grade and the eleventh grade. That means that by the time kids are eight years old, they've developed an academic pattern that is likely to carry throughout their school years, unless something comes along to change it. It's a structure that rigidly defines who's smart and who's dumb, who falls into the neat little slots of "A" students, "D" students, and so on. That means by the age of eight, most of us have it set in our minds where we fall on that letter grade scale.

After clarifying the urgency of the issue, I explained how our expedition fit with the four Great Aspirations! principles.

Belonging: For an expedition to be successful it's critical to develop a sense of teamwork, community, and belonging. Paul Schurke is a master at taking groups of strangers and crafting them into a team. Equally important is that each team member's individual strengths, weaknesses, and personality be recognized, appreciated, and integrated into the whole.

Excitement: The feeling of going to places few have seen fuels the heart and soul of each team member with the spirit of true adventure. A trip to the North Pole sparks fun, excitement, curiosity, and creativity.

Accomplishment: A feeling of optimism, overt goal setting, and healthy risk taking fuels a feeling of accomplishment. Each day we face good and bad situations. By working together as a team, we can achieve what none of us could do by ourselves.

Leadership: Paul Schurke is the trip leader. His unique blend of knowledge, skill, common sense, and quiet confidence inspires people to do what they would never consider doing. For this expedition to be successful, each member of the team will need to develop and exhibit his or her own leadership.

My proposition was to use our North Pole expedition as a publicity stunt to gain awareness of the free educational materials at the www. aspirations.com Web site. The vision was to use the North Pole, the land of Santa, to engage children and parents to come together through our journey.

The trip became the Great Aspirations! Expedition.

To make this happen, I would ask my Eureka! Ranch clients for sponsorships to fund a national public relations effort for the trip and to fund further publishing and support of organizations that help ignite the Great Aspirations! principles.

To build awareness of the expedition, we'd use the Great Aspirations! newspaper column, and my colleague and friend David Wecker, our base camp commander, would post stories about our expedition on the Scripps Howard newswire.

On the trip, we planned to use the then-new Iridium satellite network of phones and text pagers to communicate. I would call David each night, and he would write a story, which would be published as "North Pole Telegram" each night on the Web site. Family, friends, and children around the world could send each of us text messages on our individual pagers. In addition, each day a special family activity or "Great Event" (as I called them) would be posted for children and parents to do together.

Finally, syndicated cartoonist Tom Wilson was sending his loveable little cartoon character Ziggy and his dog Fuzz on the trip with us to serve as our official "spokes characters." Having Ziggy on the trip enhanced the appeal to families worldwide. In addition, via his globally syndicated cartoon strip, Ziggy would alert his seventy-five million readers of the Aspirations expedition.

After my explanation, Paul asked for the team's perspective on the charity.

I was surprised that support was universal.

Bill said, "The charitable cause gives the expedition a sense of real purpose."

In retrospect, I shouldn't have been surprised. The Great Aspirations! charity and the world of genuine adventurers are kindred spirits. Each believes in dreaming big and reaching for grand goals.

The team's support was even more impressive because they gained nothing from it financially. All of the sponsorship money went directly to the charity.

It's interesting to note that Admiral Peary's 1909 journey had a similarly higher mission. President Theodore Roosevelt wrote to Peary, "I feel that you are doing most admirable work for science, but I feel even more that you are doing admirable work for America and are setting an example to the young men of our day which we need to have set amid the softening tendencies of our time."

The meeting ended, but the conversation continued, with the adventure veterans sharing their tales of victory and hardship. Though their stories fascinated me, I felt a distance from the

Theodore Roosevelt saw Admiral Peary off. Peary's ship was named *the Roosevelt* in the president's honor.

group. Their "club" intimidated me, even as it drew my interest. I wondered if, at reaching the North Pole, I'd be a member.

Just after midnight, I went to my room and unrolled my new Wiggies sleeping bag on top of a Hudson Bay red-and-black striped blanket. I would sleep in the bag I'd take to the pole. I even opened the window a crack, thinking it might help me acclimate.

I felt good. The bag was puffy. I felt like I was inside a cloud. Then my feet hit the bottom of the bag. I could barely move in its embrace, but I slept well. The next morning, I was rested and ready.

I volunteered to help feed the dogs before breakfast. It was 7:00 A.M. as I bundled up in my new gear, pulled on my new boots, and headed to where Craig and a few others were already wrestling with the dogs. As I stepped on the outside porch the thermometer read 10 degrees above, which was mild by Arctic standards.

Entering the kennel area—a honeycomb of wooden boxes, plywood dividers, and wire fencing—I took off my mittens to free my hands to help with the dogs. Within a couple minutes, my fingers went from feeling chilled to feeling frozen to feeling numb.

I shook them to try to bring back feeling, and when that failed I quietly freaked out. Not just because of my numb fingers but because I suddenly came face to face with the stark, undeniable realization that I was in over my head. Absolutely, indisputably *waaaaaay* over my head. If I was freezing at 10 degrees, what would I do in the minus-30 neighborhood?

A barrage of anxieties shot off in my mind. *I'm a pretender, an imposter trying to pull off a colossal charade. What will my sponsors, my children, my friends say? How would I explain to them that, hey, sorry, but I found out in the nick of time that it would be far too cold in the Arctic.*

I laughed at the thought. Then I laughed at myself. "Look, dummy," I said to myself, "of course, it's going to be cold. What did you expect? Get over it."

My fear calmed a bit. For the mo-ment.

After breakfast, we all took a brisk hike through the woods. The pace was aggressive. Schurke's long deer-like legs flew through the pucker brush while I struggled to find footing on the mossy rocks. With each step, my feet slipped to one side or the other. Against those blessed with long legs, I've always been at a disadvantage. My legs are an inch and a half shorter than they should be, due to the football accident that broke the growth plate in my left hip. To keep my legs an even length, so that I wouldn't have a lifelong limp, my doctors halted the growth of my right leg.

I began to see that perspiration really is the enemy more than the cold. Sweat poured down my back like a salty Niagara. Schurke advised us to open our jackets and to vent away the heat our bodies generated.

As I struggled along, I glanced now and then at my companions. Was I totally out of synch with the situation? They looked so calm. Or perhaps they were hiding their fear better than I was. Some of them were even laughing.

For the next two days, Paul and Bill filled our heads with information. When we weren't on the trail, immersing ourselves as much as possible in the ways of Arctic camping, we watched videos of Paul's previous trips.

Then we embarked into the North Woods. It was the first time that year that Paul's dogs had been out for a run, and they were eager to pull. Chains ran the length of the sled runners to slow down the dogs, but the runners might as well have been greased with butter.

There wasn't much snow, so we went onto the lake. The dogs galloped at a speed fast enough, almost, for my life to flash before my eyes. We completed several long runs with the dogs and spent a couple nights in the woods with Paul's staffers as our babysitters. Then we went out on our own for two nights.

The dogs were rested and ready for adventure.

Craig and I became the cooks for the expedition. I don't know exactly how it happened. We may have gotten kitchen duty because we had the least experience. Or it could have been the only job we felt confident we could handle. I do consider eating one of my talents.

On the trail I found myself comparing myself to my teammates, sizing them up while sizing up myself.

I felt the same way when I worked out at Mercy Healthplex to get in shape for the trip. I'd lift one plate where others had lifted four, five, or six. It was embarrassing to set the weights lower than the guy—or the gal or the senior citizen—who had gone before me.

As my status as a high-adventure rookie became clearer to me, my fear of being exposed continued to grow. My work in

On the training trip the two rookies, Craig and Doug, got the cooking duties.

the corporate world had not prepared me for this situation. Pushing the mind to find new ideas is not at all like pushing the body to its breaking—or freezing—point.

But as my spirits hit bottom, my sense of humor rescued me. My exaggerated fears struck me as comical. I found myself laughing. Watching me laugh at myself and mumble to myself, my teammates must have been ready to have me committed. Somewhere out in the woods, I surrendered to the idea that I would survive the Arctic or I would not, but in any case, I was going.

Early one morning, we awoke to Paul hollering that the ice was cracking and we had thirty minutes to break camp. I knew it was a drill; I also knew the issue was real. I'd read of it in Admiral Peary's book *The North Pole*.

My frantic scramble to pull myself together could have been an audition for the Keystone Cops. I couldn't find my glasses, couldn't find my mittens, my boots were frozen, where were those danged glasses? It took me twelve minutes to get dressed. Paul hollered out to note each minute's passing. Somehow, thirty-two minutes later, we were off and rolling—

two sleds and eight dogs—with all our gear packed and tied down on the sleds.

In that one clumsy moment, the team came together. It was a great feeling, knowing we could work together and make things happen.

During the week I also learned how to navigate celestially. Each of us took a turn with the sextant, learning how to shoot the sun and the noon meridian. The experience reaffirmed my appreciation for modern technology, but it also made me appreciate how things were done before batteries and how the old ways invariably required one to use more of one's own resources. Paul Schurke's emphasis on self-reliance appealed to me. Slowly, almost without realizing it, I began to grow into an adventure mindset.

And just as readily, I would relapse into fear and confusion. Later that evening, I put the *Why* query to Paul, hoping to find an answer that explained why I was drawn to this challenge. Why was this little voice inside me urging, prodding, poking me to go to the North Pole?

Paul's answer didn't help, but it was a good one nonetheless. He told me that, growing up, he always wanted to be an astronaut, and the high Arctic was as close as he'd ever get to standing on another planet.

"When the plane leaves, you have this feeling of being dropped onto another planet," he said. "It's a powerful sensation. The sound and colors are amazing. The surface and environment change hourly. There is also something about the sense of total isolation from the rest of the earth. It brings your attention to things like never before."

He paused to collect his thoughts before adding, "Then again, maybe it *is* just crazy. Maybe we're just doing an incredibly grueling trek on a constantly moving surface hoping to arrive at an invisible target."

That night around the campfire, Paul ratcheted up the risk factor. He made us understand what we were about to undertake. He said he was obliged to advise each of us to get a membership in MEDJET, an insurance group that would evacuate us in case of emergency. He also made it abundantly clear that we would have no guides, Sherpas, or friendly polar bears to help us when our loads became heavy. He told us we *were* the expedition.

By the end of the week I was functioning nicely in nine-degree weather. It wasn't bad at all. I was struck by how quickly my body adapted to the cold.

When we returned to the lodge we unhitched and fed the dogs. Then, before we went into the lodge, Paul led us down to the lake for our final test: A full swim in full gear. We were to extricate ourselves on our own and make our way back to the lodge. Seeing myself as the runt of the litter, I was one of the first to volunteer.

Ready, Set, Go — and I was off...

Paul pointed to a black hole in the ice. "The ice isn't too hard," he said. "Just be sure to hold onto your ski poles. You use the points as ice picks to pull yourself out."

Then Paul gave the command: "Ready, Set, Go!" I reflexively dug my poles into the ice, thrusting myself forward on my cross-country skis. My legs shook, partly from the cold, partly from absolute terror.

As I reached the edge of the black water, I heaved myself upward, imagining myself in an arching trajectory like one of those Olympic ski jumpers I'd seen on TV, flying gloriously

My first attempt was not successful.

into the wind, almost tasting the thrill of victory.

In my mind, it played out in slow motion. Up, up, up I went—a noble Icarus of the ice. What, ho! Was I getting a smidgen of lift from the wind? Down, down, down I went, anticipating the bone-deep chill when I hit the water.

Instead, I bounced.

I bounced.

Instead of a deep hole in the ice, I'd fallen into an eight-inch puddle.

As water rolled down my back, I got super-cold.

The second time I went for a full swim.

Like the rag-dog ski jumper in the famous credits of ABC's *Wide World of Sports*, I instantly knew the agony of defeat. The wind seemed to amplify the laughter of my teammates. As I lay there, sprawled out in a freezing cold made colder by the wind, Paul decided I wasn't sufficiently submerged and casually pointed to another hole.

The wind whipping my wet clothing—coupled with my desire to put this behind me as quickly as possible—inspired me to get moving again. I skied toward another black hole and this time I went straight in, all the way under. The cold grabbed my body like a giant fist and squeezed. I broke the surface and shifted my grip on my ski poles, holding them near the point. Then I used them as ice picks to pull my soaking self back onto the ice.

Paul grinned slightly, then turned his attention to his next victim. As I scrambled the half-mile to the lodge, I mumbled to myself. Actually, I started holding a conversation with a little cartoon devil enemy of mine who loves to make me uncertain, unsure, and downright scared. The devil screamed into the wind,

"HEY IDIOT! What's the point? You could be warming your balding head on a beach in the Bahamas. Instead, you're in the middle of a Minnesota winter volunteering to be miserable. Volunteering!

And if that's not dumb enough, you're going to pay twenty grand for the right to do this."

"It's not that bad, it could be worse. At least there's a lodge to warm up in."

"There's a lodge here in Minnesota, but what about in the Arctic? What are you going to do if you fall in up there? Get out! Get out now!"

As I sprinted down the ice toward Paul's lodge, teeth clacking spastically, I wrestled with another dilemma. When I ran fast with my arms swinging, the wind chill was frigid. If I walked slowly, I could wrap my arms around myself and feel warmer but it took longer. Should I run or walk? I opted for running, hoping that the numbness I was feeling on my face, fingers, and toes would not do permanent damage.

To ignore the devil, I focused on what the admiral wrote about tenderfeet and how they handled a "wetting."

> It was with a feeling of intense satisfaction that I watched, my Arctic 'tenderfeet,' as I called them, proving the mettle of which they were made. A man who cannot laugh at a wetting or take as a matter of course a dangerous passage over moving ice, is not a man for a serious Arctic expedition.

The devil saw an opening and pushed hard at my fragile confidence, *"Be honest. You are not a man for a serious Arctic expedition."*

I tried hard to convince myself that I could do it. I told myself that a touch of lunacy, mixed with levity, is a prerequisite for trekking to the North Pole. As with any great adventure, it's not the rational thing to do. The whole idea of this trip is to see what I'm made of.

The admiral said it himself:

> The Arctic is a great test of character. One may know a man better after a short time there than after a lifetime of acquaintance in cities. There is something in those frozen spaces that brings a man face to face with himself and with his companions. If he is a man,

the man comes out. If he is a cur, the cur shows as quickly.

The devil worked this hard: *"Well I guess we know the answer to the question 'Are you a man?'"*

Before I could respond, I arrived at the lodge. I peeled off my ice-crusted clothes and rubbed my fingers to bring warmth back into the tips. I poured myself a healthy nip of Scotch but I avoided adding ice or a splash of cold water. I'd had enough of that for one day.

I knew that alcohol actually makes you colder, but the trip was finished and I felt I'd earned it. Besides, the admiral liked a nip of brandy. He carried a bottle with him on his Arctic expeditions. He wrote of how the brandy would freeze solid at minus 60.

As the rest of the team made their way into the lodge, I looked at Paul's pictures from the Arctic hanging in the lodge.

The expedition will take us over white ice, blue ice, and ice of all textures and degrees of hardness. It will be, essentially, flat and monotonous. In my romanticized notion of the North Pole, I pretended I would know I'd arrived when I saw the red-and-white striped barber's pole.

The reality, of course, is that there is no barber pole at the North Pole. It's actually an imaginary place that can only be located with navigational tools. And, since the Arctic is nothing but floating ice, the spot on the ice that is mathematically the North Pole is moving constantly. You could pitch a tent at the pole one day and be four miles away from the pole the next without ever leaving the tent.

I knew the trek to the pole would require agonizing exertion, interspersed with moments of holy terror from open water, numb fingers, and polar bear tracks that would remind us we weren't necessarily at the top of the food chain. As I sat down beside Paul's woodstove sipping my second glass of fine Scotch, I still didn't know why I was about to put myself through this harrowing ordeal. I just knew it was something I had to do.

❄

The next morning, Paul and Bill summoned us one by one to Paul's home to discuss the trip. Most conversations went quickly. Mine lasted a little longer. Paul said I'd made the cut, but he felt I needed to train more intensely to be ready, and I had just four months to get in shape.

"You could stumble your way to the pole in the shape you're in," he said, "but it will be a lot more fun if you're in better shape."

I asked what role I would play on the expedition. Handling the dogs? Navigating? Communications?

Paul smiled and shook his head. "Craig's going to be the head cook," he said. "You're going to be his assistant. It seems to be the best use of your talents."

I made it. So did all the others. Okay, so I would be the assistant cook, the lowest-level job on the expedition, mostly cooking ice into water and cleaning dishes. But in the event that the head cook was not able to perform his duties I needed to be ready to step in.

As we left the lodge and headed home, I didn't care about my role on the team. I was going to visit Santa's Land!

Chapter 3
Ready ... Set ... Go

*A*FTER LEAVING PAUL'S LODGE IN DECEMBER, I focused on fitness. When I first dreamed of going on this expedition I was a poster child for mentally fit—and a clinical case of physically unfit. I didn't want to be the caboose, the weakest link, the runt of the expedition litter, and so I changed my workout program.

Working out in full gear

Given that fitness was foreign to me, I outsourced my program to personal trainers in a six-day-a-week, often twice-a-day schedule. I lifted weights, trained as a boxer, did aerobic exercises, and took up long-distance swimming, spinning, cross-country skiing on roller skis, and running. I also did cross training in full Arctic gear. My kids thought it was so funny they volunteered to get up early and go to watch me.

Each of the trainers made me their special project. In each case, I was blunt with them. I knew I'd found the right trainer when they responded to my challenge with glee. I especially liked the ones who added a touch of sadistic humor. They took the challenge seriously. I provided an opportunity for them to really apply the intensity of their training.

My biggest challenge was learning what it feels like to work out. Over the years I had insulated myself from fitness through a commitment to not getting hurt. When I exercised and felt pain, I stopped to prevent injury.

In truth, I had been lazy. I didn't understand good pain from bad pain. I didn't understand that muscle soreness from a workout was a good thing. It meant I was getting stronger. Although I understood the basics of working out, I didn't know what it really felt like to be healthy.

The trainers had a common religion: the heart rate monitor. It's a truth teller. When my mind told me I felt tired, even though my body was capable of more, the monitor would snitch on me, and the trainers would demand more effort.

During the December training trip, I tracked my heart rate while working with the dogs and sleds. While in the snow and loaded with gear, my heart ran above 75 percent of my theoretical maximum rate. When the sled had to be pushed and pulled, my heart rate shot up to 90 percent of maximum.

As the time for the journey came near, I underwent a second heart stress test at Canyon Ranch in the Berkshires. An earlier test at their Tucson location showed that my heart and lungs were in below-average shape. Not good enough. The test involved running as fast as I could on a treadmill for as long as I could, wearing a facemask to measure my oxygen intake and my CO_2 output. A nurse stood next to me with what looked like heart jumper cables while I kept thinking, "Sell my clothes, Mabel, I'm heaven bound."

I lasted twelve minutes in my first test. On the second one I managed twenty-three minutes. Afterward, the Canyon Ranch doctor said, "I have good news and bad news."

"Give me the bad news first," I said.

"The bad news is you can't use your heart as an excuse for

not going" he said. "The good news is you may freeze to death, but you probably won't die from a heart attack. Your heart is in excellent shape."

The test indicated that I had the maximum heart rate of a twenty-nine-year-old and the VO_2 max of a man of twenty-four. Naturally, I've been mentioning these results since then to anyone who will listen.

By the time I left for the expedition I had increased the average maximum weight I could lift by 32 percent. For the first time in my life, I could bench press my weight! Not bad for a guy who a year before could only bench press 60 percent of his weight (roughly equivalent to seven small sacks of potatoes).

I was in the best shape of my entire life. Of course, that wasn't saying much.

After more than a year of intense planning and preparation, I was finally on my way, leaving Cincinnati to travel 3,523 miles to the top of the earth.

On a Sunday we flew to Edmonton, Alberta, to meet the rest of the team, and from there we flew to Yellowknife, then onto Resolute Bay, the Inuit village that served as our point of departure, from which we would fly to a point on the ice at 88 degrees latitude, where we'd be left to our own devices.

In the week before leaving, three events occurred that my imagination fanned into full-blown crises:

Crisis One: On April 8, in Orlando to give a lecture to a trade association, I awoke in my hotel room at 2:30 A.M. with a nasty sinus infection. The world outside was quiet, but my mind exploded into hyper-drive.

What if the doctor said I couldn't make the trip? What if my condition was contagious? What if the Twin Otter planes that would transport us to 88 degrees were not pressurized and my eardrums burst?

Worst of all, these internal tensions exposed a vulnerability I hadn't realized until that moment. For the first time, I understood how important it had become to me to make this trip. I had come down with an irrational, nonsensical need to stand on a piece of ice on top of the earth. I had Arctic Fever. The admiral suffered from the same malady.

> To me the final and complete solution of the polar mystery which has engaged the best thought and interest of some of the best men of the most vigorous and enlightened nations of the world for more than three centuries, and today quickens the pulse of every man or woman whose veins hold red blood, is the thing which must be done for the honor and credit of this country, the thing which it is intended that I should do, and the thing that I must do.

Later that morning, a call to my office triggered a chain of solutions. By noon, a fast-acting steroid and turbo-charged antibiotic awaited me in Cincinnati.

Crisis Two: That Saturday, I learned of a new demon: diarrhea. Jeff Stamp, a food scientist who consulted at the Eureka! Ranch, called me to report important scientific findings. He told me he'd been eating the food I would be consuming on my way to the pole—six thousand calories each day with a high dose of fat for fuel.

"Within three days," Jeff reported, "I was dehydrated and in the throws of massive diarrhea. Worst of all, the diet's high acidity caused significant exit pain."

EXIT PAIN! Diarrhea! Say what?

I remembered Paul Schurke telling me that he'd had bad diarrhea during his 1986 expedition to the North Pole. Yikes! Not only did my head feel like a truck had run over it, now I had reason for concern over discomfort in my personal hinterlands. I called my brother Bruce, who had once been brand manager for a fiber supplement product, Metamucil. In fact, Bruce had created a mascot for the product that he named Mr. Happy Bowel. It was a cartoon song-and-dance bowel that can only be fully appreciated by the medical community.

Relaying Jeff's findings, I asked Bruce's advice. Once he stopped laughing, he suggested I take a Metamucil Wafer after each meal.

"Research indicates that 80 percent of those who do, report a spectacular bowel movement the next day," Bruce said.

It was music to my ears. I bought two packages of Metamucil Wafers. Crises averted.

Crisis Three: 6:00 A.M. Sunday. No luck sleeping. Boots strewn across the living room floor.

Given that we were traveling on foot, I had to choose the right boot for the trip. I gave it a lot of thought. Waaaayyy too much thought. Each style had its virtues and drawbacks. I even had to choose what size to wear. With a larger boot my feet would be warmer because I could wear more socks. However, if the boots were too large I'd lose ankle support when skiing and climbing over ice.

I laid out all four styles of boots, some in multiple sizes. I'd tried all of them in multiple test runs, both on the December trip to Ely and a cross-country ski trip in Jackson, New Hampshire. My conclusion? Confusion. Nothing seemed to fill all my needs.

The traditional mukluks favored by the Inuit are like giant leather socks. But they wear out easily and provide little ankle support.

Most of the team was going for the big, white Moon Boots created by Paul Weber, who has been with Paul to the North Pole. They're a high-tech form of mukluk with rubber bottoms and multiple layers of insulation. They're designed to breathe and release moisture, which also means they aren't waterproof. Hands down they seem like they'd be the warmest. However, they're also heavy and don't offer great ankle support.

Then there are LaCrosse boots. They have rubber bottoms and leather uppers. They weigh a pound less than the Moon Boots. They don't seem as warm but offer great ankle support and Paul Schurke's endorsement as the right choice.

Weight is a big issue. I've read that the reduction of just one pound off your feet increases your performance by 5 percent.

And for me, every bit of extra energy and performance is going to be important.

The last option is a bizarre invention of mine. It's a multipiece system of footwear built around the New England Overshoes. NEOS, as they're called, are waterproof overshoes designed to keep stockbrokers' wingtips dry. I've added foot liners, foot wraps, and high-tech ankle braces to make them into the lightest footwear on earth. They weigh half as much as the Moon Boots. In theory they're the perfect choice. But because they've never been to the pole, their durability, warmth, and suitability have not been proven.

At 7:00 A.M., I put a different boot on each foot and ran around outside. I kept trying options until I'd been through all the boots at least once. Finally, I made my decision: I chose the most conservative option, Schurke's recommendation of the LaCrosse leather boots, and the most innovative one, the NEOS system.

I also decided to go with vapor barriers to keep my feet warmer. Vapor barriers are socks made of scuba suit material. You force your foot to sweat inside the barrier, which then

Tori, Brad, and Kristyn decorated the car for the trip to the airport.

holds in the warmth. The feeling can be a little clammy and odd, but your toes are toasty.

By 9:00 A.M., I had all my gear in the bags. Debbie and our children (Kristyn, twelve; Tori, ten; and Brad, eight) took me to the airport in Debbie's SUV, which they had decorated with balloons and well wishes. We looked like we were headed to a soccer tournament or a wedding.

At the airport, I meet up with Craig Kurz, and my longtime partner in crime, David Wecker, who would be the expedition's base camp commander in Resolute and our link to the civilized world.

As a columnist for the *Cincinnati Post*, David would translate my dispatches

I met up with Craig and David at the airport—just 3,523 miles to go.

from the ice each day into newspaper columns that would be distributed worldwide via the Scripps Howard News Service, as well as on the Great Aspirations! Web site. Should something go awry—if, say, we needed emergency supplies or a quick evacuation—he would arrange with one of the two Arctic bush-country air carriers at Resolute Bay to make it happen.

Like Butch Cassidy and the Sundance Kid, or maybe more like Abbott and Costello, David and I have shared adventures around the world. We have invented ideas for cookies, cat food, credit cards, cars, and even coffins. We've sparked revolutionary thought from the capitals of corporate America to the Imagination Pavilion at Disney's Epcot Center and some of the most historic castles in Europe.

As the idea of turning my less-than-Schwarzeneggarish self into shape for a trek to the North Pole took shape in my mind,

David was among the first to hear of it. In typical fashion, he suggested I was suffering from a polar disorder and advised me to seek help.

It was comforting to have these two good friends on the trip, but it wasn't without some anxiety. I felt a certain responsibility for them, having done a bit of a sales job to get them to take part in the expedition.

The hugs from the kids lingered longer than normal. I thought I saw a mixture of fear and excitement on their faces. Then I hugged Debbie, who has always supported my crazy schemes, like only someone who truly loves another could.

In our embrace, she whispered in my ear, "You're ready."

"Are you sure?" I asked.

"Absolutely!" she said.

I don't know who's crazier, me for getting myself involved in stunts like this or Debbie for supporting me. I guess you could say we're genuinely crazy for each other. (I know it's sappy, but as I write this story we've been together for thirty-three years, and we're still happily in love.)

At 1:32 P.M., I settled into my seat on the American Airlines flight to Chicago, the first leg of the journey. I knew I'd miss my family, but I felt pulled forward. Debbie's words washed over me. I had a feeling of peace and steadiness. For the first time in days, I slept well, dropping into a deep sleep as the plane lifted into the air.

Monday, April 12: The team assembled in Edmonton for the long trip north. Before we headed out, I had work to do on behalf of the Great Aspirations! charity. At 6:00 A.M., I began doing radio interviews at the rate of one every fifteen minutes. The expedition generated publicity, but my message was about encouraging parents to believe in their children.

I covered the country from east to west, following the time zones for the early morning commuters. I talked to Boston, Falls Church, Kansas City, and on across the country. Given the hour, I strained to sound chipper. "I'm like a kid on Christmas morning," I told the morning guy from Spokane's KXLY radio. "I'm going to see Santa Claus!"

Jon Paul Buchmeyer—the account supervisor from the aptly named Bragman, Nyman, and Cafarelli, a public relations firm I commissioned, lined up the interviews, along

We were selling radio audiences on connecting with their kids.

with dozens more for when we are on the ice. The interviews would depend on whether my expensive Iridium telephone technology functioned properly. Jon Paul, who had represented Whoopi Goldberg and Cameron Diaz, was skeptical about the prospects but excited about the potential.

To the guys with the "Al & Rich Show" on the USA Radio Network in Dallas, I said, "This is a bizarre charity. Don't send money. Please. Instead, sit down and spend ten minutes with a child. It'll have more of an impact on that kid than any dollar amount ever could."

To make the Great Aspirations! charity work, we have to generate publicity. And I'm the charity's P.T. Barnum. My problem is that we can't claim any firsts, other than the fact that Alan Humphries would be the first Irishman to walk to the North Pole. Granted, I might have pitched myself as the first life member of the International Jugglers Association or MENSA to make the trip, but who would care?

Jon Paul met us in Edmonton to tape "B roll" footage of the trip. TV stations don't do stories if they don't have video to go

The team, except for Mike Warren and Corky Peterson, posed for photos at Rabbit Hill.

with them, and once we hit the icy trail to the pole, it would be impossible for us to provide it. So Jon Paul wanted to have footage in the can to offer any stations that might show interest.

He planned to tape the team slogging along in the snow. Unfortunately, when we pulled into Edmonton, the snow had melted—and the 40-degree temperature didn't promise to offer more. But the resourceful Jon Paul had the New York staff make phone calls throughout the area and found a ski resort called Rabbit Hill that had snow machines. They still had a dusting of snow on the ground and they could make more if we needed it.

I nervously approached Paul Schurke about taking the dogs and a sled to the ski resort to cook up some Arctic-y footage.

Paul understood. He also realized that the team might be less enthusiastic about the idea. Paul worked a little marketing magic and presented it to the team as a tune-up trip, a sort of last-minute dress rehearsal.

No one bought it. Some members of the team weren't interested in staging a situation. One suggested we might as well stage the entire expedition, phoning interviews to radio stations across the world, waxing on about the cold, grueling the conditions as we munched blueberry muffins in our hotel rooms. Two days later, when we were dropped on the ice at the 88th parallel, some of us would think that wouldn't have been a bad idea.

Paul, Alan, and Celia watch the scene. Alan thought it was a bit absurd.

Rabbit Hill was really more of a bunny hill. But at least it offered some snow. Three camera crews came along to film us—the PR firm's team along with crews from two of the Canadian television networks.

We put on our bright red expedition jackets, covered with seventeen sponsor patches. We scrambled in the snow as

Paul gave the "experienced explorer" take on the trip.

we'd been trained to do, making our actions look as realistic as possible. The only hitch occurred when a black Rottweiler appeared out of nowhere as Alan ran a dog team and sled past the cameras. The dog chased Alan, nipping at his leg when suddenly the nine sled dogs caught its scent and turned on it. I've never seen a big bad Rottweiler run away as fast as that one did.

The crews then filmed Paul Schurke, asking him what it's like to go to the North Pole. Paul gave the big-picture perspective: "The North Pole has often been compared to a horizontal Everest. It has the same extremes of climate and remoteness."

Then they interviewed me as the head of the charity. Jon Paul

"I'm scared to death," I explained.

had briefed me on what to say, but in the anxiety of the moment, my response didn't come out as I expected. Over a shot of the dogs barking, the announcer said, "The dog team is ready to go. But the man behind this expedition may be having second thoughts."

Then the camera turned to me and I said. "I'm scared to death. To be perfectly honest, it is, absolutely terrifying."

Not exactly the bravest statement I could have made, I guess. But at least I was honest.

Before such challenging expeditions, it's common to engage in a ritual of gathering and selecting gear, a practice that probably dates back to prehistory, when cave dwellers squatted around fires chipping away at flint spearheads, selecting the truest arrows, restringing bows, assembling food caches, and articulating their anti-cipations in jag-ged streaks of war paint.

Back at the hotel, Paul told us to exam-ine our gear and make our final selec-tions on what we would take. I had spent hundreds of

Bartlett (in the center) had a real "toughness" to him.

hours and thousands of dollars searching for the most effec-tive gear. From long underwear to high-tech communications systems, I had given a lot of thought to my equipment, and I enjoyed going through it one last time, picking the things I most needed.

I looked again with pride at the expedition jacket with its patches. In the weeks before leaving, I'd put it on many times to see how I looked. I even had my picture taken in it before the trip. Real explorers definitely have a look about them that says they're serious, and in the photo above, Bob Bartlett looks like a rug-ged explorer. In the pic-ture of me in my winter gear, I don't evoke quite the same ruggedness. However, I was more interested in promotional power anyway, publiciz-ing the roles that Ziggy and Fuzz would play on the trip.

Never in history had an explorer posed with two cartoon characters — Ziggy and Fuzz.

Though posing with cartoon characters may not seem appropriate for an Arctic explorer, I think the admiral would have gone along with it. When it came to raising money and generating publicity he was very aggressive. He endorsed cigarettes, ammunition, Pianolas, rifles, pencils, razors, watches, toothbrushes, whiskey, toothpaste, socks, and cameras. He even promoted the "Peary coat," a heavy fur greatcoat that he designed.

When it came to selecting gear, the admiral was very much a scientist. He tested everything. He described the importance of preparation this way.

> Thorough preparedness for a polar sledge journey is of vital importance, and no time devoted to the study and perfection of the equipment can be considered wasted.

That evening, Paul called us together to review key issues and talk about gear. He opened two gun cases. "Each sled will have a gun," he said in a serious tone. "They're to be used in the case of a polar bear attack. It's unlikely, but you need to know where the guns are. Just in case."

The more he talked, the more my fear grew.

He then showed us his gear. We were most impressed not by what he had but by how little he had. He was taking a few spare clothing items along with a mug, plate, and spoon tied

Paul's gear was amazingly sparse. Mine weighed twice as much.

by string to a bowl, a pee bottle for use during the night, and a small copy of the New Testament. That was it. I lifted his pack, then mine. I was aghast. Mine was at least twice as heavy. No, probably three times.

Paul made it clear that no team member should bring more than twenty-five pounds of personal gear—pack and all. He said that the three most important items were those that related to protection for your eyes, hands, and feet.

"On every trip, I've ended up with mild sun-blindness from the reflection off the snow," he said. He also said he always wished he'd packed more liner socks and liner gloves.

I wasn't sure about my footwear, but I was confident about my protective gear for eyes and hands.

After my local Lenscrafters manager had called their store in Anchorage for a recommendation, I bought two pairs of prescription glasses each with an extra polarization coating.

As for hand protection, I had two favorites—a pair of hand-made wool mittens I'd bought on Prince Edward Island and a set of Plunge Mitts designed by Paul's wife, Susan. Equipped with two inner liners, they look like the giant potholders. Susan designed them especially for polar treks.

Paul closed the meeting by telling us to ready our gear for final inspection. When he checked my pack, he said it seemed a little heavy. "Do you really need all this stuff?" he asked.

After he left, I unpacked the pack, looking for things to eliminate. I felt the anxiety building again. What should I leave behind and would I regret leaving it when I was at the pole?

The admiral wrote about the importance of keeping gear as light as possible.

> Careful attention must be paid to even the slightest details. Everything should be just as light as it can possibly be made. For the number of miles a party can travel depends on weight carried. Every reduction that can be made conserves mental and physical energy.

As I sorted through my gear, my anxiety built into a full-scale panic. Admiral Peary would have called it an attack of Tornarsuk, the Arctic Devil.

Tornarsuk was the god of the Inuit underworld. The Inuit believe that all departed spirits reside in the underworld, beneath the land and sea. Their souls are purified in preparation for their travel to the Land of the Moon—or Quidlivun—where they find eternal peace.

The early European explorers translated Tornarsuk into a Satan-like being to create alignment with the Christian view of the world of good and evil. In time, the name became slang for Polar Hysteria.

In medical journals Arctic panic is technically listed as Piblokto. It's a feeling of being possessed, a simultaneous mania and depression. It feels like an urgent need to do something, anything, coupled with an inability to make a move. In the worst cases of Piblokto, victims tear their clothes off and run naked outside.

Fortunately I was not at that stage.

I was, however, clearly "possessed" by fear. I knew the fear was irrational, that it made no sense, but I couldn't stop it. Panic took control of me.

Obsessively, frantically, I began swapping out my gear—my metal bowl for a plastic one, a special knife engraved with the expedition logo for a Boy Scout pocketknife. With all the gear removed from my pack, I realized that the pack itself was part of the problem. Instead of picking a mid-size pack, I'd bought an oversized one because I figured it would be easier to pack in the cold. As I held it I realized there had been a real reason why Paul had suggested the smaller one.

It was 7:00 P.M. as I tore open the Yellow Pages and found Valhalla Pure Outfitters. Thirty minutes later, after borrowing a rental car and driving into town, I was in front of the store.

I sauntered inside, trying to act like a real explorer, following advice Paul Brown, founder of the Cincinnati Bengals football team, gave his players when they scored: "Act like you've been there before."

I approached the two staff members behind the sales desk and said, "Hi, I'm going to the North Pole." They looked up and laughed. "We know," the lady said. 'We saw you on the news."

My television comments about being "scared to death" apparently made quite a hit in an outfitter store.

Forgetting my poise I said, "I really need some help. I'm missing some key gear."

Telephone (780) 414-0414
Fax (780) 439-4199
e-mail:
edmonton@valhalla-pure.com

7920 - 103 Street
Edmonton, AB T6E 6C3

http://www.valhalla-pure.com

I tried to act like a pro. But they'd seen me say on TV that I was "scared to death."

A staffer named Matt, a real outdoors fanatic, looked at my list. First, he found a backpack that weighed half as much as mine. Figuring that I probably needed help, he made the all-important adjustments to the waist belt and the multitude of straps to reduce stress on me and my back.

Next, he got a balaclava—a sort of portable hood that protects your neck, head, and face. I'd never cared for these, perhaps because of my distaste for neckties. In my role as a creativity guru, I'd called them neck tourniquets, horrible pieces of apparel that served only to cut off the flow of oxygen-rich blood to the brains of corporate executives. But I was heading for a world far removed from the corporate boardroom, one where protection of neck and face is critical.

Long johns—I had medium weight and ultra heavy. After seeing Paul's gear, I wanted a pair of lightweights, especially for skiing. A pee bottle—Paul had been persuasive about the value of having an extra water bottle that could be used as a urine receptacle during the night to eliminate the need to leave the comfort of one's sleeping bag.

The gaiter and long underwear were easy choices. The pee bottle was a bit more difficult. What size would I need?

I immediately rejected a thirty-two-ounce bottle because it was the same size as my water bottle, and I definitely didn't want to get the two confused. They had a smaller bottle, but the top was small, and I was concerned about aim. After some digging in the back of the store they found me a sixteen-ounce bottle with a wide mouth. Eureka!

Selection of the right pee bottle was challenging. Later I would learn that I made the wrong choice.

Heading back, I felt myself start to relax, feeling that I was finally ready for the expedition. Resolving the gear issues gave my mind a space to relax.

I decided to take a swing through Edmonton before heading back out to the airport. I stopped at a bookstore to buy a book to take with me. I went to the information desk and asked, "If you were going to the end of the earth, what one book would you take?"

The clerk gave me a blank stare.

I tried again, "If you were on a deserted island what one book would you want to have?"

"I don't know," she said. "Maybe a poetry book or a Bible." She pointed to the self-improvement section, figuring, I guess, that I needed it.

I ended up buying a book of Ben Franklin quotes, Franklin being my personal hero. I figured that if it didn't inspire me, I could burn it for heat or, in a pinch, use it as toilet paper.

As I walked toward the checkout I picked up a New Testament. I figured that if it was good enough for Paul it was good enough for me. Besides, given the emotional roller coaster I was riding, it might help calm my mind.

I returned to the hotel at around 8:30 P.M. and carried my gear to my room. I was feeling good—too good. As I moved my gear into the new pack I suddenly realized that I'd lost my mittens. My big, blue, double-insulated plunge mitts were missing. I tore through my bags, my jackets, my gear, turning everything inside out.

The mittens were critical. I had to have them.

I backtracked. I'd had them at the ski resort that afternoon. I remembered taking them off to demonstrate the satellite phone. I was up and out of the room, running down to the truck that had taken us to the resort and back.

I pawed through the truck and the dog crates. Nothing. I ran back upstairs to look again. Nothing. Then back to the truck again to look under the seats and beneath the sleds. Nothing.

Tornarsuk the fear dragon appeared again.

I called Paul's room and asked if he'd seen my blue plunge mitts. Nope. I called Craig, then David. Double nope.

After one more trip to the truck and back I was in a state of panic.

I had no recourse but to call my new friend Matt at Valhalla Pure Outfitters.

"Hey, it's me again, do you have any really really warm mittens? You do? Excellent! What time do you close? In ten minutes? Uh, um, okay. Do you think it would it be possible for someone to bring a pair of those gloves to me? It would? You're awesome, man!"

Twenty minutes later, I had a spanking new pair of two hundred-dollar mitts. I gave Matt a hundred-dollar tip. I also gave him a Great Aspirations! Expedition patch and my eternal thanks. He seemed happier with the patch than the money.

Tuesday, April 13: It was 6:25 A.M. My blind terror from the previous night's exertions had worn me out, giving me six hours of uninterrupted sleep, the most I'd gotten in five days. The curse of my missing mittens had turned into a blessing. Amazing.

But a sudden spiral of doubt started turning again. What if I didn't have the energy to make this trip? What if, despite all my training, I really wasn't ready? What if I was just totally nuts? One conclusion seemed clear: I had no business being on this trip. None whatsoever.

I opened one of the notes Debbie and the kids had secretly packed in my bags. Without me finding out, they had packed a collection of small, folded notes in every nook and cranny of my pack. I had found them the day before and placed them all in a plastic bag. I'd decided to open one whenever I really needed a boost of confidence. This seemed like one of those moments.

I grinned at what I read:

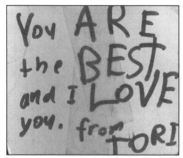

My wife had the kids secretly stash notes in my backpack.

My wife Debbie's support for this crazy idea went far beyond what would be considered reasonable.

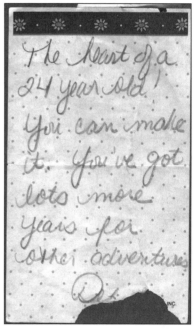

Instantly, I had more courage. My family's faith in me was greater than my faith in myself.

At breakfast, in front of the whole team, Paul asked about the status of my blue plunge mitts. Terrific, I thought. Expose me as a total fool for losing my mittens.

With a big, pearly white, totally engaging smile, Paul told me he'd found them in the truck and put them in the spare clothing bag.

What a relief! On second thought, what the hey?!?! If he'd found my mitts in the truck, then, well, you get my drift. What kind

Paul found my mittens and enjoyed the site of watching me panic. I didn't mind being the "fool" as long as I had my mittens.

of psychological magic was he working now? What lesson was I supposed to learn? Or was my role to be the entertainment for the team?

I remembered something Paul had said in an interview in the *New York Times*. "Trips are too predictable when everyone's a veteran. It's much more interesting to watch a bunch of people who are still trying to figure out what to do." It looked like I would be providing lots to watch.

By 7:30 A.M., we were packing the dogs, sleds, and gear at Canadian Air Cargo. It took two hours to load it all onto the shipping pallet that would go into the plane.

The scene was a bit chaotic.

Paul was negotiating on the fly, so to speak, with the Canadian Airways representative, working to make sure all our gear was loaded. The issue was weight. The airline was used to this game. The seats had been removed from the front half of the passenger compartments. A set of doors on the side of the plane allowed for loading pallets. Our eighteen dogs in their crates with our sleds filled one pallet. There were

The dogs were loaded into kennels and onto a pallet.

also several pallets of perishable goods like eggs, lettuce, and bacon.

At 11:30 A.M., we finished loading, and I took my seat in the rear for the flight through Yellowknife to Resolute. I've never seen so much carry-on luggage before or since.

A woman in front of me shrieked when I went to put my bag in the overhead compartment. "Watch my donuts!" she hollered. She must've been packing six dozen.

I settled in next to Paul Pfau, the last person to join the expedition. A deputy district attorney in Los Angeles, Paul had been climbing mountains for thirty years. He'd led four expeditions to the summit of Mt. Everest. In fact, he was climbing Everest—"gratefully so," he says—when his colleagues stood in the global spotlight prosecuting the O.J. Simpson murder trial.

You meet the strangest people on an Arctic expedition.

Eager to talk, I shared some of my anxieties. I asked Paul how he dealt with fear.

"It'll be good to be home," he responded.

Huh?

He spoke with quiet intensity. I felt like I was listening to Yoda from *Star Wars*. Certain phrases rose to the surface:

The front of the plane held the pallet with dogs and gear.

"Honor the process ... Do your best each day ... Burst your comfort zone ... Value each step ... Make each day's steps better than the steps you took the day before."

He was on a roll, and I listened intently.

"Focus on both the big picture and the small details ... No detail is too small ... Never underestimate what goes on in your head and heart ... Goals are wonderful, but staying alive is the real goal ... On the adventure you'll find yourself getting into a rhythm, but it'll still be nice to be back. It'll be good to be home."

I madly scribbled notes. Maybe somewhere in all this, I might get the answer to why I was obsessed with taking this crazy trip.

"The overall experience of such an expedition keeps feeding you—whether it's good, bad, or in between—until the day you leave this planet," he said. "For me, there's been an ever-changing motive for taking on major challenges. Over the years, this has evolved into the pursuit of intangible, enriching experience."

I kept scribbling, not wanting him to stop. And he kept going, speaking in ornate phrases, as if he'd prepared the talk before we left.

"The act of climbing a difficult mountain results in the convergence of the physical, mental, and spiritual realms," he said. "I expect to experience the same sense of coming together here. I know the Arctic zone is a wonderfully beautiful part of the planet and anticipate that it will yield the kind of enriching experience that's been a life force for me. And I know it will be one of those ever-enriching experiences that will stay with me forever."

Our conversation lasted nearly an hour. In some ways, what Paul said disturbed me. Who were these crazy people? In other ways, I found it fascinating.

I dozed briefly, then was awakened by a flight attendant offering café Franklin—a combination of coffee, brandy, and whipped cream. She said it was named after the "famous polar explorer Sir John Franklin." I flinched. He was "famous" because he DIED. He was killed along with 128 men in the greatest disaster in the history of the North and South Poles.

I mumbled to myself, "I don't want to be *that* famous!'

Three-and-a-half hours later we arrived in Resolute Bay, Nunavut.

A deep penetrating cold blasted us as we left the plane, the temperature standing at minus 5 degrees. With the wind chill, my temperature gadget, a special tool that measured temperature and wind speed, read minus 35 with the wind. It was my first hint of the incredible cold that would envelop us around the clock.

We unloaded the dogs, ran out two lead lines, and clipped the dogs to them. Keeping the dogs separated on the line makes it harder for them to fight each other. Sled dogs constantly test each other for dominance, which means they can break into a fury with no warning.

We trotted into a mechanic's shop to warm up. Inside, Paul discovered that in the chaos of leaving the plane, he had left behind a small pack, one containing maps, contact information, our radio codes, his sextant, and other critical information.

We looked at him with fear in our eyes. This was a huge

Resolute Bay has a population of not quite three hundred, except for the "silly season" when fools like us make attempts at the North Pole or go polar bear hunting.

problem that couldn't easily be solved. The plane with Paul's bag had already departed for its return trip south. It wouldn't return for a week.

Paul seemed to go away for two minutes. He stood next to us physically, but his mind was focused elsewhere. He remained calm, calling on some strength apart from himself. Then, as quickly as it had risen, his wall of isolation fell away.

"Worse things can happen," he said.

Bill Martin offered to check with the tower to see what might be done. Paul nodded, and we slowly left the mechanic's shop, heading for Resolute Bay, where the view is of another world—an utterly stark alien-looking terrain, whiteness cast in a pale blue glow of the endless sunlight of the Arctic spring.

Resolute has a population of not quite three hundred people, most of whom are Inuit. Except for in the summer, snow stays on the ground year-round. There are no trees for lumber, no materials for making concrete or cement blocks—only snow and gravel. Every nail, every piece of gum, and shred of toilet paper has to be shipped here.

To give you some idea of how cold it is, you need a jack-hammer to dig a grave. The permafrost in this part of the world starts at ground level and goes straight down at least two thousand feet. And when a grave needs to be dug, even with a jackhammer, it takes a strong man three days to do it.

Residents live primarily in prefabricated dwellings that look like corrugated metal cylinders and lay sideways and half buried in the snow. Each house typically has a polar bear hide stretched out on a wooden frame to dry or a frozen seal carcass lying in the snow. Or both. Once a day, the woman of the house steps outside bearing an axe. She chops off a piece of seal meat, carries it back inside, and cooks it, usually by frying or boiling it. I'm told seal tastes like fishy beef, but I didn't try it—primarily because of that description.

Dan Leaman, the senior administrative officer of Resolute Bay, has spent the past twenty years putting together a history of the town and surrounding region. He said the Inuit were believed to have come to the Western Hemisphere from Asia, across the frozen Bering Strait between Russia and Alaska, sometime in the 1400s. It's believed they moved east into the Canadian prairies and forests.

The first Inuit in Resolute Bay were imported in 1954 by the Canadian government, during the height of the Cold War. Six years earlier, when the area was deserted, the Canadian and U.S. governments established a joint Arctic weather station here and two years later stationed troops from the Royal Canadian Air Force and U.S. armed forces.

"There was an issue of sovereignty," Dan said. "To establish sovereignty, you need people to live there. And, of course, everyone was afraid the Soviets would invade from the other side of the pole."

The first sixteen Inuit to come to Resolute comprised three families. They were accustomed to living off the land. But the game in northern Quebec and on Baffin Island had dwindled due to a string of hard winters. And the Canadian government painted a picture of good hunting, fishing, and trapping up north.

"It was quite a sales job," Dan said. "The government wanted to establish a civilian work force to support the military presence, both here and on Ellesmere. They enticed the Inuit, and then gave them extremely poor accommodations. The Inuit came to call themselves 'relocatees.' It's one of the sadder chapters in Canadian history.

"Of course, when the Inuit arrived, they saw this place was not the utopia they'd been promised. And they were told that, if they didn't like it here, they could always go back to Quebec and Baffin. But when they asked to go back, the government wanted money to take them. And they had no money. They were stuck."

So they adapted. They learned to hunt polar bear and narwhal. A second group of Inuit arrived a couple years after the first. Their sons and daughters married and had children. Today their grandchildren buzz around on snowmobiles, listen to music on compact discs, and guide wealthy hunters from Germany, Brazil, and the United States on polar bear hunts. Resolute is limited to thirty-seven bear kills a year, some of which the Inuit keep for themselves, some of which they offer to hunters from the outside world. The hunters pay about twenty thousand dollars each for the privilege, which just happens to be what we're paying to travel across the ice.

One of the most bizarre ways that the village makes money is by providing automobile companies with a place to do extended test drives in secret. While we were there, a bright red Audi TT Roadster prototype was driven twenty-four hours a day on the loop from the village to the airport and back in an endurance test. It was strange to see a fancy sports car whizzing around in a flat, Arctic wasteland of ice, and I tried to take a picture, but the driver stopped the car and said it was a new prototype and that photos were not allowed. In retrospect, it appears the Audi team didn't do enough high-speed driving. The model being driven in Resolute would eventually face recalls and lawsuits as a result of handling problems at very high speeds.

By the end of the twentieth century, the Inuit elders worried about the younger generation drifting away from the old culture and speaking English more fluently than the native Inuktituk language. But with the establishment on April 1, 1999, of the Canadian territory of Nunavut—the Inuit word for "our land"—they were hopeful they could begin to control their destiny.

"This is our home now," says David Oingoot, who was a teenager when his parents brought him here to live. "It was hard at first, but we learned. Now we have made this place our own."

We set up our base camp at the South Camp Inn, run by a wily and eminently hospitable Tanzanian ex-patriot named Aziz Kheraj, although everyone called him Ozzie. His wife is an Inuit woman named Aleeasuk Idlout, who is considered the most skilled polar bear hunter in the Great North.

Spring is the time to travel in the Arctic. That's when you have maximum daylight, although it's also when the ice is most active. The locals call the spring the silly season—as in when silly fools from around the world take a crack at the pole. I realized I was one of those silly fools.

Within hours of settling in at our base camp, Craig and I felt panic taking over. The cold was ridiculous. Stepping outside to make a test of the Iridium phone was like walking into a giant freezer. The cold hit my body and face like a wave of water—only this was pure freezing cold air. Soon it submerged me in cold. My fingers turned into fat, frozen sausages as I tried to work with the phone.

On the call home, I did a spin job: Things are great, we're pumped. We're ready. Three Twin Otters will be taking us north soon. What, me worry?

While the rest of the team prepared for the trip the next day, Craig and I took a walk around the village. As we crunched along the road that circles Resolute, the bottom of the sun sat on the horizon. We shuddered as we stared into the distance— a stark, desolate expanse of white, a place like nowhere we'd ever been before.

During our walk, we came upon four children, all with shiny black hair and big brown eyes. Wearing parkas with fur-trimmed hoods and mukluks, they played in temperatures equivalent to minus 35 degrees Fahrenheit, with the wind chill.

I asked to take their photographs, and they posed gleefully, making faces and hamming it up, like kids anywhere might do. One child, a girl about four years old with a runny nose, came along riding a tricycle, pedaling furiously to check out the two strangers.

I asked if she was cold. She shook her head as if she'd never heard a sillier question. Then, having given us the once over, she happily rode off, oblivious to surroundings that were, for us, hard to endure even on our short walk.

The rookie in Resolute. It was cold. But what had I expected?

The kids buoyed our spirits and made the place seem less forbidding, but as we continued our walk, our conversation grew forced. We commented on what we saw but avoided the real subject on our minds: Our anxiety over the all-consuming, inescapable cold.

I did learn, however, that we shared a secret. We'd both felt serious pain during training and had been advised to see a sports medicine specialist. I suffered soreness in my hip, while Craig hurt his knee while running on a patch of ice. In both cases we'd been advised to have surgery, which would have meant canceling the trip.

We'd both found relief from the pain through the same chiropractor, Dr. Eric Eiselt, and we laughed at what a dumb "guy thing" it was to avoid the doctor, putting our bodies at risk.

When we returned to the South Camp Inn, we saw David soaking in the scenery from the windows.

"It's alien out there," he said. "Looks like a completely different planet."

We learned there had been no word on Paul's pack. We had to face the fact that our efforts to recover it probably wouldn't succeed. And I had to find a way to face up to my fears about the trip. My emotions raced up and down like a runaway elevator. All things considered, the mood was somewhat bleak as we passed the time in the icy metropolis of Resolute.

Chapter 4
The Longest Day...Part One
WEDNESDAY, APRIL 14, 1999

I AWOKE TO THE SUN SHINING THROUGH THE WINDOW above Paul Schurke's bed at six in the morning. Beside the bed sat Paul's backpack. I blinked hard, not quite sure what I was seeing.

It was like Christmas morning. How could it be there? Canadian Air flew to Resolute only once a week.

Paul awoke and, seeing my astonishment, said, "Just a wonderful bit of serendipity."

Huh?

The message about the missing pack had been radioed to the plane. The crew gave it to a bush pilot they met in Yellowknife who miraculously was flying to Resolute Bay.

"Incredible!" I said.

"It was an inconvenience," Paul replied. "It's never good to become too tied to your possessions."

The impossible nature of Paul's luck reminded me of something his wife said when I asked if she was ever afraid for him: "Paul has an angel looking out for him. No matter what happens, miracles occur when he's in the Arctic."

I hoped his luck rubbed off on me.

And speaking of rubbing, as I rubbed my fingertips I noticed a tingling sensation—the first sign of frost nip, the result of the short walk I'd taken outside the night before.

The South Camp Inn functions as a launch pad for any crazy attempting to make it to the pole, a simple place with some strange characters—sort of like the cantina scene in *Star Wars*.

British actor Brian Blessed was there with a team attempting to ski to the magnetic North Pole. The magnetic North Pole is the spot where the compass points. It is actually about six hundred miles south of the geographic North Pole, around which the earth rotates. Therefore, while we traveled to the geographic North Pole our compasses pointed south.

Brian had built a successful career playing "big" characters like King Lear, Long John Silver in *Return to Treasure Island*, and the Baron in the stage adaptation of *Chitty Chitty Bang Bang*. With his booming voice and theatrical manner, Brian held court during meals at the South Camp Inn with tales of his three attempts to climb Everest. His reputation as an adventurer was such that Jon Krakauer consulted him while writing *Into Thin Air*.

To the beating reggae rhythm of the CD *Tropical Escapes*, Randy Reid, the cook, served me the biggest breakfast of my life—six eggs, twelve pieces of bacon and sausage, and four pieces of bread. Feeling stuffed, I passed on the fresh oranges.

With a slight Jamaican accent, Randy said, "Hey, mon, don't turn up your nose at these oranges. They're the last you'll see for a while." I grabbed two. It should be noted that Randy isn't actually Jamaican, he's from Detroit, but in the wacky world of the high Arctic, it didn't really matter.

The most unsettling part of breakfast was the stuffed, nine-foot-tall polar bear in the corner of the kitchen. I didn't need the reminder.

As we ate, Paul told everyone to bring some dry socks. "We'll be on the plane for over six hours, your feet will sweat. You don't want to jump on the ice with wet feet."

Craig looked at me and said, "Another detail. What others aren't we aware of?"

"That's half the adventure as a tenderfoot," I said. "Figuring out what the others know that you don't."

Craig loaded a dog onto the plane.

At the airport we started packing everything onto three Twin Otter DHC-6 airplanes, the workhorse of the high Arctic. The Twin Otter has a non-pressurized cabin, a cruising speed of 185 miles per hour, and a range of nine hundred miles. One of its major virtues in this frozen world is that it can land and take off on an extremely short fourteen hundred-foot runway.

The DeHavilland Corporation began producing Twin Otters in 1966, building 844 in all. It's such a reliable plane in cold-weather regions that, today, used Otters sell for up to twenty times their original price.

It was the most expensive flight I'd ever taken—and with the worst service. The flight up to 88 degrees cost Paul Schurke over eighty thousand dollars. The fabulous, bargain-basement price was made possible through free-market bidding between Borak and First Air Service. If you want to go to the pole, you need one of them to take you there.

The cabin of our plane was roughly five feet wide, five feet tall and eighteen feet long. Half of the nineteen seats had been taken out to make room for our gear, sleds, and dogs. Since there was no room for the dogs' portable kennels, they were clipped to the few remaining seats.

A Twin Otter carries a twenty-five-hundred-pound payload, max. The fuel and pilots take approximately nine hundred pounds of that total. Each flight is calculated to the last pound. On a flight from Eureka to the pole, the planes have to refuel at a fuel cache located at 86 degrees north in order to make it the pole and back to the cache. There, they refuel again for the flight to Eureka, where they fuel up yet again for the return to Resolute.

The Aspirations Expedition logos on the team jackets gave me courage.

As we loaded dogs, sleds, and gear onto the planes for our trip to the frozen Arctic Ocean and the trek to the North Pole, the enormity of the challenge ahead hit me full force. It scared me, big time, but I somehow had arrived at a level of acceptance. Or maybe it was resignation. In any case, it was too late now to back out.

While snapping a few pictures on the tarmac at the tiny Resolute Airport, I caught a glimpse of five members of the team, with their backs facing me, dressed in their red expedition anoraks, the five round white Aspirations Expedition logos shining like headlights. The moment reminded me of our goal, and it gave me courage.

Before getting on the plane, I talked with David.

"I don't think you'll need this—but if we need help on the ice, you will," I said, handing him a zip-lock plastic bag containing forty thousand dollars.

"Hey, thanks. If you need me, I'll be in Bermuda," he said. "No, really. What's this?"

"If we need to get out, cash talks," I said. "This should be enough to get one of these Arctic bush pilots to come rescue us."

"I'll put it in the safe deposit box," David said. "No, wait, there aren't any safe deposit boxes. Okay, I'll hide it in my underwear drawer."

"Just keep it in the plastic bag," I pleaded.

With that, we hugged, and I was off to the plane.

As I crawled to my seat, I could see my breath. The vibrations of the engine sent a buzz up through the seat, and I looked down to see a dog poke his head up between my legs. Another dog leaned against me to my right.

The captain welcomed us to First Air.

"There are two exits in the back of the plane, although one is blocked with your gear," he said.

I gave David the bag with forty thousand dollars cash—in case we needed a plane quickly. It turned out to be a good decision to have the cash.

"There are two fire extinguishers in the cabin; however, this is a nonsmoking flight. You'll find survival gear in the tail of the plane with an emergency beacon. I'm sorry to say there will be no food or beverage service on today's flight, but if you have something good, feel free to share with the pilots."

At 9:38 A.M. we took off. David stood on the edge of the runway waving his potholder plunge mitts as we passed over him.

It would be nine hours till we reached our starting point on the ice.

The Roosevelt locked in the ice for the long winter night

The journey already had seemed long, but it was nothing compared to Admiral Peary's. To be in position to attack the pole in the spring, he had to leave New York City with his ship, *The Roosevelt*, the previous July. He spent the summer working the ship past icebergs as far north as possible.

The ship was then set into a cove and frozen into the ice for the long winter night. The ship was custom built with steel crossbeams in the hull to prevent cracking under the pressure of the ice. To prevent his expedition team and Inuit guides from going "crazy" during the endless dark of winter, he kept them busy hunting musk ox, seal, and walrus for food. They also spent the winter preparing clothing and sleds.

My feet chilled from a combination of the plane's cold floor and my legs being folded like a pretzel for hours in a child-size seat. I removed my boots to massage my feet back to warmth. The view was stunning. On the horizon, the blue of the sky faded to pale, presenting the mere hint of a horizon.

Directly beneath us was Ellesmere Island with its mountain ranges and towering cliffs painted with snow. Between the ranges, the snow seemed to have the texture of a flowing river.

Maybe the most precious gift my son had ever given me

Shining seams of glacier blue ice oozed down the mountains like thick glassy veins.

I opened another note from my family, this one from Brad, my eight-year-old. It included a little plastic knight with the words "Here is this knight to save the day." I smiled as I moved the arm that holds the sword up and down.

After four hours, the pilot announced our approach to Eureka, the world's northernmost nonmilitary airstrip, ham radio station, and weather station. It's also the last piece of quasi-civilized hard land before the Arctic Ocean.

We landed in bright sun with a bump, a shimmy, and a skitter.

We woke the dogs and crawled out of the plane. We unloaded the dogs first so they could stretch their legs and relieve themselves. I snapped some photos of the scene for the pilot to take back to Resolute for posting on the Great Aspirations! Web site.

Suddenly I heard a cry for help from Michael Warren, "Doug, Doug, please help. Help!" He was gripping the end of the dog line, and I ran to him and grabbed the end of it. Suddenly, he let go, leaving the line loose for a moment, and the slack line signaled the dogs to run. I was carried away, nearly horizontal, as sixteen dogs yanked at once.

Hearing the barking chaos, Alan and Paul came to my rescue.

After getting the dog line stretched out again and wrapped around some fuel drums, I went back to Michael and asked why he let go.

He pointed to his feet. A perfect streak of yellow smeared his perfectly white Moon Boots. In the chaos of unloading, the dogs had peed on his boots.

My tension from the past few days melted in peals of high-pitched, out-of-control laughter, which, I'm sorry to say, didn't exactly make Michael feel better about the yellow stain he would be living with for the next few weeks.

I returned to shooting photos. At one point I set down my mittens on one of the fuel drums to get a better hold on the digital camera. When I picked them up I realized that the drum had some unfrozen jet fuel on the top. And now my mittens smelled of it.

My first instinct was panic. I'd smell that fuel for weeks. My second was laughter. The absurdity of Mike being worried about the stain or me about the smell became clear at once.

We took off again at 1:20 P.M. As the plane reached cruising altitude, I unfolded an e-mail David had given me that morning. It was from Tom Wilson, the cartoonist who draws Ziggy. As I mentioned earlier, his readers would be following our adventures in the comic strip, and so we named our sleds "Ziggy" and "Fuzz." We planned to race them to the pole, adding a bit of fun for readers following the trip on the Web site.

In the comic strip, Ziggy was taking a snowman to the North Pole so he wouldn't melt.

Tom's e-mail to the team read, "God speed, O intrepid explorers. I've given Zig and Fuzz strict instructions to look after you and to bring you all home safely. I'm proud to know you. Have an ICE trip."

Tom's note drove home the odd, somewhat twisted nature

of our endeavor. Here I was in the company of seasoned, hard-core explorers, traveling to the top of the earth, the entire time orchestrating a global P.T. Barnum-style publicity stunt.

For the first time in weeks, I felt myself starting to relax. The laughter from the yellow boots, my own mishap, and Tom Wilson's note combined to anchor me in the reality of the situation. I believed for the first time that things would be all right, that somehow, I would survive the ordeal ahead.

We chose to begin our adventure at 88 degrees because the controversial part of Admiral Peary's 1909 trip to the North Pole began at that latitude. Peary started his quest with twenty-four men, nineteen sleds, and 130 dogs. He used a leapfrog approach, having five separate teams take turns breaking trails, building igloos, and leaving caches of food and fuel for the teams following behind. That approach is used in the Tour de France, when a teammate rides in front of the team captain, allowing the latter to draft, helping him conserve energy for the race to the end.

NASA uses this approach when sending rockets into space, with the first and second stages sacrificing themselves to propel the capsule into the great beyond.

Explorers use it to climb Everest and other great mountains. Teams establish a series of base camps, relaying gear up the mountain in preparation for the final assault.

Paul once told me that virtually all explorers owe a debt to Peary because he was the first to use relays to achieve a goal.

Through my window as the Twin Otter made its way north, I gazed at ice, ice, and more ice. Huge pressure ridges and icebergs formed what looked like steppingstones from the air. The view was hypnotic, an endless pale patchwork of hues and tones ranging from bright Caribbean blue to the whitest of whites. It was at once perfectly beautiful and totally fearsome to behold.

The earlier laughter about Michael's boots and at my own near panic about the fuel-soaked gloves continued to relax me. I pulled a pack from the stack of gear, leaned my head on it, and settled in for a midafternoon nap.

Chapter 5
The Longest Day...Part Two

WEDNESDAY, APRIL 14, 1999

A BUMP JOLTED ME FROM SLEEP. After several groggy moments, I remembered where I was and what I was doing. Outside the window, the view looked different from before I fell asleep. Where the ice near the shore had been cragged in ridges, now it looked like old linoleum—a sheet of white riddled with cracks.

My weather gauge indicated no wind in the plane and a temperature of 77 degrees. I held my Global Positioning Satellite (GPS) device beside the window and saw that we were flying at 146 miles per hour at an altitude of 10,600 feet. It located us 370 miles from the North Pole—or 3,153 miles from the spring warmth of my home in Cincinnati. The time was 4:43

Left to right: Corky, Randy, Doug, Celia, Paul P., and David G.

P.M. Eastern Standard Time. It also indicated that there was no sunrise or sunset here. In this part of the world, spring is a time of constant daylight.

I'd slept for ninety minutes. I scribbled some notes in a special journal I'd purchased for this trip, one with coated paper that would be waterproof. I'd also packed lead pencils, which, unlike ink pens, wouldn't freeze in the Arctic.

I amused myself by using my GPS to track our progress. Peary, however, had to use a sextant to measure the altitude of the sun, then do a series of calculations and look up data in a set of charts to determine his location.

At 87 degrees, or 207 miles from the pole, our pilots began looking for a place to land. Putting a plane down on this terrain is a gamble, one that requires a good deal of experience and a pinch of luck. Planes have been known to break through the ice on landings—not often, but it has happened. Landing on the ice can be quite jarring even when everything goes well.

The mood in the plane tensed. Celia tried to take the edge off the moment with a joke. "Attach your static lines," she hollered.

Everyone chuckled, but the cloud of nervous anticipation still hung over us.

I pulled on my boots and my jacket.

If the ice was too rough and the pilots couldn't find what looked like a safe landing spot, they would fly back to Eureka. And that would be that for the Aspirations Expedition.

Our plane banked to the left to give our pilot a better view. Our copilot chewed his fingernails—not an encouraging gesture for the team. The radio crackled between the three planes, and though I couldn't make out the words, I could hear the tension in their voices. I could feel it building in my body. Taking my pulse, I noted my heart pounded at 150 beats per minute.

At 6:40 P.M., my GPS put us at eight hundred feet. The pilots still searched for a suitable landing spot. Three minutes later, both pilot and copilot stretched to look at a spot below and to the left, where one of the other planes attempted to land. Success!

At 6:42 P.M., our plane sliced a stomach-jarring turn to the right. The pilot told us to hold on tight.

Another minute and still more turning, more banking to the left and then the right so both pilot and copilot could look.

Two more minutes, the tension squeezing us. Both the pilot and copilot craned to look out the left window to watch one of the other planes try to land.

A visible sigh of relief from both pilots—one plane down safely.

At 6:46 P.M. the GPS read three hundred feet. We jerked sharply to the right, heaving people and gear to one side.

Another minute passed. Then the pilot shouted, "Here we go. Hold on tight, it looks very, very bumpy."

As the plane skimmed a few dozen feet over the ice pack, what had looked relatively smooth from the air looked rough and ragged as it flew past the window.

The plane bounced once, twice, three times as its landing skis kissed the ice. Then it settled into a continuous bouncing and bucking rhythm. My GPS read 6:48 P.M. and thirteen feet above seat level—the theoretical distance from my seat in the plane, through the ice below to the surface of the ocean below.

As soon as the plane skidded to a stop, we jumped up to unload.

"Quickly!" Paul shouted. "We've got twenty minutes. Anything not off in twenty minutes goes back to Resolute."

The pilots kept the engines running. If they shut them off at 25 below zero, they might not get them started again. And there's no AC power available for a jump-start.

It had taken an hour to pack the plane. Even broken down, each sled had to be lifted at just the right angle to get through the cargo door. Each dog had to be lifted down and attached to the lead line.

In addition to helping haul our gear off the planes, I was charged with testing our Iridium satellite phone. At the time of our expedition, Iridium technology was state of the art in communicating from anywhere on earth. It's made possible by a global network of low-orbiting satellites—like a cell phone on steroids. But it had not been tested in the high Arctic. My first priority was to confirm the phone worked in this forsaken place. If it didn't work, I would send it back to Resolute on the plane. If

The Iridium phone and waterproof case

it worked, I would return one of our two radios, keeping one for a backup.

Radio communication is highly dependent on atmospheric conditions and works best for short messages and emergencies. I set up the phone with speed dials, intending to call my wife's cell phone. She would relay the message to Kari, who would post a notice on the Aspirations Web site that we had landed safely.

On the plane, I had done my best to script a poetic, Neil Armstrong-like message. I settled on, *"Aspirations Expedition has landed—with faith and optimism, we seek our dreams."*

I turned on the phone and tried pushing the buttons through my gloves. No luck.

Paul shouted, "Does that phone work or not? The pilots have to get moving!"

I pulled off my right glove and, with my bare hand at 25 below zero, I pushed the buttons to call Debbie's cell phone, rehearsing my message again as I dialed.

The phone rang once, twice, three times.

"Hello," Debbie answered.

"Hi, Deb. It's me."

"Hi—hold on a minute."

Hold on? I'm calling from the other side of nowhere, and she tells me to hold on?

I was spending five dollars a minute on the first telephone call from the high Arctic, and my wife *puts me on hold!*

The site of the first phone call from the high Arctic.

To be fair, at the moment I called, our son Brad was going up to bat in a baseball game and our dog Missy had just eaten a child's sandwich—plastic bag and all. With Brad yelling, "Hey, Mom, watch!" and the kid who lost his sandwich crying, Deb couldn't focus on the call.

Given who was put on hold, I knew my status in the family. In the stir, my Neil Armstrong-like message faded away.

When Debbie came back to the phone I hurriedly reported that we were safe on the ice.

"I gotta go," I said. "The planes have to take off, and I need to load the spare radio on the plane. I love you."

"I love you, too," Deb said, sensing my urgency. "Brad just got a walk. I'll tell Kari you're down. I love you so much. I'll send messages to your pager. Please be safe."

That was the content of the first phone call ever made from the high Arctic.

I put the phone aside and placed a waterproof case containing one of the radios back on the plane.

Then I joined the team to watch the planes depart. The planes bumped up into the air and banked to the south. We

The planes took off and it got very, very quiet and cold.

watched until they were specks on the horizon.

Then we fell silent. Very silent.

I turned to take in the scenery. All I could see in any direction was white ice, a pale blue sky, and a white sun. It was like an OmniMax theater times two.

As I came down from the adrenaline rush of landing and getting the gear off the planes, the cold hit me like a fist. Though the glare of sun on ice was bright and white, the cold cut through everything. It was very, very cold—a new definition of cold. So cold there should be a different name for it. "Cold" didn't begin to express this feeling. A cold that could throw you on your back and step on you. Hard. My temperature gadget read minus 54 degrees with the wind chill. The top of my mouth felt like it was flash freezing with each breath.

"Welcome to the big time," Bill Martin said, putting a hand on my shoulder.

Sure enough, I was sixteen hundred miles north of the northernmost hunk of Alaska.

I was standing on the Arctic Ocean.

There was no turning back. There would be no shortcuts. The only option: go forward.

I was reminded of the Norwegian explorer Fridtjof Nasen, who would destroy the snow bridges as he crossed Greenland to discourage himself from turning back.

The contrast between hearing Debbie's voice and the obscene glare of white and relentless cold brought to mind what the admiral wrote as his ship left civilization.

> Behind me now lay everything that was mine, every-thing that a man personally loves, family, friends, home, and all those human associations which linked me with my kind. Ahead of me lay—my dream, my destiny, the goal of that irresistible impulsion which had driven me for twenty-three years to hurl myself, time after time, against the frigid Great North.

I had to get moving to generate some heat. Fortunately, we had much to do. Our gear lay in a tangled heap. The dogs were tethered to two long lead lines. The tents had to be set up, the sleds assembled, the gear organized.

My teammates would stay in three of what Paul referred to as Himalayan Hotels. Craig and I would stay in the cook tent, the one Paul called the Siberian Chalet. Fancy names for Spartan accommodations.

The Siberian Chalet cook tent is a novel contraption inspired by a Russian design Paul discovered when traveling over the Bering Strait from Russia.

First, we shoveled out a hole about twelve feet in diameter for the center of the tent, leaving benches around the edges for seating and to support the cook stoves. Then we set up cross-country skis around the perimeter, sort of like teepee poles, and placed on them a circular metal frame set, creating a frame-work. Next, we stretched a black nylon parachute-like cloth over the framework. Finally, we packed snow high around the outside of the shelter to hold the cloth in place.

Set properly, it became a modern igloo, with the entrance slightly below the surface of the snow to keep out the wind. We piled the snow from the hole behind the stoves, leaving plenty to melt into drinking water.

When the planes left, this was the chaotic scene on the Arctic ice.

After we set up our cooking facility, Craig began firing up the Coleman stoves—not a simple matter. In ultra-cold conditions, the white gas used to fuel our stoves was quite temperamental, and the stoves were old and trail-battered, monuments to Paul's frugal nature. They required repeated efforts to get them to ignite.

When the stoves finally lit, I shoveled snow into the pots to make water. With the kettle on, I slipped out of the tent to check the progress with sled assembly.

We had four dogsleds—two ten-footers and a pair of five-foot mini-sleds. Paul's plan called for each team of nine dogs to pull a large and small sled. By dividing the load between two sleds, we could more easily manhandle them up and over pressure ridges—huge walls created when vast pans of ice push against one another, creating walls of fractured ice that rises up twenty feet or more. Instead of having to push a thousand pounds over the ridges, we would push six hundred pounds in the first sled up to the top of the ridge, and then the weight of the first sled going down the ridge would help pull the four hundred-pound second sled over the ridge.

Unlike a product made from a special mold that could break and be useless, these homemade sleds were bolted together. When a strut or brace broke, Paul simply cut another piece and rebuilt it. We'd learned how the sleds went together when we took them apart in Edmonton to pack for the trip. But in the frigid temperature, assembly took much longer. A dropped bolt or nut became a major challenge.

David Golibersuch stood next to the second sled to be assembled. He stared off into the distance as if in a daze.

"Are you okay?" I asked.

"Just a little cold," he said. "Having trouble feeling my hands and feet."

"You'd better get moving. Go for a run or do that thing Matthew Henson advised in his book on the Peary trips, where you wave your arms like a windmill."

With that, David went off for a jog, his arms waving around. It was quite a sight. I helped for a short while with the sleds, and then returned to boiling snow.

We talked about naming each of our camps. I suggested we give each night's camp a name; otherwise, they would simply be recorded by date, longitude, and latitude. We settled on a name for tonight's temporary settlement: "Camp Serendipity," in recognition of Paul's good fortune in getting his bag back from the plane.

English author Horace Walpole is credited with coining the word, "serendipity." He defined it as an unexpected and accidental discovery of something positive that no one had looked for. The return of Paul's pack fit the bill. We'd lost hope of getting it back. Its return was an unexpected blessing.

Given the runaway flood of emotions that I'd been experiencing, I was all in favor of being peppered with serendipities.

Around 9:00 P.M. Eastern Standard Time, I prepared to make my first call to the Aspirations! Expedition phone center. The

plan called for me to contact them each evening around that time, using a phone bridge established by one of our sponsors, Quest Communications.

The conversation mostly would be between David in Resolute Bay and myself. Whatever had happened on the trail that day, I'd pass along to him, and he would translate my gabbing into a daily North Pole Telegram for the Aspirations Web site and into a newspaper article for the Scripps Howard News Service and the Universal Press Syndicate.

Kari McNamara at the Eureka! Ranch in Cincinnati took part in case we needed help with technical support issues, as did Jon Paul Buchmeyer in New York City to discuss media interviews and publicity strategies.

Finally, my wife and kids could listen to the calls, as could my parents in Florida. At the time, my mother was undergoing aggressive treatment for cancer. I had offered to cancel the trip, but she insisted that I go. My mom was a teacher for many years and supported the Great Aspirations! program.

I dialed my first call. It was immediately disconnected.

My second call connected but only momentarily. I sputtered just a few words—"It's cold. I'm cold. It's very cold."—before the phone disconnected.

I dialed again and again. Each time my concern increased. I'd put the spare radio on the plane because I had judged that the phone would work. But now it wasn't working well at all. I wondered if I'd made a major rookie mistake.

I also laughed, imagining what David must be thinking. If I couldn't get through, he'd be stuck trying to extract a North Pole Telegraph from, "It's cold. I'm cold. It's very cold."

I dialed once again.

This time, the connection stayed solid. While the connection lasted, I felt like I was talking to my echo. The words moved slowly.

When I listened to the recordings later, I realized I was the one who was slow. My mind was not working at full speed. At one point, I explained how I had been talking to Debbie at Brad's baseball game. David asked me the name of Brad's team.

I hesitated, and then Kari said, "The Ravens."

Too late, I tried to cut her off. "Wait, I know, don't tell me," I said, after she had said the name not once but twice. "The Ravens, that's their name," I finally said.

David asked me to describe the scene. My response: "What people anticipate the cold will be like, they're right. But there is no way you can understand how incredibly beautiful the colors are. The whites and blues are spectacular."

David asked, "How is the team holding up?"

"The shift in temperature is severe," I said. "It's a shock. Alan said the other option he had was a Caribbean vacation. He's wondering if he made the right choice. We're all joking about the other warm places we could be instead of here in the middle of the Arctic Ocean."

I handed the phone to Paul for a more complete description of the terrain.

"As we left Eureka, there was lots of open water," he said. "As we headed north, there were fewer leads or open cracks in the ocean. It looks beautiful. We're in an area of older pressure ridges with smaller pans of ice about a quarter mile across, surrounded by hedgerows of six- to eight-foot pressure ridges. To the north as we landed, I could see some fresh sea ice. When we get to it, we'll find out if it's strong enough to travel on.

"It's nicely cold, which is good as it keeps the ice solid. If the wind came up a bit, it would be pretty ugly. As it is, the fresh sea ice will be as smooth as a skating rink. But that may or may not be safe. If we can go on them, that's the gravy train."

David asked again about the team.

"It'll take a few days to acclimatize," Paul said. "It's gone surprisingly smooth to this point. We didn't have a single poop on the plane. That's a record."

I took the phone back and worked through details with the public relations team in New York City. Karen from Jon Paul's office reported that the Associated Press, New York *Newsday*,

North Pole

Bistro

Best "glop" at the top of the world!

Quite possibly the first time an expedition had its cooking "branded."

and the *Chicago Tribune* had picked up the story and were directing parents and kids to the Web site.

When the call ended, it was time for dinner. The human body readily adapts to conditions. Cold stimulates the appetite, and increased food intake sparks a higher metabolic rate and thus increases heat production. The Inuit have so adapted to the cold that researchers have found that their natural metabolic rate is some 25 percent faster than people in warmer climates.

The menu at the "North Pole Bistro," as I branded our cook tent, was a gourmet feast of what we lovingly called *glop*. Each recipe began the same but ended differently. A pound of butter was tossed into a pot of boiling water. The high Arctic is the one place where a high-calorie diet is a good thing, and nothing has more calories per ounce than fat.

Fat-based flavors created gourmet glop.

Craig tossed in some precut beef along with egg noodles. Voila! Pasta glop.

On this expedition, we lived gourmet. Some friends at Wild Flavors in Hebron, Kentucky, had created a set of special flavorings for us to take on the trip. By and large, commercial flavorings are concentrated then dried. For us, Wild Flavors spray-dried flavors onto pure, unadulterated fat, resulting in flavors with a real kick—more flavor and more calories!

We've given each of the flavorings a name and label for each person. Tonight's dinner: Paul's Polar Perfect Lasagna!

Flavor aside, the absolute best part of every dinner was the *heat*!

The team gathered in the cook tent, bringing their foam sleeping pads as seats. During dinner, the discussion inevitably gravitated to a single topic: The cold. As we sat in our circle, we took turns expressing how !@#$% cold we were.

Craig called it "a beautiful hell."

Our co-leaders made lame attempts to comfort us.

"It'll get better," Bill said. "You just have to give it time."

"It'll take time for your body to adapt to the cold," Paul said. "Soon you'll barely feel it."

Say what?

Ceila's response echoed my thoughts: "I really believe it'll get better," she said. "I really want to believe."

Alan was more honest: "I have no idea how I'm going to survive for two weeks or more."

After dinner, as we focused on building the sleds, Craig got hit by Tornarsuk, the Arctic Fear Dragon. While squatting at the cook stove, he had partially cut off the circulation to his legs.

His face paled white with fear, and his shoulders hunched like a turtle's shell. His arms curled around his body in an attempt to hug warmth into himself.

"Are you cold?" he asked me.

"Of course I'm cold. It's minus 54!"

"I can barely feel my feet. I don't know if I can do this. This is crazy."

I knew what he was feeling. I'd felt it in Edmonton. A total sense of hopelessness, a feeling of panic tinged with temporary insanity. I could see in his eyes the feelings I'd felt. I knew, too, that he was projecting himself into the future, asking himself all the "what if" questions: What if I can't carry my weight? What if I turn out to be the weak link?

Earlier, Craig told me he wanted to be seen as a leader on the trip. He wanted to perform at a high level and not have to be "dragged" to the pole. My anxieties were different. I was concerned about letting down what I hoped would be millions of children and parents who would be following the trip.

I worked to jolt him out of his dark mood. With great animation, I declared, "You're not blaming me for selling you on this trip, are you? It was your choice. And don't forget you're paying big money for the pleasure of standing here on the ice, freezing your butt off, eating fatty food. What a deal!"

He grinned a bit, and I suggested we go for a run to generate some heat. We ran a half-mile or so down the ice. The neighborhood was pretty boring—ice upon ice. The running got our blood circulating, slowly but surely stoking Craig's feet with warmth. By the time we returned to camp, he had slain the Fear Dragon, at least for the moment. And I had learned a bit more about my own reaction to the cold.

During this time, the rest of the team put together the sleds. Assembly was a painful process. Struts and boards that normally fit easily required extra effort to fit in the ultra-cold. Screwing nuts to bolts was especially painful. To hold the nuts we had to take off our mittens and use only our thin nylon liner glove. The nuts were so cold they burned through the nylon like a spark from a campfire—a burn in the form of a frigid cold like nothing we'd ever felt before.

After hours of work, I looked at my watch and was surprised to see that it was 1:00 A.M. The time caught me by surprise, not because we were having fun, but because the sun looked the same as when we landed four hours earlier.

By 1:45 A.M., the sleds were assembled.

We stepped back and studied our handiwork. Paul reverted to his Zen master self. "It's Earth at its utter innocence," he said, reflecting on the vast landscape around us.

My first thought was that it looked like hell frozen over. I kept that thought to myself.

Out of the wind, my temperature gadget now read 25 below. My teeth chattered.

Turning to the cook tent, Craig and I prepared our sleep systems and went for another quick run to warm our bodies before slipping into the non-comfort of a minus-25 degree cocoon of a sleeping bag, which felt like slipping into a giant icicle.

I climbed into my bag and shook my legs and arms as quickly as I could, not because I was shivering, but because I was trying to avoid the cold.

After about ten minutes, I checked myself. My toes and arms felt cool but not frigid. Five more minutes of the horizontal rumba, and I had heated up the bag to the point where I could sleep with a modicum of comfort.

I pulled my knit cap over my eyes to block out the sunlight coming through the tent walls. Having been up for about twenty hours, I was relieved to see that long day finally come to an end.

Sometime that night, a message came through on my pager:

Thanks for making me first!
Glad you're down safe. Hope
you're warm enough. Enjoy
your glop. Ravens win 9-0.
Have fun and 'Godspeed,
Doug Hall.' Luv Deb. 4/15.

www.Aspirations.com
has audio from this day's phone call

Chapter 6
And We're Off!

THURSDAY, APRIL 15, 1999
Distance to travel to the North Pole: 200 Miles
Temperature: -15 F

...THANKS TO EL NIÑO... YOU'VE BEEN AROUND A LOT LONGER THAN YOU SHOULD'VE, BUT NOW MIGHT BE A GOOD TIME TO TAKE YOUR VACATION!!

Follow Ziggy LIVE on his Great Aspirations trip to the North Pole at www.ASPIRATIONS.com!

*A*ROUND 8:00 A.M., I woke up disoriented, my legs and torso wrapped in the sleeping bag like a mummy. My hat covered my eyes, and when I reached to pull it off, I bathed my face and neck in a cascade of snow and ice. *What the!?!?*

In the super-cold, my breath had frozen into a lace-like object of art across the small opening in the top of the sleeping bag. My movement shattered the ice, delivering a sting of frigid cold before I was even fully awake.

Craig was working the stoves, beating them into submission, coaxing them to start.

With as cheery a tone as possible, I said, "Good morning, Craig." He didn't respond so I said it again.

"Morning," he said. "How'd you sleep? Were you cold?"

In truth, I'd slept well. After my little sleeping bag dance, I was actually quite warm inside my Wiggies ultra-thick, double-layer, ground pad sleeping system. I toned it down a bit, guessing that Craig had not had a good night

"Not bad," I said. "It's going to take some time to get used to this. Maybe by the time we leave I'll have it down pat."

Craig didn't seem to hear me, focusing instead on the stove, pounding it and mumbling in frustration. Exasperated, he poured fuel into the center ring of the burner and lit it.

A two-foot flame shot up next to my nylon sleeping bag inside our parachute-covered tent frame. I scrambled out of my sleeping bag, worried he might set the whole place on fire.

But his pyro approach worked. It warmed the burner, allowing the fuel to vaporize into a super-hot blue flame.

I got ready to do my duty as chief water cooker. As with all great culinary endeavors, the key to cooking water is to use the finest ingredients. In the case of the high Arctic, this means gathering clean, fresh ice and snow that contains no salt

One stove for cooking food, one stove for melting snow and ice into water

and no hint of the color yellow. You also have to be careful with your utensils. In the gourmet kitchens, the chef's knife is indispensable. In the Arctic, the tool of choice is the shovel. But here again, one must be mindful of where the shovel has been—careful not to choose one that has been used to clear dog droppings.

It's often said that a watched pot never boils. But given that twelve inches of snow melts down to an inch of water, the process of cooking water requires constant vigilance. Every three to five minutes, another shovel full of snow must be added to the pot.

Around 9:30 A.M., the team started wandering into the cook tent. The two questions of the morning are repeated with each new person: "How did you sleep?" and "Were you cold?"

The answers are fairly consistent: "I slept horribly," and "I was freezing." Again, having slept well and warm, I said nothing. Then again, I might actually have been cold and not known it. I'd slept so little in the past week, I was totally exhausted.

Craig made breakfast, an Arctic version of a Western omelet—rehydrated eggs, mixed with meat and potatoes. He didn't attempt a pretty fold, but no one complained.

During breakfast, Paul seemed distracted—more than his normal absentminded self.

After breakfast, we packed up to begin our journey. Around 11:00 A.M., three pagers rang. At this point, the hardened Arctic explorer lost it. Paul had put up with having his polar jacket adorned like a NASCAR driver with corporate sponsor patches, not to mention having his sleds

I might have gone a bit overboard with logos.

decorated with the Ziggy and Fuzz comic strip characters. But the Iridium pagers I'd given everyone were the last straw.

Paul called everyone for a meeting.

"I'm all for technology," he said in a serious tone, "but we've got to do something about these #$*@ pagers. I woke up three times last night with pagers going off. We're here to get away from all that, and having pagers beep is wrong, very wrong."

As he ranted, a pager suddenly erupted into beep, beep, beep.

We all laughed, breaking the tension.

Paul sensed a lack of support. For all of us, our pagers supplied a tremendous source of encouragement and connection to our lives back home.

Paul then said, "Can we at least turn them off at night?"

Someone suggested we switch them to "silent" at night, which seemed like a reasonable idea. Everyone nodded, though Paul clearly felt that his escape to nowhere was being poisoned by civilization.

"So we agree about this?" he asked.

Paul gave a lecture about pagers.

With assorted grunts of agreement, the team went back to packing.

About fifteen minutes later I asked Paul if he'd checked his pager.

"No" he said, and pulled it from his pocket and paused.

Unlike us city folk, who relied on electronic connection as a daily lifeline, Paul lived unplugged at the end of a dirt road in Ely, Minnesota.

I took his pager and showed him how to check for messages. He had four.

As he read them I sensed a softening in the hardened Arctic explorer. His disdain for the electronics melted as he got hugs and kisses from his wife, Sue, and he learned that his daughter Bria had received all As on her report card.

By noon, the dogs were harnessed and the sleds loaded and ready. Before heading off, Paul gave us a quick lecture about how long it had taken us to break camp.

"We'll never make it to the pole leaving at noon every day," he said. "We've got to be better about getting started."

I felt pangs of guilt. I'd been slow in packing. Then I remembered that in the book about a previous Schurke polar expedition, *To the Poles by Dogsled and Ski*, by Joseph Murphy, the exact same scene occurred the first morning.

> We did not get off until late, far too late if we were to reach the pole in time. Schurke was disappointed in our slowness, saying we had to move out more quickly in the future, or we would never make it.

Corky, David, and Paul Schurke took off on skis first. Then Craig and Randy started their dog team with Bill and Paul Phau on the mini-sled behind them. Alan and I manned the second team, with Mike and Celia towed behind us on our mini-sled.

The start was fast and furious. We crossed a flat pan of fresh, smooth ice, and the dogs were full of energy. I thought, **HEY, THIS IS PRETTY EASY.** Alan and I stood on the sled's back runners, enjoying the view as we flew across a smooth surface.

The dogs took off at the start.

Our exhilaration didn't last long. After a quarter mile, we hit a stretch of older ice that looked like an earthquake scene—ruptures of ice sheets scattered as far as we could see.

I quickly learned that Alan and I had no control over the sled. A smooth ride quickly became an out-of-control freight train. The dog team ahead of us slowed, but our team sped along, our dogs passing the first team to the right, seeking the lead.

Actually it wasn't the lead they wanted; they wanted to play. Or maybe they wanted to fight with the team ahead of them. Craig hollered out, fearing a massive dogfight, followed by a massive crash once the teams were side by side.

Alan and I hit our sled's foot brake as hard as possible, to no effect. As our dogs passed, Craig grabbed a collar and tried to divert them by running them to the right, away from his team. I jumped from my sled and scampered up front to help him, my boots flopping and jacket flapping.

It felt like I was in a scene from an old Western movie, trying to chase down a stagecoach, except I didn't have a horse.

Dogs barked and humans yelled. Craig stumbled trying to keep up with the dogs while I slowly lost ground. Finally the combination of the rougher terrain, Alan's braking, and Craig's

The dogs lived to pull.

hold on our lead dogs brought the run to an end without a serious crash.

Craig had every right to be angry. Alan and I had lost control of our sled. Instead, with a big bright smile, Craig said, "Welcome to the Arctic."

I mumbled an apology and told him it wouldn't happen again. I grabbed the collar of Narpa, our lead dog, and waited as Craig returned to his team. This time, Alan and I made sure to leave a healthy distance between our teams.

Our progress slowed as we bumped and skittered through the ruptured ice field.

As Alan shouted "Gee" for the dogs to go right and "Haw" for left, I became the runner, sprinting ahead when the dogs headed off course or running in front when it looked like a fight might break out between them.

I probably didn't have to run in front of or next to the dogs as often as I did, but when I ran, I felt warm. When I stopped running, I'd feel great. Then the "blob," as I called the cold, would slowly engulf my arms, legs, head, and torso. From all directions the blob chilled my entire body, leaving me no choice but to get off the sled and run hard to stoke the fires of my internal heat engine.

The dogs seemed to know the value of movement as a source of heat, too. They pulled tirelessly. Out of respect for them, I would like to include their names here.

Pulling my sled were Palasi, Rock, Carhart, Giggle, Ellesmere, Baffin, Makwa, and my lead dog, Narpa. Ellesmere and Baffin were brothers from the same litter and would run only when harnessed side by side.

The dogs pulling the other sled were Atti, Dusty, Otis, Beaufort, Sydney, Mawson, Lumi, and in the lead, Slava.

Five years earlier, on a winter survival trek in northern Minnesota, Paul's sled dogs had included Mawson, as well as Ellesmere and Baffin. Mawson had been a junior dog then, but now he was one of the top dogs in the pecking order.

The Inuit dog is considered the Sherman tank of the mushing world. The dogs developed within the Arctic cultures that employed them as draft animals. They can pull twice their weight. However, the more weight they pull, the more energy they use. If you push them too hard, they are known to go on a work stoppage and just stop running. It's called "dog burnout," and at that point the trip is over.

The dogs can pull our sled loads for weeks on end. However, adding the weight of one to four humans can create serious overload, which is why we're supposed to run behind or beside the sleds, riding them only when we're on smooth, new ice. But running in big moon boots while wearing winter gear grows very tiring very quickly, and there were times when some of us rode the sleds to grab a rest. The issue would cause a ruckus later in the trip.

Canadian Inuit dogs were clearly the mainstay of Arctic transport for thousands of years. But when the snowmobiling frenzy swept the Arctic in the late 1960s, the dogs fell into disuse and the breed all but disappeared. In recent years, however, it's making a comeback in Greenland and the eastern Arctic as villagers have taken a renewed interest in this central element of their cultural heritage.

These dogs live to pull. Their pulling instinct is so strong

I couldn't imagine a trip like this without dogs.

that they need little training. Young dogs are first harnessed at about eight months of age. Each one is with a seasoned veteran for training, but within minutes, they dig their paws in and their line goes taut as their pulling instinct clicks on like a light.

There are three "roles" on a dog team.

The two dogs closest to the sled are called the wheel dogs and are the strongest. They take the brunt of the force when the sled turns.

In front of the wheel dogs are two to five swing dogs. They form the core of the "pack" and are neither the strongest nor the smartest.

The lead dogs run at the front and are the smartest. These dogs can follow voice commands, set the pace for the team, and pick the best path.

The lead dogs are usually female.

I don't believe it's because females are naturally smarter than males.

That's not it at all.

Putting the females in front gives the male dogs something to chase.

Because of their strength and ability to thrive in extreme conditions, Canadian Inuit dogs were selected to power the first expeditions to reach the North Pole (Robert Peary in 1909) and the South Pole (Roald Amundson in 1911).

Like their cousins, the Arctic wolves, they have extremely strong pack instincts, and the pack hierarchy is always changing. Many of them will not run together without fighting for dominance. Think of the dogs like a group of teenage brothers and sisters and you get the idea. The mood swings are just as huge, as are the attitude problems.

I quickly learned that I didn't understand them. When a dog fought with his partner, I moved them around in the team until by trial and error I found a peaceful arrangement.

The dogs fight with each other but rarely with humans. They're very friendly and easygoing as long as they understand that you're the lead dog of the pack. If you show weakness, they will take advantage by tangling their lines, not running hard, and being generally disrespectful.

Their thick double coats and toughness allow them to thrive in extreme conditions. In fact, they pull harder in colder weather. They're accustomed to eating snow for moisture and, when night comes, they curl into a ball, wrap their tails over their nose, settle into the snow, and sleep soundly. They all pop up with the slightest hint around camp that sleds are being loaded, anxiously pawing the air as if seeking to be the first to be harnessed

The Norwegian explorer Sverdrup is thought to be the first European explorer to understand dogs. His view was that explorers were most effective when they viewed the dogs as equals. He found that Inuit dogs were least responsive when treated as a beast of burden.

The beauty of the place overwhelmed me. Where the jungle provides a patchwork of thousands of greens and the desert its varied brown tones, the high Arctic provides an infinite variety of whites and blues.

As the sleds made their way across the ice I was on fire. The excitement of actually traveling as Peary did came full force to my mind. He loved the Arctic.

> The lure of the North! It is a strange and powerful thing. More than once I have come back from the great frozen spaces, battered and worn and baffled, sometimes maimed, telling myself that I had made my last journey thither, eager for the society of my kind, the comforts of civilization and the peace and serenity of home. But somehow, it was never many months before the old restless feeling came over me. I began to long for the great white desolation, the battles with the ice and the gales, the long, long Arctic night, the long, long, Arctic day, the handful of odd but faithful Inuits who had been my friends for years, the silence and vastness of the great, white lonely North. And back I went accordingly, time after time, until, at last, my dream of many years came true.

I became engrossed with the excitement of being on a real expedition, living in a world I'd only imagined, where everything is possible.

I took off my outer jacket, then my heavy fleece, then my lighter fleece. Though it was 15 degrees below zero, I felt warm

I was so warm from running that I started dropping layers.

from running and from exhilaration, living the motivational slogan "heat comes from within."

We crossed a half dozen one- or two-foot pressure ridges, just speed bumps, really. The dogs scrambled over the top, I ran to the front, grabbed the sled and popped the sled nose over the ridge, letting it crash down the other side.

I felt incredible.

Time stood still.

We passed beautiful ice sculptures that seemed to have been carved by an artist. We saw frost ferns, created from a single salt crystal, looking like tiny fir trees, one to two inches in height, sparkling like Christmas tinsel.

The bright sun and clear sky fueled my energy, but in time, I started to feel a chill and my strength faded. I pulled on a light fleece to shake off the cold.

We traveled slowly, more because of our inexperience than the conditions. We floundered like so many stooges on the ice—dogs running up the backs of others and lines getting tangled as the dogs sorted out their leadership issues. Mostly, we stopped to adjust our clothing as one team member would grow either too hot or too cold.

Craig and Randy climbed over a pressure ridge with skis on.

About five in the afternoon, we stopped for a rest. I reached inside my pack and dug out my GPS. In our first run with the sleds on the Arctic ice, we had traveled about six miles in five hours, about 1.2 miles per hour.

A baby crawls faster.

Craig walked up beside me to check the distance. His attitude had changed. No longer filled with despair, he was positively cheery. "Isn't this incredible?" he said.

"Awesome," I replied.

"It's great to be moving," he said. "When we're moving, I go into a zone. I feel like I could travel all day."

I agreed. After months of preparation, it felt good to be moving forward.

Then he offered a little confession. "Last night I almost didn't go to sleep," he said. "I was worried about my feet freezing while I slept."

"You did seem a little crazed last night," I said. "I especially liked when you did the turtle thing with your shoulders." With that I pushed my shoulders up to my ears and made a funny face.

We both laughed and got ready to get moving again. It was a short conversation. Not much of anything really. But in the Arctic, as you travel with your body bundled from head to toe, you replay the least little thing over and over again in your mind.

In the next hour, I replayed our conversation and found myself smiling over and over at the same exchanges.

As we moved north we were winding our way from side to side around chunks of ice. The landscape looked like the aftermath of a landslide, with rocks rolled from some Arctic mountain onto the ice valley.

Soon it all changed. We moved from the valley of ice boulders to the super highway of the Arctic. Paul's luck had struck again. He found a fresh frozen lead, about a week old by his estimation. The ice was as smooth as a hockey rink. Paul yelled for everyone to get on the sleds and for the skiers to grab hold of the lines that drag behind the sled. The idea is that if you stumble and the sled gets away from you, you're supposed to dive on the dragline and act as a human anchor to get the sled under control. This is only an issue on smooth ice. Most of the time, a slow walk is faster than the dogs pulling up and over the ice rubble.

The dogs hit a full gallop. Off we went, zooming northward.

After about an hour, the highway ended. Before us loomed a twenty-foot pressure ridge. Paul decided it was a good place to make camp.

We'd traveled about four miles in an hour, three times faster than we traveled in the first five hours. And in six hours, we had traveled some fifteen miles but with all the zigging and zagging we'd actually moved ten miles closer to the pole. I was struck by the results. Here we were, a team of Arctic rookies, and in just six hours we'd moved ten miles closer to our goal.

On my first day in the Arctic I realized that critics who claimed the admiral's sled speeds during this portion of his 1909 expedition had been exaggerated clearly had never been here. According to the admiral's records, his speed on The Last Dash was about double his speed up to that point—twenty-five miles per day versus twelve.

Experience indicates that there is nothing remarkable about the admiral's sled speeds. The ice near the pole is significantly easier to navigate than the massive pressure ridges near shore. For example, Paul Schurke's and Will Steger's epic trip from land to the pole took them twenty-one days to cover the first 120 miles. They covered the last 125 miles in five days, the same number it took the admiral to travel 135 miles.

The admiral's speeds were very realistic. Our team of Arctic rookies with sleds weighing one thousand pounds had traveled ten miles toward the pole in just six hours. Peary, traveling with the world's best dog mushers and with sleds weighing just five hundred pounds, had traveled twenty-five miles in twelve to eighteen hours.

As we hit camp everyone set into action. Two wire lead lines were staked out, each end drilled into the ice or anchored around a large ice flow.

Everyone helped with the dogs.

It was an ugly experience. As I attempted to unbuckle the dog harnesses, my hands froze, hampering my manual dexterity. I felt like a bumbling idiot. Adding to the misery, the dogs, knowing that food soon would be served, gyrated in four directions simultaneously. Factor in the occasional dogfight and you have one painful half hour of work.

Once the dogs finally settled down, we turned to setting up tents, feeding the dogs, and cooking dinner.

Tonight it took about an hour to set camp. A miracle compared with the five or six hours it had taken the night before. Craig and I made chicken, rice, and mixed vegetables. Again, there were no complaints. It appeared that anything hot and packed with calories would suffice.

Around 8:00 P.M., I dialed into the phone bridge. Without the slightest nod to amenities, David said he wanted to get right to the North Pole Telegram. It was clear I'd done a poor job of reporting the day before.

Nice hearing from you, too, David.

"Right," he said. "So what happened today?"

With that, I reported that we had arrived safely at what we were calling Camp Aspirations!, in honor of the charity.

Then Kari checked in, asking which team was ahead, Ziggy or Fuzz.

Huh?

"The teams, Ziggy or Fuzz, which is leading?" she asked. "I need to put it on the site."

I didn't know what to say. It was the last thing on my mind.

She didn't give up so I said, "Fuzz started out fast, and then Ziggy took charge. But then Fuzz used his canine connections to make it work."

I wondered what Admiral Peary would think of reporting on the progress of comic strip characters.

The call lasted about forty minutes. David drilled me for details of the day, while Kari wanted to know what to do with the Web site. I'd been out of touch for a day and a half and already I was having trouble focusing on the charity and the Web event. For me, survival was of greatest importance. I was also overwhelmed with a sense of isolation

I pleaded with David to encourage more messages, more notes.

I said it over and over. Seeking to get the message through, I explained how Celia had received a page with Sunshine from Florida. I'd held up my hand to feel for warmth.

Alan had received a "Dear John" page from a girlfriend. He thought it was a joke but not wanting to take chances, he asked David to give the lady a call.

David didn't understand my pleadings. "I think your brain is scrambled," he said.

Jon Paul in New York brought good news. "The B roll we filmed at the ski resort in Edmonton ran on NBC in Los Angeles last night."

Excellent! We were getting some good coverage.

Near the end of the call, I then learned of a new challenge. Mike Comeriate or "NASA Mike," as he called himself, had suddenly appeared in Resolute and wanted to visit us. Before the trip, I'd learned on the Internet about NASA Mike's Cool Space educational outreach program. I had flown to meet him at the NASA Goddard Space Flight Center in February to discuss ways that we might partner. I left the meetings very confused about what he was doing. He talked about many things: taking ice measurements, finding information on global warming, making a phone call from the North to the South Pole, bringing water from the South Pole to the North Pole, doing an educational Web cast to students.

In the weeks between my visit and the trip, NASA Mike's plans changed constantly. One week we were working together, the next we weren't. I eventually tired of the roller coaster and turned him over to Paul Schurke, who made a tentative agreement that we would share flights with him to and from the pole. NASA Mike's team would fly to the pole, and part of our team would fly back on NASA Mike's planes. In addition, we would play host at the pole, cooking for them and letting them use our tents and gear.

I didn't believe it would happen, because it seemed that NASA Mike didn't have the funding to get to Resolute. Clearly I'd been wrong. However, his chaotic ways had not changed. On the satellite phone David had lots of questions from NASA Mike about which airline to use to fly to the pole, what weight was allowed, what gear to bring and on and on.

I changed the subject to something of more urgent need for me—keeping the batteries charged for the Iridium satellite phone. I had a solar charger, but when I set the batteries and the charger outside the cook tent, they went from full to one-third in an instant because of the severe cold. We had planned a drop of new supplies at 89 degrees, so it was important to talk specifics of what to do should the phone run out of power.

"Here in the cook tent, it's like 60 degrees," I told Kari. "Maybe if I run the battery into the cook tent, that'll help."

Kari had another idea. "What if we got you some of those packet hand warmers, and you wrap one up with the phone to keep it warm?"

After forty-three minutes the call came to an end. I knew that Debbie, our kids, and my parents were listening so I gave a quick "love to all," hoping they'd get it.

I wanted to say more but didn't want to sound like an adventure wimp. I'd been on the ice for just twenty-four hours, but all I could think about was getting to the pole and getting home. The sense of isolation and perpetual cold overwhelmed all other concerns. It was hard to hit the power button to turn off the phone.

As I put the phone away I couldn't believe the difference in how I felt when talking on the phone. It was like I was here and there at the same time.

We'd traveled fifteen miles despite not getting going till noon. We'd gotten lucky hitting that northward super high-way of a lead.

As I put the phone away Bill laughed and said, "Where'd you get 60 degrees in the tent?"

I look at the thermometer on his jacket. It read 36.

The tenderfoot mistake gave everyone a good laugh. When you're in the super-cold, 36 degrees feels like room temperature.

After the entertainment of the phone call we gulped our glop of chicken, rice, and mixed vegetables—a fine meal. Everyone ate ravenously, scraping the pot clean again and making clean up easy.

As we prepared to hunker down for the night, Paul cautioned us about where we'd been so far and where we had yet to go.

"We're on the gravy train," he said. "The wonderful Arctic has rolled over and shown us her soft white underbelly."

I'd be fine with riding the gravy train all the way to 90 North.

We went to sleep with 185 miles to travel.

www.Aspirations.com has audio from this day's phone call

Chapter 7
Welcome to the Mountains

FRIDAY MORNING, APRIL 16, 1999
Distance to travel to the North Pole: 185 Miles
Temperature: -17° F

© 1999 Ziggy and Friends, Inc. /Dist. by Universal Press Syndicate

...i GUeSS iT ReALLY
iSN'T POSSiBLe TO
eSTABLiSH A LASTiNG
ReLATiONSHiP WiTH A
SNOWMAN !!

Follow Ziggy LIVE on his Great Aspirations trip to the North Pole at www.ASPIRATIONS.com!

*F*RIDAY MORNING BEGAN MUCH FASTER than the day before. By 8:00 A.M. we enjoyed a hearty glop of bran, granola, apple, and strawberry flakes with lots of brown sugar. I ate extra granola and bran fiber to prevent diarrhea.

We kicked off the morning with a couple of great runs, catching two super highways of smooth new ice. We flew along. Okay, maybe not flew—in the Arctic, speed is relative. We traveled at about two to three miles an hour. On cross-country skis, a leisurely pace is five miles an hour; in the Olympics, they cross-country ski at fifteen miles per hour.

We stopped for a ten-minute break about once an hour, just long enough for me to drink from one of my two one-liter water bottles and to create a small patch of yellow snow.

The first five minutes of each break were the most enjoyable moments of the day. The relief from continuous exercise felt tremendous and for five minutes I didn't feel tired or cold.

The next five minutes were among the worst moments. The heat generated by the aerobic activity died out and the cold set in. The perspiration in our clothing became a heat thief, stealing warmth from our bodies twenty-five times faster than air.

We stopped a little longer for lunch—more for the dogs than for ourselves. I used today's stop as an opportunity to fiddle with my footwear options, swapping leather boots for my contraptions.

Balancing the sled over a ridge and over a gap

I switched as quickly as possible. First I put on silk liner socks, and then the wet suit booties made of neoprene to seal in sweat, creating a water bath. Next I tugged on thick wool socks, followed by ankle braces. Over those, I added another layer of wool socks.

Finally, I pulled on the New England Overshoe, known as the NEOS.

The process took time. I ended up rushing to get them strapped on as Paul called for us to load up again. Just before we took off, Paul spoke again about our good fortune to that point:

"We've hit the *Jeopardy* Daily Double," he said. "We need to cover as much distance as we can while the going is good. Any day, we could be hit with a storm."

That afternoon, those words ran through my head over and over again as the conditions turned bad. We encountered twenty-foot pressure ridges that we had to climb over, pulling the dogs and sleds with us. I was on the front sled, again with Alan, as part of team Ziggy. Our sled weighed about six hundred pounds, gear and all. Our trailer sled, with Mike and Celia, weighed about four hundred pounds.

For perspective, the sleds used for the Iditarod, the famous Alaskan dogsled race, weigh well under a hundred pounds.

Given his experience running dog teams, Alan was our musher. I was the runner, his loyal assistant. Whenever we stopped, I ran to the front of the sled and grabbed the collars of the lead dogs to keep them from turning around and starting a dogfight.

On the first major pressure ridge of the day, I scuttled to the front, climbing on boulders of ice. The giant ice sheets that formed the ridge were scattered at every angle imaginable, making it tough to find firm footing for leverage as I pulled the sled forward. The dogs also scrambled for footing, but they have four feet instead of two, so they're much faster at it. I pulled as hard as I could, while Alan pushed the sled from the rear.

The third pressure ridge was especially devilish. Alan and I tugged and pulled but nothing worked. The sled stood still. We called Celia and Mike to help us, and lifting with all our might, we inched the sled forward. My back ached. Worse yet, we often slipped on the ice chunks and fell. And though the snow looked beautiful, it was hard as rocks—ice rocks. The bruises mounted, though I did avoid twisted ankles, sprained wrists, and a wrenched back.

Finally, we reached the top, but we still faced the other half of the battle. The climb up was 80 percent work and 20 percent danger. The ride down would be 20 percent work and 80 percent danger.

Alan held the break while manhandling the back end of the sled, and I used my legs as a sort of a battering-ram steering system. From the right side of the sled, I extended into a spread-eagle, with my right hand gripping a tie-down rope in the front and my left on the back of the sled. My legs stretched out at a diagonal angle to the front right of the sled.

As the dogs picked their way down, I used my legs to jolt the sled to the right or left to find the cleanest path for our descent.

Done right, the feeling is sheer exuberance. It's an immense rush, crashing down with the sled, bouncing from ice block to block to the bottom. Imagine sledding off the second story of your home, and you'll have a good idea what it's like.

Done wrong, it gets ugly real fast.

Later that morning as we came down a pressure ridge I hesitated a moment too long and collided with a block of ice. The dogs did the sensible thing and split the block, with half the team going to the right, the other to the left.

That left the sled to crash head on.

After recovering from the collisions we had to move the sled. It's against the nature of the Inuit sled dog to go in reverse; they're bred to move forward. But we needed to go backward before we could go forward.

Alan took the front left side of the sled, and I took the front right side. With a one, two, three, we strained to lift the front

I hesitated and the result was a head-on collision with the ice. Fortunately there was no audio with this photo. Alan was saying $%x#!!!

of the sled. Nothing happened. It was wedged tight. The sled itself was sitting at a 30-degree angle, the nose tipped downward. We had no choice but to push the sled backwards along with the dogs, then lift the front nose of the sled and slide it to one side of the ice block.

By now the team in front of us was getting cold and impatient. They'd made the right choice coming down and were waiting for Alan and me to get our act together.

I knelt down and imagined I was one of those Russian weight lifters I'd seen on *Wide World of Sports*. With a mighty lift, the sled went back, up, and over.

I looked at Alan, who had clearly lifted a lot more of the sled then I had. "Good thing I did some weightlifting to get ready for this trip," I said. With a grin, he said, "I'm in favor of it. If you want to do a little more in camp tonight to prepare for tomorrow, that'd be okay, too."

As the runner—or "Arctic Cowboy," as I christened my job—I helped kick-start the dogs. When the sled stops, it takes extra energy to break the friction and get it started. I would go to the front and pull back on the dog line to generate some slack. Then, on Alan's signal I would let go of the dog line with one arm and pull as hard as I could on the front of the sled with the other.

Once the sled starts moving, it usually keeps moving. Sort of like life. The starting is always the hardest part of any task.

About midday, we were winding our way through rubble—the snow soft, the sledding was slow. For what seemed like the four-hundredth time that day, I ran out front to start the dogs. This time my foot slipped into a hole. At that moment, the dogs caught better traction and the sled lurched forward. As I fell backward I pulled the sled to the right—right on top of me.

Down in the soft snow I went as the sled ran over my chest. I reached up immediately to cover my head, feeling the weight of the sled running over my body. As the sled passed over, I started to get back on my feet. Then I heard Celia scream, and I turned to look. The tow sled headed right at me.

I dove face first into the snow. Before it hit me, all I could think of was the brake. Please don't be standing on the brake, I thought.

Each sled is equipped with a brake at the rear. It's a jagged piece of metal that's attached to a spring, which the driver can stand on to slow the sled's forward progress. If Celia or Mike were standing on the brake, the snow would soon be red with my blood.

Their sled ran up and over me.

I pulled my head from the snow.

I'd survived.

Fortunately, Celia and Mike were smart enough to jump off the sled to reduce the weight.

As I dusted myself off, I laughed. I could see the headline: "Tenderfoot Flattened by Arctic Dogsled Mishap."

I asked Craig if he caught the moment with his camera.

"Sorry, missed it," he said.

"How could you?" I said. "That could be my most exciting moment of the trip.

"Something tells me you'll have more of those moments," Alan said.

Considering the terrain, Alan and I were lucky that day. We dumped our sled just once—and into soft powder at that. We could easily have dumped twenty times. And if we'd dumped onto hard-packed ice, we could have done serious damage to the sled.

Sometimes when we kick-started the sled by pulling on the dog line, we caught momentum and moved right along. Other times we nudged forward just a few feet. It's a depressing experience to move thousands of pounds of dogsled a foot at a time.

We crossed over snow that had the consistency of soft Styrofoam carved by the wind into undulating waves, frozen into the Arctic landscape. Alan joked that he felt a little seasick. In truth, the waves are a key part of navigation. In general they run east to west. Thus, traveling north is often as simple as traveling at a right angle to them.

When the dogs needed a little motivation, we had someone ski or run in front of them. They love to chase. That afternoon, Craig ran in front of our sled. When the dogs hit a smooth spot, they ran over him. It didn't take him long to become good at jumping out of the way whenever he heard the dogs bearing down on him.

I spent much of the second day removing clothing and putting it back on, zipping and unzipping, seeking a thermal balance between the heat I generated from movement and the relentless cold. Too much clothing, and sweat built up. Too little, and a deep chill sank its claws into me. I had twenty-four different layers I could take on and off: nine layer options for my chest and legs, five for my feet, my hands, and my head. I found myself endlessly fiddling, always too hot or too cold.

Tori, Kristyn, and Brad helped with frozen taste testing.

Lunch was what I called Dining ala Pocket. We all had stuffed various foods in our pockets, where it was easy to access. For my appetizer, my lower right pocket provided a couple handfuls of peanut snack mix. My main course came from a pocket inside my fleece—that day it was slices of salami and pieces of cheese. I kept them in the inside pocket to prevent them from freezing. Dessert from my lower right pants pocket: crispy M&M's. Yum.

In preparation for the trip, my kids and I experimented with finding out what treat could survive freezing. We bought a couple dozen treats and stuffed them in the freezer. The next evening we had a 'taste off' and found that only Crispy M&M's didn't get rock hard.

We also liked the miniature Snickers, which were small enough that when frozen they'd fit in my mouth like a hard candy. At first I was embarrassed by my selections, as the veterans brought various PowerBars and PowerGels to use for energy. But I preferred the Snickers bars.

The other lunch food was Wintergreen Pemmican. On Peary's trips, they ate real pemmican, a condensed food made from beef, lard, and dried fruit.

On Schurke's trips he uses a modern variation created by

Joe Bodewes, at Wintergreen Lodge. *Self* magazine called them the Godiva of Granola Bars. Here's the recipe:

Mix together:
    5 ¼ cups regular oatmeal (not instant)
    1 ½ cups chunky peanut butter
    ¾ cup brown sugar
    2 sticks butter
    ½ cup corn syrup
    1 ½ cups chocolate chips
    2 eggs

Optional: 1 cup raisins, 1 cup sunflower seeds, and ½ cup honey

Press into 9 x 13" pan, bake at 350 for 25 minutes.

Cut into bars while slightly warm. Enjoy!

As we came into what would be our campsite for the night, I checked our progress. We'd gone nearly nineteen miles. Our pace in the afternoon had been about one-half mile per hour. We might as well be riding six-hundred-pound snails.

"That's the hardest nineteen miles I've ever done," Alan said, venting his frustration.

During dinner, I talked to the mountain climbers in our group—Paul Pfau, Bill Martin, and Mike Warren. They agreed that this was a totally different experience from what they'd done before. When you climb, they said, you use intense energy and then you rest to acclimate to the altitude. Here, you run the whole time. It's like running a marathon. The constant movement created a burn in my legs that never seemed to go away.

As we unpacked the sleds to retrieve the cooking gear, we found that two fuel canisters had sprung leaks, probably from crashing over the pressure ridges early in the day.

This was not good news.

In the Arctic, fuel is the most valuable of all commodities.

With fuel, you can turn ice into water, cold into warmth. Without it, the trip would be over.

As we gathered for dinner, it was clear that the day had taken a toll on everyone. Some had taken a physical beating—Alan had a major bruise on his leg that he "iced down" in the cook tent.

As 8:00 P.M. neared, I dialed into the phone bridge. It connected, and David came on-line.

"I just got back from the weather station," he said with a note of urgency. "There's a very big front coming in from Alaska. If it keeps moving the way it is, you guys are going to be in for some bad weather in about two days."

I found myself stuttering as I tried to hide my terror. "Are you, uh, serious?"

Then I did what any rookie would do with overwhelming information. I passed the phone to Paul.

At that moment, with the tension at its greatest, the operator chimed in with a formal introduction for the call. She played an inane jingle and formally announced the beginning of the call. The whole time—probably twenty seconds—we chomped at the bit for details about the blizzard.

David tells me that bad weather is coming.

"Good evening and welcome to your Quest Communications conference call. I'd like to turn the call over to Mr. David Wecker and Mr. Doug Hall."

The absurdity of the situation was incredible. If a blizzard hit, we weren't going anywhere. Massive winds would drop the temperature into the deep freeze.

David repeated the weather information to Paul, who nodded. My untrained eye noticed a glimmer of trepidation in his expression.

Then when it seemed things couldn't get worse, I learned something else.

"David, quick question," Paul said. "Last night, an airplane came over our camp about two in the morning. It was a Twin Otter. Do you know if the Malaysian group was picked up? I'm curious because if that plane went up to pick up the Malaysian group, that was our resupply plane. If so, that would be a wash."

Paul was more concerned about the resupply than the weather. If we had bad weather, we could be stuck for a week, and without new supplies we could face a serious shortage.

The rest of the call brought good news. The radio interviews in Resolute had reached about ten million people. All of Canada saw our news story. The BBC also picked up our story. And ABCNews.com had confirmed interest in doing a piece about us.

We were reaching millions. My crazy plan was working. And maybe the publicity might connect to a parent who might download some material from our Web site on Dr. Quaglia's teachings and help make a real difference in the life of a child.

The conversation turned to the continuing soap opera with NASA Mike. David was having trouble getting the straight story from him on his flight plans. It didn't bother me, but it was fun listening to David whine about it. He can be quite creative in his complaining.

Paul didn't seem bothered either. The plan, as best as we could tell, was to meet Mike and crew at the pole. Paul hoped to send back some sleds and humans on the planes that delivered NASA Mike, which would reduce our final load on the return. In exchange, Paul would pay a portion of the flight cost, and we'd host Mike's team at the pole for a day or two.

As I hung up, exhaustion and fear overwhelmed me.

The previous two nights I'd been shivering because I was cold and scared to death. On this night, I was exhausted and scared. Exhausted from the beating I'd taken and scared to death by the approaching storm.

The menu that night was black beans and rice with tortillas and taco flavoring. While Craig cooked the rice in one pot and the beans and taco mix in another, I fried the tortillas in butter. During the call, David had suggested that in honor of our Mexican dinner we should name our location Camp Cancun.

The naming of camps after sponsors was just one of many perks Peary offered to those who gave money to support his expeditions. Money and the pursuit of sponsors were two topics that constantly plagued polar explorers. Peary and Amundsen, credited with the discovery of the South Pole, were both in debt on their final journeys.

According to Amundsen, no one but an explorer could appreciate the agony involved in raising money for a polar expedition. He claimed for years after arriving at the South Pole that the burden of seeking financial support nearly broke his constitution.

Books and lectures provided the primary sources of funding beyond outright begging for donations. Ernest Shackleton of Antarctic fame said, "Lectures sold books, books sold lectures, and newspapers sold both. Particularly when you come home from an expedition with a big hurrah."

Not everyone loved the stage, however. Arctic explorer Charles Hall of Cincinnati (no relation—I checked) once said, "Lecturing is the curse of my soul."

The admiral was a vigorous speaker. It's said that he once did some 140 lectures in a one hundred-day period. It was a primary source of his fundraising for future expeditions.

www.Aspirations.com has
audio from this day's phone call

Chapter 8
Welcome to the River District

SATURDAY, APRIL 17, 1999
Distance to travel to the North Pole: 166 Miles
Temperature: -44° F

Follow Ziggy LIVE on his Great Aspirations trip to the North Pole at www.ASPIRATIONS.com!

A WICKED COLD MORNING. Icicles that had formed from our breathing during the night hung from the ceiling of our tent. I slid out of my sleeping bag grudgingly, pried my feet into my frozen boots, and went for a walk to relieve myself. Fortunately, my daily doses of Metamucil made the process fast and efficient.

In the cook tent I learned that Paul had put the stoves on rations. With the broken fuel cans we needed to conserve fuel. He told us to use only one stove instead of two. I cooked the water and Craig made breakfast. I then paused for my favorite moment of the day—my cup of Brain Brew coffee. Brain Brew is no ordinary coffee. It's the private blend of my Eureka! Ranch. It's crafted from a collection of four beans, and in a blind taste test with two hundred consumers it beat Starbucks two to one!

Real explorers frown on consuming caffeine. Paul Schurke has written "No sugar or caffeine should be included in standard rations. These stimulants throw your body's metabolism on a roller-coaster ride of booms and crashes, which over the long run can have very detrimental effects."

Caffeine is also thought to be a diuretic. The more you drink the more you have to pee. Paul says for every cup of coffee you drink you should drink a cup of water to make up for it.

Everyone on the trip had gone decaf.

Except for me.

I'm passionate about the bean. It's well proven to give you energy. In fact, the impact of caffeine on performance is so great it's actually banned in Olympic competitions. It's also a thermogenic, meaning that it raises your heartbeat and core body temperature. Yes! Liquid heat!

Finally, not only does it kick your body in gear, it also helps you think smarter and more creatively. Once I tested the impact of three cups of coffee on a participant's ability to invent big ideas. In a forty-five-minute test, the caffeinated group invented 40 percent more ideas than the decaffeinated group. Note: there was no study of after effects.

The big challenge in the high Arctic is finding a way to brew a proper cup. After much testing I settled on a sort of reverse French-press system. Inside my plastic Brain Brew cup I inserted a plastic filter cup with a heaping tablespoon of Brain Brew.

After adding hot water I covered the cup with a wooden

disk, which kept the heat in while the coffee brewed. After about five minutes—voila! Intense, robust, eye-opening java!

I tied the disk to the mug with a nylon cord so I wouldn't lose it in the snow. Debbie and the kids decorated it, so just looking at it provided some warmth.

Cleaning up coffee grounds can be a mess, but in the Arctic I just let them freeze, and with a snap of the filter they popped out in a lump.

Absolutely nothing in the world tasted better than a cup of hot Brain Brew coffee when it was 44 below zero.

As the coffee finished brewing I held the mug close to my face with both hands. Ever so slowly I lifted the disk and inhaled the aroma. What an incredible experience.

The aroma awakened and restored my soul. Ever so gently I took my first sip, rolling the coffee around my mouth from side to side, front to back, relishing the heat, the flavor, and the harmony of the beans—first the notes of the Java from Java, followed by the pure Columbian and the distinctive twang of Tanzanian Peaberry (the only coffee bean that grows as a half bean), ending with the high notes of authentic Hawaiian Kona, the king of coffees and also one of the most expensive.

The admiral was on my side of the caffeine debate, sort of. He considered tea a critical component of Arctic travel. The admiral said, "Tea is an imperative necessity on such a driving journey."

To add a piece of proper civilization to the effort, I also eat half a chocolate biscotti. In the Arctic, biscotti packs a crunch that is not often experienced. I allocated half a biscotti a day, but they'd gotten crushed in my backpack so I ate a handful each morning.

The combination of chocolate crunch and Brain Brew coffee is orgasmic.

In Saturday's landscape, the previous day's pressure ridges gave way to open water, called a "lead." When the ice folds up into the air to form a pressure ridge it has to come from some place. That place becomes open water. The energy it must take from the tides and winds to set the mass of ice in motion is hard to imagine.

The first lead was about thirty feet across. We turned to the west and traveled about a quarter mile to find a place to cross it.

In the afternoon I switched places with Craig and put on skis while he worked with Alan on the big red sled. I was excited about skiing. I did a lot of cross-country skiing as a youth growing up in New England and had visions of skiing in the front, navigating and leading the team. Soon the visions appeared to be delusions. I was totally incompetent. I couldn't get a good kick with the skis, couldn't keep my balance over the ice blocks, couldn't keep up with the dog teams. I kept falling farther and farther behind on even the semi-smooth terrain, not even close to the high speeds we got on fresh frozen leads. I had expected skiing to be an asset, only to find it a frustration.

In the middle of the afternoon we came to another river of black water. We turned to the west and traveled for about one mile until we came to a spot where the lead seemed crossable. Soft but passable ice had formed where the lead turned.

Up ahead I saw Alan steer his dog team to cross the ice. The ice suddenly gave way and four dogs fell into the water. Alan rushed to the front of the sled and grabbed the dog line and began pulling the dogs out of the water.

As he pulled at the dogs, the ice under him gave way. He dropped instantly into water up to his waist. By holding onto the dog line he saved himself from completely submerging.

"Fuuuuuuuuck meeee!!!" he screamed.

Team members dashed from all directions, but Alan didn't wait for help. Any other weight on the fractured ice would only worsen his situation. With one arm holding the line, he reached with his other arm for hard ice. He then grabbed farther up the line and slowly pulled himself up and out.

He cursed up a storm—not about being wet, but because he thought the icy water might have shorted out his pager or his manhood. When he checked, he found the pager working and his manhood, other than some major shrinkage, in good shape too. He let out a huge laugh.

A few members told him to change clothes immediately to prevent hypothermia, but Paul said it would be better if he skied hard for an hour or so to get his temperature up before changing clothes.

Craig took the big red sled by himself and Alan grabbed the skis. After about an hour we stopped for him to change his socks and put plastic bags between his outer boot and his now somewhat dry inner socks for added warmth.

Corky, Randy, Paul P., Celia, Bill, Paul S., Mike, Alan, Doug (Craig took the photo)

He said the experience was invigorating, adding that he had feared falling into the water and now having done it he felt free of that fear.

Looking at his ice-crusted pants, I wondered how I would respond to such a situation.

When Alan changed his boots, I took the opportunity to change mine as well. I was having a hard time skiing with the NEOS, which were lightweight but even with the brace my ankles didn't seem to have enough support for skiing on the rugged terrain.

I changed back to the LaCrosse leather boots. However, as they had been sitting in my pack, they were now frozen stiff in a collapsed form. I loosened all the laces and got my feet in. Then I tied them as best I could. When the leather warmed from the inside out as I skied, I'd have to retie the laces a number of times.

I hoped I'd ski better wearing the leather boots.

I soon learned that the problem was not my footwear.

The problem was me. I couldn't get the hang of Arctic skiing.

The ice rubble made me cautious. The bruises from the falls made me cautious. I looked like a child just learning to walk. Or a senior citizen shuffling along using ski poles for canes.

All I could think was: "This is not the way it was supposed to be." I had visualized myself flying across the landscape. Instead, I was tentative, unsteady, and scared I was going to fall onto the rock-hard blocks of ice.

The freezing cold—minus 44 degrees with the wind chill added to my frustration. I'd always thought wind chill was only something created by weathermen to hype their reports.

Skiing in ugly terrain. Here Celia fell on the rock-hard ice.

I was now a believer. From here forward, I will only report the wind-chill-adjusted temperature.

Wind amplifies the cold. It's also sneaky. It can find a crack or crevice in clothing and instantly put neck, hands, or torso in a deep freeze.

My breath froze instantly. An inch of ice covered the front of the balaclava on my face, which made breathing difficult.

Later that afternoon Randy put a foot through the ice, soaking his boot. He was wearing the big white moon boots, so the liners absorbed the water instantly. That one boot used to be half a pound heavier than a leather boot, but was now about two-and-a-half pounds heavier, having absorbed about a quart of water.

Unfortunately, that afternoon we hit the mother of all leads. Westward we traveled along the river of black water that flowed to our right.

Admiral Peary was stopped for six days by an open-water lead that nearly ended his 1909 expedition.

> The open water was about a quarter of a mile in width, and extended east and west as far as we could see when we climbed to the highest pinnacle of ice in

We traveled west in search of a way to cross the lead.

the neighborhood of our camp. The lead had opened directly through the heavy floes, and, considering that these floes are sometimes one hundred feet in thickness, and of almost unimaginable weight, the force that could open such a river through them is comparable with the forces that threw up the mountains on the continents and opened the channels between the lands.

All the next day we were still there beside the lead. Another day, and we were still there. Three, four, five days passed in intolerable inaction, and still the broad line of black water spread before us. During those five days I paced back and forth, deploring the luck which, when everything else was favorable— weather, ice, dogs, men, and equipment should thus impede our path with open water.

Only one who had been in a similar position could understand the gnawing torment of those days of forced inaction, as I paced the floe in front of the igloos most of the time. It was a harrowing time, that period of waiting. Altogether, I think that more of mental wear and tear was crowded into those days than into all the rest of the fifteen months we were absent from civilization.

After traveling about three miles to the west we came to a bend in the water. Paul declared it a great place for camp. Seeing that the water at the bend had a very thin skin of ice on it, Paul said, "We'll build an ice bridge and hope for the best overnight."

"An ice bridge?" I asked.

"We'll slide pieces of ice out onto the thin ice. If we're lucky they'll freeze overnight and create a steppingstone bridge."

As I set to work digging the hole for the cook tent with Corky, Paul's words went through my head over and over. If we're lucky? What kind of carefully planned strategy is that?

Before I could get far with the digging Paul stopped me.

"Let's get the stoves going immediately," he said. "Without waiting for the cook tent. I want to get folks to bed early

Paul had the idea of building an ice bridge over the lead.

tonight. Having dinner outside without the warmth of the cook tent, they'll go to bed faster."

Then he said, "I also want to test your fancy pot to be sure it's paying its way. Convince me that it really boils water faster."

I'd invented the pot with the help of Jeff Stamp in my office and Paderno, a cookware company. Instead of a flat bottom, it

To build the "Siberian Chalet" cook tent we dug a hole and then used skis to hold up the frame for the covering.

had a giant indent, sort of like a bundt cake pan with the center pushed up about a third of the way from the bottom. The theory was that by increasing the amount of surface area in the bottom of the pot and by concentrating heat in the tunnel, we'd melt snow into water faster.

The Paderno Polar Pot was specially designed to melt snow faster.

The only problem with the pot was its weight, which was almost twice as much as the other pot.

We'd tested the pot in Cincinnati on our gas range, and it was definitely faster than a flat-bottom pan. Paul, however, was concerned about its weight versus worth. He didn't care if Paderno Cookware was a sponsor.

"If that pot doesn't do what you say it does out here it's going to Davy Jones's locker," he said, meaning we'd throw it in the river next to the campsite.

We set both pots on burners, loaded both with snow, and cranked the burners on full throttle.

Then we waited. Watching a pot boil is especially painful when you're thinking about what you're going to say to your sponsor later on. The pot had been handcrafted by friends at Paderno Cookware, located on my beloved Prince Edward Island. They make some of the world's finest cookware and when asked to create a polar pot they produced a gem.

As the first load of snow melted we saw no difference. I was getting worried. I looked for a sign that Paul was kidding.

I didn't see one. The team was feeling a little beaten up, and Paul seemed ready to make the pot "walk the plank" as a motivational example.

I shoveled another load of snow into each pot. Then another. Watching. Waiting for a sign.

I said a little prayer. *"God, I know it's not polite to ask for your intervention in the life of a pot. But, if you're so inclined, if you have a spare moment, I would appreciate a little help here."*

The pots were filled about a third of the way with water, just above the center cone of the Paderno pot.

Then the snow added to the Paderno pot melted faster. Soon I found myself adding snow twice as often, three times as often to the Paderno pot.

The Paderno pot probably didn't melt the first load of snow faster because it was so much heavier that any gain in heat transfer was lost as the metal soaked up the heat. However, once the snow melted into water, the center cone acted like a heat amplifier. The snow melted as it floated by the cone, and the center cone created a natural circular flow, rising in the center and sinking to the outside.

The pot filled with boiling water in *half the time!*

"It works, it works," I yelled as I did a little dance across the ice.

Paul smiled.

As the water boiled he asked me to help build the ice bridge. We grabbed chunks of ice weighing fifty to seventy pounds and slid them onto the thin skin of the lead, as if we were curling.

When we finished it was time to eat. Dinner tonight: mashed potatoes, ground meat, green beans, and Doug's Burger and Bacon spice. Folks loved it. Then again, standing on the side of a pressure ridge at 40 below zero, anything hot tastes great.

Later, I called into the phone bridge. As the cook tent wasn't finished yet to protect me from the wind, I kept walking to try to stay warm.

I asked first about the storm.

"It looks fine," David said. "It's moving away from you. All you'll get is a dusting of snow and winds of twenty miles an hour or so."

I called for details on the storm.

"Twenty miles an hour?" I said, a bit louder than I intended. "At these temperatures that would put it at minus 60 something with the wind chill."

Who hired this idiot as base camp commander, I wondered.

Ugh. I hired him.

There is no way he could understand the consequences of the wind.

As the phone call continued I suddenly heard my wife speaking to my eight-year-old daughter, Tori. A mistake had been made at the phone bridge and their phone extensions had been made "live" tonight. Ordinarily they could only listen.

"Hi, Deb," I said.

"You can hear me?" she said

"I love you love you love you, Daddy," Tori said. "I listen every night and get to talk about it to my class."

Kristyn, my nine-year-old daughter, added, "Did you get my page? I love you."

It was wonderful to hear their voices. But it was also hard.

The frigid cold of today and the ugly skiing had taken its toll. If I spent too much time thinking about home it might destroy what little concentration I had.

After saying "hi" to the family I returned to telling David about the activities of the day. I told of the cold, the wind, and Alan and Randy's dips in the water.

Mostly I explained Paul's crazy plan to use ice blocks as steppingstones across the softly frozen lead. If the ice was still soft in the morning, Paul planned to walk the gear across in relays and then run the sleds over empty.

As I described the plan I could hear Debbie gasp. The call ended with a message from Tori, a favorite saying we had when I tucked them into bed.

In our camp set up, we had three tents for sleeping and one work tent.

She said, "Daddy, don't let the bed bugs bite. See you in the morning light! Yea!"

About ten minutes after I hung up, my pager vibrated. It was from Tori. *"Dad, Hey, I hope the ice bridge works and dogs are not too afraid of it. You can do it. I hope you are having fun. Love, Tori."*

As Craig and I got ready to sleep we talked about the state of the team. During the day I'd been totally absorbed by my problems. During dinner it was clear that everyone was suffering similar if not worse issues.

"Some people are really having a tough time," Craig said.

"Today was ugly," I said. "But it's still early in the trip.

What will it be like in a week?" I was beginning to understand what Paul meant when he said adventuring is life in fast-forward and how trips like these offer a concentrated source of personal growth.

"I find myself going through rapid ups and downs," Craig said. "Everyone is. I just hope no one cracks."

We talked for a while about the stress of the trip. I mentioned how frustrated I'd been with skiing. We also laughed at Paul's plan to "get lucky" overnight with the creation of a steppingstone bridge.

It struck me that high-adventure trips often involve getting in position for lucky breaks. In life down south, we do a lot of planning under the illusion that it creates greater certainty. Here in the Arctic, there was no illusion. Luck was an open and planned-for strategy. Paul's deep experience gave us the ability to better play the odds.

We both pulled our hats over our eyes and cinched the hoods on our sleeping bags, leaving just a small breathing hole. Sleep came quickly.

www.Aspirations.com has
audio from this day's phone call

Chapter 9
The World of White

SUNDAY, APRIL 18, 1999
Distance to travel to the North Pole: 152 Miles
Temperature: -60° F

As I savored my morning mug of Brain Brew, Paul entered the cook tent and said the ice bridge looked good. However, the weather to the north looked bad, and it was coming our way. We needed to cook breakfast as fast as possible.

We made a quick honey and cinnamon oatmeal.

I made the mistake of talking more than eating and the oatmeal froze in my bowl like cement. A splash of hot water brought it back to edible.

Paul checked the ice bridge again as we loaded the sleds. The wind blowing at twenty miles an hour gave us an effective temperature of minus 60! I read once that the military considers minus 40 as extremely dangerous.

To give you some idea of the impact of cold, think about this: How long does it take you to go to the bathroom? A minute, two minutes?

In the arctic at minus 40, skin freezes in just a couple of minutes and at minus 60 it freezes in about thirty seconds. Going to the bathroom, therefore, is fraught with risk. The six most commons areas for frostbite are, in order: feet, hands, ears, nose, cheeks, and penis. Despite this list, after returning from her morning bathroom stop, Celia said, "For the first time in my life I have penis envy."

Alan, being the only single man on the trip, was particularly concerned about this appendage after his dip in the ocean. After his little swim he kept a fleece cap in his pants to, as he said, "guard against frostbite on the one extremity I would hate to lose above all others."

One last piece of trivia about all things bathroom: I read in one explorer's book that if skin freezes to metal the best solution is to urinate on it. You'll be free immediately, and you won't mind the aroma because in the super-cold there are no strong smells.

When we were ready to move, Paul called the team together and asked for volunteers.

Volunteers?

I don't exactly know why, but before I could stop myself I volunteered.

"What do you need?" I asked.

"The ice is just barely strong enough for us to walk on," Paul said. "I'd like to lay down ski poles and skis in an X pattern across the ice. Then I'll have folks put skis on and walk on top of the crossed poles and skis. This will spread out their weight and reduce the chances of breaking through."

Paul asked for volunteers to help shuttle gear across the ice bridge.

"What do you need a volunteer for?" I asked.

"We don't have enough skis to lay on the ice and go across. I need someone to relay the skis back after some have crossed. You'll have to cross five times."

I felt myself swallow hard. "Sure, whatever. I'll do it."

Being one of the smallest on the trip, I figured it was my responsibility to volunteer. In fact, the admiral had a decided preference for small men.

> Small, wiry men have a great advantage over large ones in polar work. The latter require more material for their clothing and usually eat more. Large men take up more space than small ones, necessitating the building of larger snow igloos. Every pound in weight beyond the maximum requirement tends to lessen a man's agility; in fact, renders him clumsy and more apt to break his equipment. And the decided disadvantage which a large man is under in crossing new ice is apparent.

At the least, I figured this might earn me a little respect from my teammates. Maybe with this tiny act of courage I could become a real explorer. I also remembered the story Peary wrote about crossing a lead like this.

I told the men that it was each man for himself; that to help each other meant death for all. I was the heaviest so I knew I would probably go first. I took off my deerskin coat, rolled it into a bundle and dragged it on a string behind me. We started, walking wide and some fifty feet apart. I did not dare to lift my feet. I glided one slowly past the other. There were undulations from every man. Twice my toes broke through the ice. This is the finish, I said to myself. I heard a cry. "God help him, which one is it?" I muttered as I continued on. I reached the edge of the ice and looked along the line. Every man was there! As we looked over that film of ice we could see a dark crack cutting our bridge. We had crossed just in time.

Walking across with the first group, I saw that the chunks were frozen hard but the ice around it was so thin you could see through to the water below. The first few steps were pretty wet as water seeped up through small cracks as we walked. The ice felt rubbery, buckling with each step, like walking across a trampoline.

The crossing took only a couple minutes, but it seemed like it took half an hour. When we reached the far side, I grabbed an armfull of skis and started the return trip. The weight of our first trip had softened the ice even more. The bounces were bigger and water slushed on top of the ice, splashing around my boots when I stepped.

I reached the shore, tossed the skis, and turned around for the next lap.

Halfway back on my next return with skis, I heard a loud crack to my right. My weight was causing a chain reaction of cracks. I widened my feet to spread my weight even more, and I picked up the pace ever so gently.

When I reached shore I leaped up. I'd done it. I'd made four trips across. One more to go.

Paul stood on the north shore and called for us to toss snow onto the ice to make it look less "black." The dogs are smart and they naturally avoid going toward the water. They'll shy away if they think they might fall in.

Left on the southern side of the lead were Randy, Craig, Bill, and I. We each took a sled. Paul was on the other side holding two long ropes, one tied to the front of each of the dog teams.

Paul whistled for the first team of dogs to charge. The team-mates on the other side ran as fast as possible while pulling the rope to guide them across. By pulling the rope they kept the dogs moving, preventing them from veering off. Also, if the sled crashed through the ice, they'd be able to help pull it out.

On our side of the ice we gave the sled the biggest push we could muster. Speed was crucial. Sir Isaac Newton's laws of motion declared that the faster we moved forward the less downward pressure there would be from the sled.

It worked. First one set of sleds, then the other, cleared the lead without crashing through. The four of us then skied across, picking up the skis and ski poles on the ice as we skimmed across.

The release of tension and sense of accomplishment were immense. I was ready to hit the pub, have a pint, and tell of the victory.

To Paul, it was just another bump in the road. Just another minor problem solved.

I felt good. Too good. The admiral had warned about the dangers of feeling too good.

> When things are going too well, Look out! The Arctic
> Devil is only sleeping.

After the difficulties skiing the day before, I moved back to the sled with Alan. The pressure ridges were smaller but more chaotic.

Most were about ten feet high; however, the blocks of ice were bigger and spread farther apart so I ended up straddling and sometimes leaping from block to block.

On the fifth major ridge of the day, the sled slid sideways toward me, and I came down hard on a particularly big block, slamming my right knee into the ice. Pain knifed through me.

When I stood up to walk, my right leg buckled. I set the leg

The sky closed down as the storm came in.

again and gently put weight on it. It held up, but a sharp pain cut into my knee with each step.

"Are you okay?" Alan asked.

I nodded. "Just hurt my knee a little," I said. I immediately wondered why I hadn't admitted to the pain. Had I become "infected" with this macho explorer role so much that I'd lost touch with reality?

Fortunately, I was working the right side of the sled, so I could stand with my left foot on the runner. My right leg was supposed to kick and push, but with the pain I managed little more than going through the motions

Then things got even uglier.

The horizon lowered and darkened as the storm from the north hit us—a storm like I'd never experienced before or since. We were soon wrapped in an all-out blizzard unable to discern up from down, lost in a swirl of white all around us.

The snow blew horizontally and right at us, the wind whipping directly into our faces. Though I didn't use my temperature gadget to check the temperature or the wind, I know it was significantly colder than the minus 60 I'd recorded that morning.

Cold air cut through my body. My face burned with it. Corky's beard grew icicles. When I blinked, my eyelids stuck together or, rather, tried to freeze together. Cold crept in first at the tips of my toes and fingers and moved toward the core. I wiggled my toes and fingers to bring warmth back into them.

And still we marched on.

The admiral spoke of moments like this one:

> In the black moments of absolutely hopeless obstacles, of supreme physical discomfort, of threatened catastrophe, I have hugged my dream to myself and said, "This is but for the moment. I shall win out yet. And when the end comes, I can knock at the gates on the other side, and with head erect, offer as my passport, "I have made good."
>
> Were I a ragged beggar in the streets today, without a friend in the world. I could hug my dream to myself and feed and warm and clothe myself with the thought "I have made good." And when the end comes, I can knock at the gates on the other side, and with head erect, offer as my passport, "I have made good."

It was a white-on-white world. This photo was not overexposed.

Paul Schurke had another way to motivate us. When the going got tough he would keep us going by chanting, "How do you eat an elephant?"

This question was our cue to shout in response, "One bite at a time."

Around 11:30 A.M. the dog team just stopped.

Alan yelled into the wind at them and still nothing.

"They don't know where to go," I said, yelling above the din of wind and snow. "They've lost the trail. And we can't see the team in front."

It was a terrifying moment. We stood in the middle of a whiteout at 60 to 80 below zero with no teammates in sight, completely lost thousands of miles from home. The white world around us looked like heaven but felt like hell.

I trudged to the front to help guide the lead dogs, dropping to my hands and knees to feel around for the ski tracks. Nothing. The dogs were right to stop. We were not on the trail of the other team.

I wandered farther on my hands and knees, feeling the ground for any sign of the other team.

Nothing.

We were lost and blind, trying to feel our way to safety.

The dogs were pointed to the left so I took that as a clue. I crawled along beside them, feeling the ground. Finally, about fifteen feet back from the front of the dog team I found the ski marks. The team ahead of us had taken a near 90-degree turn to the left. Our dogs had missed the turn and gone past it before coming to a full stop.

I pulled the lead dogs and started walking in front of them, stopping every dozen feet to be sure we were still on the trail. In the terror of being lost, I'd forgotten about my knee. Now that we were back on the trail, I felt the stabbing pain again, jolting up my leg with every step.

I looked into the white ahead of me for the red jackets of my teammates.

I felt very isolated, even from the members of my team. The hood pulled tight around my head created a tunnel effect, while my two hats muffled the roar of the wind and all other sound. I couldn't hear and could hardly see Alan and the others behind me. On and on I plodded, stopping from time to time to be sure we were still on the trail.

After about an hour we found the team. They were on the backside of a huge block of blue ice. Paul Schurke was bundled up like a mummy, his head covered in his fur-lined hood, the rest of the team bunched into a huddle to conserve warmth.

"And I thought the ice bridge was going to be our biggest challenge today," Craig said.

"This is incredible," I said. "I hurt my knee earlier and it's killing me."

"Can you walk on it?" Craig said.

"Yeah, it'll get better," I lied and smiled. As I smiled the wind whipped between my teeth, flash-freezing the surface of my gums.

Paul explained that normally on a day like this, navigation can be difficult. It's impossible to set a bearing on the forward path when you can't see more than ten feet.

A pressure ridge was used as a windbreak from the relentless wind.

"Today it's easy," he said. "The wind is coming directly from the north. Wherever your face hurts the most, that's the direction we need to go."

I tried stretching out my knee. I tried bending it.

As we left the rest stop, I realized that I couldn't keep up with the sled. I soon gave up and drifted to the back of the pack where I became a slogging mule.

As the sleds moved forward, I lumbered along, wincing with each step of the right leg. Every step felt uncertain. With the snow blowing in our faces through a white-on-white world, we had no depth of field. It was hard to tell if a surface was hard or soft, if it would hold or collapse under the weight of a step. Sometimes I post-holed down to my knee through soft snow. Other times I hit a hard surface, jarring the knee. Worse yet, sometimes I hit the edge of a hard surface and careened left or right as I lost balance.

As the wind blasted us, my mind slowly wafted away, losing focus, even losing awareness. I would find myself suddenly wrenching into consciousness as a jolt of pain shot up from my knee, like waking from a dream. When I awoke I would be surprised to find myself in this strange, punishingly cold place. I teetered in and out of consciousness, sleepwalking in a whiteout. I couldn't discern the difference between the pack ice and the sky—there was no horizon line. I felt numb except for the pain in my knee. My mind twisted with contradictory emotions—frightened and uncaring, nervous and despondent.

Tornarsuk had taken over. Terrified of being left behind, I also wanted nothing more than to lie down in the snow and stop the endless trudging. Like a cancer, the negative energy grew throughout my muscles.

I stumbled up to the team at a rest break, the last person to arrive. I slumped down on an ice block to rest, lost my balance, and fell over sideways into the snow. I could hear my teammates talking around me, but their words blurred into nonsense. Though they were right next to me, they seemed remote, as if in some parallel universe.

I let out a great exhale and actually thought this might be it. I might not ever get up again. What a place to die—lying on your side in a whiteout.

Though I was scared, I was ready to give it up and die at that moment.

To give you a sense of how bad I felt, a little over two years later I would be in New York City, a few blocks from the towers when they got hit.

It was horrific. Ash and papers blew everywhere. For hours an average of seventeen sirens a minute went past the hotel where we were ordered to stay for our safety. But 9/11 is the second most scared for my life I've ever been.

The worst was that day lying on my side on the ice.

I felt I was at death's door. The thought of getting up and continuing the journey was more than I could take. Though sick with fear that I would never get up, I also wanted nothing more than to lie there forever.

Bill Martin sensed my situation and came over to talk to me. He asked about the charity, about my family. He kept asking me questions, one after another. I must have babbled some answers or grunted or I don't know what. I have no memory of how I responded.

I was on the ground, second from left, my pack in the foreground.

He reached out his hand and pulled me to a sitting position. He and Alan then forced me to drink a full water bottle—thirty-two ounces of warm Tang. Yes, Tang, as in the dried orange-juice powder made famous as the choice of astronauts.

It's appropriate that Tang was popular in the high Arctic because astronaut Neil Armstrong told a friend of mine that the North Pole was the closest to being on the moon you could be on earth.

You may turn up your nose at the thought of hot Tang, but let me tell you, it's pretty incredible. The aroma of the hot orange awakens your senses, and its bright orange color brings joy to one's eyes in a world of white, white, white.

In the frigid conditions I had neglected to keep up my fluids. I was dehydrated, exhausted, and hurt, and in my weakened physical state, Tornarsuk slithered into my brain.

Every morning each of us ladled hot water into two thirty-two-ounce plastic bottles with Tang, lemonade, or other powdered drink mix. For extra insurance against freezing, we placed the water bottles in our packs upside down on the side closest to our backs to use heat from our bodies. We stored the bottles upside down because water freezes from the top first. If the bottles were stored cap up, the lid would freeze shut.

Even at 20 to 60 below zero, if we do all of the above, in the afternoon we still had liquid to drink—it's cold, but it's still liquid. If we tied the bottles on the outside of the pack to get to them quicker or placed the pack on the sled instead of wearing it, then the water freezes solid even inside the insulated wraps that surround the bottles.

I reached into my pack for my water bottles. Today they were both full. I'd not taken a drink all day. In the terror of the whiteout I'd forgotten to drink.

"Doug, I want you to drink a full bottle," Bill said. "Now!"

I had no energy for fighting so I drank. My mind knew that if I drank I'd feel better.

Nevertheless, I told Bill I didn't think I could go on.

He said, "Don't worry. We'll do it like we do on the mountains. We're going to reduce your focus. I want you to walk behind me focusing your energy on my feet. Step exactly where I step. Focus only on my feet."

When we started moving, that's what I did. I kept my eyes focused on Bill's feet.

Right foot.

Left foot.

Right foot.

Left foot.

Hour after hour, I walked. In a deadened stupor. My head down, my eyes glued to Bill's feet. It was a walking nightmare. White on white. The ground and the sky all one.

Every now and then I looked up for a sign that we were stopping. Praying that we were stopping this madness and camping for the night. But we didn't stop.

In the afternoon, I found myself better able to concentrate. My head started to come back to me. I stuck with Bill for the afternoon. In time the wind slowed and visibility returned. However, it didn't seem that there was any stopping Paul Schurke. He just kept going.

To entertain myself and keep my mind from sinking again into the clutches of Tornarsuk, I sang. The only song that came to my mind was "White Christmas." Making things worse, I couldn't remember all the words. So I sang, "I'm dreaming of a White Christmas just like the ones I used to know. Where the treetops glisten and mmm...mmm.... And I hummed the melody until the chorus came around again, when I launched another spate of singing, "I'm dreaming of a White Christmas...."

I sang over and over and over again. A form of whistling in the dark, I guess. A way of calming my fear and making this terrible day in this faraway place seem at least a little bit like home.

About 6:00 P.M. my White Christmas death march came to an end.

As I slipped off my pack, Bill put a hand on my shoulder

and said, "Today you're an adventurer—not a novice or a rookie. You're now a member of the fraternity."

I immediately thought of the Groucho Marx line: "I don't want to be a member of any club that would have me as a member."

If this was the first ritual for joining the adventure fraternity, I had no need to reach the next level. I was happy to stay a junior member.

Incredibly, we traveled farther that day than the day before—14.3 miles versus 13.4. We now had 138 miles to go.

We had moved west from a longitude of 87.07 on the first night to 90.06. Because the prevailing current pushed the ice from west to east we turned west whenever we hit open water to counteract the flow. However, the westerly flow was not strong during our trip, so we'd moved west. It's not much distance up here, but when you wrap the distance around the globe, the result is we'd moved from being directly above Pensacola, Florida, to being above Minneapolis, Minnesota.

As we set up the cook tent, Paul told us, "Make the cook tent extra large tonight, we might be here for a while."

The storm that had hit us, the one that to me seemed like the worst on earth, was just the beginning of what could be in store.

The wind had set the entire ice cap floating south. When I checked my GPS, I realized for the first time how fast we were floating south—nearly four miles per day. While we slept we could lose a couple miles! I knew that we were floating south, but given how hard each mile had been today, it was very hard to deal with this realization.

Today's battle with the ice bridge and the storm brought an even larger realization: getting to the pole was not a sure thing. In fact, it was more likely to be an unlikely thing. The fact that Paul had made it four out of five times now seemed even more miraculous to me.

The storm had given us all a pounding. David Golibersuch was so beaten up mentally that he talked to Paul about being pulled out when the resupply plane came in a couple days.

Craig, however, was in an excited mood. He'd worked one of the big sleds by himself for most of the day and had kept the dogs moving pretty close to Paul up and down the pressure ridges. And his energy was contagious. The more I worked with him in our Arctic kitchen the better I felt. It sounds trite, but it's true—energy creates energy. The more enthusiasm I felt the less I felt the spirit of Tornarsuk within me.

Dinner that night was chicken, broccoli, and pasta with Craig's CEO pesto flavor.

Inside the cook tent, the steam was intense. The heat felt good, but while we enjoyed it, the water vapor was absorbed into our clothes. The more water our clothing absorbed, the colder we'd feel when the stove was turned off.

Paul opened the tent door to let out some steam and carbon dioxide. A common mistake when cooking inside a tent is allowing the buildup of gas. The admiral wrote about a near asphyxiation in an igloo.

> The Inuit were overcome by the lack of oxygen and the fumes of alcohol while Macmillan was preparing tea. Weesockasee fell back as though asleep. Macmillan surmised the cause and kicked the door to one side. In about fifteen or twenty minutes they came around all right.

As Paul vented the tent he glanced outside. "Look, a parahelia," he said.

Para what? I thought.

And followed everyone out of the tent to see. While we'd been eating, the sun had come out, and rainbows arced around both sides of it. Sort of a rainbow parenthesis. As I soon learned, it's a common occurrence in the high Arctic.

What a day. From the depths of whiteout hell to a magnificent rainbow.

❄

At 8:00 P.M. I called David. Remembering the echo of my family speaking the night before, I was very conscious of my tone of voice. I didn't want to scare my family. Before the call I had done my best to get folks laughing. It worked.

When we connected David jumped right into the conversation.

"How ya doing? How ya doing, sport?" he said.

"I'm doing okay," I responded. "Quite an adventure today."

"I can hear the ambient sounds in the background. And the people sound much better than what I was getting last night. The mood sounds much better."

Well, my spin job worked. Then again, of course we sounded better. We were no longer walking in a whiteout that looked like a fog of skim milk and felt like the worst deep chill on earth.

I quickly changed the camp name from White Christmas to Camp Parahelia, figuring it put a better spin on a horrible day. And I couldn't figure out how I would explain my singing of "White Christmas."

David asked about our health.

The quick report:

Frostbite—Mike, Randy, Bill, Craig, Doug, Corky on his nose.

Diarrhea—Corky.

Hemorrhoids—Paul.

Alan had a black-and-blue bruise on his thigh and had put on it, of all things, a bag of ice.

Kari asked about what Great Event to post on the Web site. I really didn't care. I was focused more than ever on surviving.

"Pick one on cold." I said. My interest in Web site details was way down on my priority list. I had to figure out how to get my act together or get myself out of this place.

I passed the phone to Paul to give a more professional report on the day.

"We're all recharging after a tough day," he said. "It pushed people over the top, and they responded excellently. They're getting rehydrated. It was a big day to make miles in horrendous conditions, in a blizzard."

Clearly David was bored in Resolute. He decided that even though we were talking on the telephone it should be more disciplined. I'd given him the title of Base Commander and it had gone to his head.

He'd decided that we should say "over" when we were finished talking.

"It will make it sound more professional that way," David said. "Over."

Paul played along.

"Any word on NASA Mike? Over," Paul said.

"Nothing new," David said. "Have lost contact with him. I can't reach him. John Paul or Kari can't reach him. Over."

"Let us know when you learn something. Over." Paul said.

When I took the phone I didn't see the humor in David's joke.

"I'm not saying 'over,' David." I said. The truth of what an ugly day it had been came out in my reaction. I also had something else on my mind.

Selling the family at home that all was well

"We need to immediately set up for David Golibersuch to talk to the school that he spoke to before the trip," I said. "It's important. Very important that we make this happen."

I was hoping that David got my message. David Golibersuch looked like I had felt earlier in the day. Only he wasn't pulling out of it. He, too, had a combination of physical and mental problems. On the first night he'd gotten badly frostbitten on his hands and feet. Now with the added burden of the mental breakdown from the day, he had given up hope.

He was losing his mental grip on the situation. His mind was spiraling into a deep Arctic depression. My hopes were that the phone call could bring him back. It could give him a purpose to keep trudging forward in this deep freezer.

I ended the call with a special pleading for more messages to our pagers. I was trying to tell my wife that I needed her contact to give me strength. I was trying to do it without sending an alarm to the kids or her.

"There is nothing more enjoyable than when you're traveling along and you feel vibration in your pocket," I said.

While we finished up the phone call, my pager vibrated.

After hanging up I pulled out my pager. It was a message from Debbie.

> "Sounds like a rowdy crowd. I'm trying to make you vibrate while you're talking. Luv Deb"

I smiled and thought—What a woman! Just when I needed her she was there to boost my spirits.

We were all pretty beaten up from the day. Some of the folks wanted to take a rest day to regroup. Others wanted to keep moving forward. I was in the second camp. I wanted to get the thing over with as soon as possible, and with the southern drift we could lose as much as six miles if we stayed for two nights and a day.

We compromised and decided to sleep for a couple of extra hours, having breakfast at ten instead of eight.

As I wrestled myself into my sleeping bag I thought of the admiral. He didn't use a sleeping bag for two reasons. First, he was concerned about weight. When we sleep we give off about two pounds of water a week. The water weight is absorbed in our sleeping bags, making them heavier and heavier as the trip goes on. Instead of a sleeping bag, he made his clothing loose enough that he could simply pull his arms inside and sleep in his clothes on a piece of fur laid on the floor of his igloo.

It felt like the old *Mutual of Omaha's Wild Kingdom* TV Show. David was like Marlin Perkins in the warm studio, and I was like Jim Fowler out in the wild. In this photo David was kind enough to interrupt his meal to take our call.

The second reason he didn't use a sleeping bag was because he was concerned the ice would open up on him. He'd had a close call with the ice opening in the middle of the night and didn't want to be dropped into the Arctic Ocean inside a sleeping bag.

I was just dropping off to sleep when I heard the ice creaking and groaning close by the igloo, but as the commotion was not excessive, nor of long duration, I rolled over on my bed of deerskins and settled myself to sleep. I was just drowsing again when I heard some one yelling excitedly. Leaping to my feet and looking through the peephole of our igloo, I was startled to see a broad lead of black water between our two igloos and Bartlett's. Awakening my men, I kicked our snow door into fragments and was outside in a moment. The break in the ice had occurred within a foot of the fastening of one of my dog teams, the team escaping by just those few inches from being dragged into the water.

With these thoughts in mind, I drifted off to sleep. Lots of what ifs...what if I fall through the ice...what if my knee doesn't heal...what if the ice opens in the middle of the night... what if the weather turns bad again...

www.Aspirations.com has audio from this day's phone call

Chapter 10
We're Not Alone

MONDAY, APRIL 19, 1999
Distance to travel to the North Pole: 138 Miles
Temperature: -21° F

*M*ONDAY MORNING I WOKE UP FEELING BRUISED AND BATTERED. The extra couple hours of sleep helped, but they also left me very stiff.

My knee felt better. As I stood up, I felt only a dull pain, which I could treat with a few aspirin. However, the rest of my body ached. My back ached from lifting and tugging the sled. My arms and legs felt as though I was recovering from a huge workout.

Craig said his throat hurt and asked if mine hurt too.

"Yeah, my throat hurts, my feet hurt, my legs hurt, my arms hurt, my head hurts."

"Sorry I asked," Craig said. "I can't resist pulling my head down into my bag, to breath warm air, but then it ends up all wet inside the bag."

"I've tried breathing through a face guard," I said. "That seems to work."

As we packed our gear, folks entered the cook tent. I put snow on the stove to melt. Everyone talked about the whiteout.

"I hope it doesn't get any harder than that," Alan said.

"Yesterday I bit off as much as I can chew," Corky said. "Not more than. I now know my limit."

"If we really knew our priorities, we wouldn't be here," Mike chimed in.

"When we started this trip I thought that not getting to the pole would be a disaster," Randy said. "After yesterday, survival is the priority."

The negative feelings began to build momentum. I tried to lighten the mood by saying, "And just think, we all volunteered for this."

No one smiled.

It took Celia to break the chain of thought with her trademark humor. "It's a humbling damn experience when you pee all over yourself at forty-five years of age," she told us. "The last time I did that was when I was six years old. I stood in the middle of the road and peed and my mom said it was okay."

I asked Paul why we had traveled in what had seemed like impossible conditions.

"Because we could," he said. "We need to find an airstrip. The weather was bad, but not bad enough to stop us. If you can travel, you do. The next day might be worse. The weather could become a full-blown storm."

Yesterday wasn't a full storm?

Celia and Alan protect their noses from frostbite.

I pushed for more perspective on traveling in bad weather. "When you push the envelope you start to know what you can do," Paul said. "It's the great gift of the Arctic—once you do it, you know you can. What I'm most proud of is that we didn't get more additions to our frostbite collection. It's critical that we find a space for the plane to land. If the resupply plane flies by and can't find a safe landing strip, they'll fly back and we're out of luck."

Bill came into the cook tent looking a little beat up.

I thanked him for his help the day before.

"On a trip like this you learn your priorities," Bill said. He spoke of his friends who had died on the mountains and of how days like yesterday brought them to mind.

It was an emotional moment. I stopped taking notes. It doesn't matter anyway because words would not do justice to Bill's feelings. Standing in the cook tent, the stove hissing, all of us were quiet except Bill, whose words put yesterday into perspective.

Breakfast was eggs, broccoli, and mozzarella cheese. Craig went a little crazy with the cheese, resulting in a stringy, chewy breakfast.

The food restored us and put everyone in a more positive mood.

"Every step forward is one less step I have to take the next day," said Corky, eager to get started.

"Isn't it amazing what sunshine does to your mood?" Bill said.

My frustration with the stringy breakfast intensified when I tried to clean the pot, which had a thick coating on the bottom and sides. At 20 below the cheese cemented to the pan.

I'd been taking myself too seriously. My daughter's note brought me back to reality.

As I sat sipping my second cup of Brain Brew coffee, (it was a two-cup morning) I wondered what was I going to do that day. Two days ago I'd given up on skiing because I failed at it. Yesterday I'd given up on pushing the sled because of my knee. I was running out of options.

Before I reached a decision, I opened another of the notes Debbie and the kids had stuck inside my gear. My daughter Tori wrote, "Have fun playing in the snow."

Have fun?

It struck me first as funny, then as sad. Here I was on an adventure of a lifetime, and I'd lost my naturally optimistic outlook. I'd forgotten all about having fun.

I chuckled. Hey, there's no reason for me to not have fun while I froze to death. I was reminded of a conversation I'd had with Paul back in Minnesota as we were preparing for the trip.

I'd asked him what he saw as the secret to success.

"Success is about enjoying day-to-day contentment," he said. "My focus is on enjoying the here and now rather than focusing on future goals. The key to achieving that kind of success is making your work as much like your play as possible. That means at an early age finding what you truly love. Find a creative way to turn play into work. Play is a timeless endeavor. When you make your play your work, you can reach a Zen-like existence."

As I sipped the rest of my Brain Brew, a weight lifted from my shoulders. Tori's innocent view and Paul's philosophy restored me. It was like I'd gulped a healthy serving of Popeye's spinach. Instead of feeling sorry for myself, I saw the opportunity to play.

"I'd like to ski today." I said to Alan.

"That's fine," Alan replied. "You weren't much good working the sled yesterday."

As we loaded the sleds I felt excited for the first time in days. I was ready to play in the snow and let go of my adultness. Ready to stop worrying about what others were thinking.

I wasn't Doug Hall Great Explorer. Or even Doug Hall Explorer in Training. I was an ordinary, overweight, middle-aged guy who was going to play in the snow.

I strapped on my skis, and without thinking too hard about life, where I was, or what I was doing, I headed down the trail to give the dogs something to chase.

The footing was horrible. In between patches of smooth snow stood small chunks of ice that needed to be navigated. It was a long way from my favorite cross-country ski resort—the Trapp Family Ski Lodge in Stowe, Vermont—where you move like a slot racer

Thanks to Tori's note, I recaptured the mind-set to be a skier.

on a racetrack, across the valley and even up the mountain behind the lodge. But instead of being tentative, I launched myself into skiing.

With giant pushes I leaped bumps like they were ski jumps. I went out of my way to bushwhack up and down a seven-foot mogul. When I fell, and I fell a lot, I forced myself to laugh. Before long I found myself laughing without forcing.

The trail conditions should have been discouraging. We faced lots of open water and ended up traveling west a number of times to find a place to cross.

By midmorning as my body learned the rhythm of Arctic skiing, I was up front with Paul. He made skiing look effortless, but although I took two strides for each one he took, with my new confidence and energy, I kept up with him. For the first time on the trip I was actually, genuinely, truly having fun!

The snow sparkled in reflections of the sun. The sky shone a deep Caribbean blue.

Tori's note ran over and over in my head: "Have fun playing in the snow."

Paul moved on ahead of me and then stopped to bend over. As I reached him it was clear he was looking at some kind of animal tracks. He looked up and with a grin said, "It's good to know we're not alone."

"You're nuts!" I said. With even more feeling than he probably heard.

"Incredible," he said. "Polar bear tracks. Probably about two days to the left of us. Or in front of us. Or behind us. It's hard to tell which direction they went."

I stared down at the big footprints. Footprints the size of pie plates.

"It's good to know we're not alone," Paul said.

It was hard to comprehend the idea of anything living out here.

Paul figured they were the tracks of a male and female. The largest set probably belonging to a male weighing about nine hundred pounds. His tracks were twelve inches long and nine inches wide. A big male polar bear can have feet as big as fifteen inches, so this one wasn't as big as they come. But he was big enough for me. I looked at the tracks—the bear's tracks and mine. If a bear approached, I was clearly the underdog.

We were there during mating season for polar bears, which would last until about the middle of May, and male polar bears are more aggressive during mating season than at any other time of the year. For the most part, polar bears are merely curious. Even when they fight over a seal carcass, one of them usually gives up before getting seriously hurt. During mating season, it's a different story.

"Our chances of seeing a bear are slim," Paul said. "They're really shy of dogs, and the howling should keep them away."

Of course that assumes that you're near the dogs and not a mile behind on skis.

I'm hoping that the male bear is happy with his female companion.

When the teams caught up, members vented reactions ranging from fear to frustration to excitement. Paul reviewed bear-safety precautions. He mentioned the two guns, the twelve-gauge pump shotgun and the .308 caliber rifle. Each had been loaded so that the first four shots would be flares, which would create a loud bang to scare the bear away. The next two shells in each gun were rubber slugs, designed to encourage the bear to go elsewhere. The last two shells were real.

Paul fired a test shot with each gun.

Polar bears are thought to be descendents of grizzlies. Over the past couple of hundred thousand years they've adapted to living on the ice. They have white fur for camouflage, black skin to absorb heat, and lots of fat for insulation. They can run as fast as twenty-five miles an hour. Big ones can only do so for a short distance, while smaller ones can go for a mile and a half without stopping.

Somebody repeated the old joke about running from a polar bear: "You don't have to run faster than a polar bear, just faster than the slowest team member."

It reminded me of the episode from the classic TV show *Cheers*. Cliff and Norm, two of the Boston bar's regulars, are seated at the end of the bar describing what Cliff called the Buffalo Theory.

"Well, you see, Norm, it's like this. A herd of buffalo can only move as fast as the slowest buffalo. And when the herd is hunted, it is the slowest and weakest ones at the back that are killed first. This natural selection is good for the herd as a whole, because the general speed and health of the whole group keeps improving by the regular killing of the weakest members.

"In much the same way, the human brain can only operate as fast as the slowest brain cells. Now, as we know, excessive intake of alcohol kills brain cells. But naturally, it attacks the slowest and weakest brain cells first. In this way, regular con-

Skiing along behind Paul

sumption of beer eliminates the weaker brain cells, making the brain a faster and more efficient machine. And that, Norm, is why you always feel smarter after a few beers."

It was our longest day of traveling. I got into a rhythm and for the first time relaxed enough to feel the tedium Arctic explorers had talked about in their books. My emotions had gone from manically excited the first day to terrified to a touch of boredom.

I caught up with Paul who was looking for a path through the ice rubble and asked, "What do you think about when you're skiing?"

"I work out trip details, sing songs, but mostly I go to my happy place," he said.

But before I could ask what he meant by "happy place," he took off.

For the next two hours I wondered about happy place. What did he mean? I thought about it for the next two hours, like Luke Skywalker decoding Yoda's riddles.

Happy place. Is it a meditation? A chant? An incantation?

At this temperature, in these conditions what could be a happy place?

Finally I gave up thinking and just skied. Instead of thinking I simply let my mind wander, skipping from memory to memory.

I traveled to other cross-country ski experiences. One moment I was sixteen and skiing in the woods behind our house in New Hampshire with my brother Bruce. Next I was bushwhacking up to the top of Hall's Ledge in Jackson, New Hampshire, where my forefathers settled. As my mind skipped along, I was soon at Trapp Family Lodge in Vermont, teaching my kids how to cross-country ski. I remembered the sights, sounds, and smells of the lodge.

The connections with kids reminded me of going to a small pond behind our house to try out the kids' brand-new ice skates. Luckily, none of them had skated much before. They didn't realize that falling down could hurt, and no one told them that skating is supposed to be difficult, so they weren't afraid to try it. And once they were on the ice, none of them wanted to leave. They slipped and slid and laughed until the sunset turned the sky a glorious orange and pink. It was like something out of a storybook. The scene so impressed the kids they decided that from that point on they would refer to that small body of water as Sunset Pond.

As I skied along I remembered watching the stars come out when we slipped off our skates for the trip back home. I laughed as I remembered the kids chattering on in anticipation of sharing the experience with their mom.

While I was skiing in the Arctic, my mind ran a three-dimensional movie about laughing and having fun with the kids and with cross-country skiing.

I came back to the Arctic when I heard Alan yell for help getting over a pressure ridge. As I reached down to unbuckle my skis, I realized that when I stopped thinking, I had discovered the happy place.

Happy place is about nonthinking. It's about letting one's mind wander, freely, unbridled, letting the memory cells fire one after the other. Sort of a random movie screen of memories, dreams, and mindfulness.

Late in the afternoon we traveled down a canyon of ice. The ice had split apart and then frozen into a smooth surface about six feet wide between walls of ice from four to twelve feet high.

We traveled a little longer than usual to find a runway for the resupply plane that would provide more dog food, fuel, and food the next day.

About 8:30 P.M. we stopped to make camp. Checking my GPS I found it was our best day yet. We'd covered 19.6 miles.

As I took off my backpack, I noticed that my fleece jacket was covered in snow though it wasn't snowing. The fleece fabric was taking my sweat and wicking it to the outside where it froze. The wonder of artificial fibers!

At dinner Craig made up for his stringy breakfast chew fest with a dinner of spaetzle, beef, mixed veggies, and Corky's Steak and Onion Spice. The team loved it, proclaiming it the best yet. Then again, where else are you going to go for dinner?

Our evening phone call focused on the news of polar bear tracks. We also reviewed plans for the resupply flight, which we were sharing with Pen Haddow, a British explorer who was currently at the North Pole. A television station in Malaysia had run a contest to take the winner anywhere in the world. Two brothers had won and decided they wanted to go to the North Pole. Pen had been hired as their guide. After the plane picked up Pen, it would stop near us for the resupply.

The snow on my jacket was from sweat wicking to the surface.

The plane needed a good landing space, and we reported that the strip was two thousand feet long with ice at least three feet thick with one inch of flat snow.

The plane left Resolute that day for Eureka. The key constraint on a successful connection was weather. David would send us a page in the morning to tell us if the plane could make the trip north.

Other news from the call included NASA Mike. He was driving David crazy. He kept designing new travel itineraries like he was making plans for shore visits from a cruise ship.

"I told NASA Mike to forget it, the deal's off," David said.

"Whatever," I responded. "So the food and fuel are on the plane?"

"Right," he said. "The dog food and the fuel."

"What about the green bag—the other food bag?"

"Oh no," he said. "Sorry. I missed it. I didn't know."

This was bad news, especially for Craig and me as the cooks. We had plenty of food, but we needed powdered drinks to add to the water bottles. Our Tang supply was very low.

When Paul took the phone he went over more logistics.

"We'll be taking out a small sled and film, less than fifty pounds," he said. "David Golibersuch will not be taken out. He's staying."

It had been touch and go with David, but Paul felt he could make the journey. Alan told me later that he felt David should leave on the resupply plane. Other team members felt the same.

David brought great news on the Great Aspirations! charity publicity. *CBS This Morning* wanted to have the first call from the pole, and the *Chicago Tribune* ran a big story on the trip.

The *CBS This Morning* element was a big deal. When one major outlet agrees to a story you can leverage that coverage with other media sources. If all went according to plan, we would soon have a major newspaper offering a front-page feature, and we'd also get a magazine article.

Jon Paul said, "Get ready for major interviews from the pole. It's going really well."

Kari reported, "We have some seventy-five thousand people a day on the Web site."

In the Internet dark ages of 1999, those were huge numbers.

In addition to the major outlets, we were getting a lot of coverage in small towns. The story caught the imagination. At this rate we might reach millions.

I ended the call with a quick message to my family, who I hoped were listening: "Love to Deb, the kids, Brad, Tori, and Kristyn."

David signed off with, "Good night, don't let the polar bears bite."

As I hung up, I noticed discontent among the troops. While I had gone to my happy place during the day, others hadn't. The whiteout had beaten up everyone pretty badly, and rather than rest and recover, we'd put in our longest journey of the trip. Members debated the need to take a full day of rest, weighing it against the miles we'd lose drifting south.

Again we compromised. We'd sleep late and make tomorrow a half day of travel. If all worked out right, the resupply plane would arrive around noon before we started moving.

As the conversation continued I walked outside the cook tent to check on the battery charger. Kari had built a solar battery charger, and I had placed it outside during dinner, aimed at the sun. We had enough battery power for our nightly calls, but if I could make the charger work, we'd have freedom to make more calls.

I saw that we couldn't leave the charger out over night. Unlike at home where the sun traveled across the sky in an arc to the south, in the Arctic the sun traveled in 360 degrees around us. Every hour it moved 15 degrees. If I left the charger aimed at the sun at night, within three hours it was aimed at an angle of 45 degrees. It also appeared that the battery wasn't charging. The icon was barely visible.

With the batteries so cold, it was hard to get a charge. Maybe if I got them really warm, then wrapped them in insulation, I could get a couple hours charging in the morning. I decided to put the phone and batteries in my sleeping bag for the night.

www.Aspirations.com has
audio from this day's phone call

Chapter 11
Houston, We Have a Problem

TUESDAY, APRIL 20, 1999
Distance to travel to the North Pole: 119 Miles
Temperature: -12° F

Follow Ziggy LIVE on his Great Aspirations trip to the North Pole at www.ASPIRATIONS.com!

*T*HE ALARM ON MY WATCH RANG AT 7:00 A.M. I turned it off and rolled over to continue sleeping. I didn't have to get up until 10:00 A.M. to start cooking snow. But at 8:00 Bill, Celia, and Mike came into the cook tent and woke me up to do an interview with the *Gainesville Sun* and a Florida radio station. I gave them the warm Iridium phone from my sleeping bag. Craig and I stayed in our sleeping bags during their interview.

They finished around 8:45 and headed back to their tent to get some extra sleep. I put the phone back in my sleeping bag to warm it.

Around 9:00 I felt an urge to pee. I ignored it for a while. Hoping it would go away.

By 9:30 I had no choice.

I had to get up.

But I didn't want to get up.

Then I remembered my pee bottle. I'd not used it yet but figured it was time to embrace the entire explorer experience. I unscrewed the cap and soon enjoyed true relief. Relief that turned to horror when I realized that my bladder was bigger than the bottle.

The bottle ran over into the inside of my sleeping bag. Yuck, I thought. But I didn't have long to feel that way—because soon true terror exploded through me.

"Shit, shit, shit, shit" I screamed, hopping up in my sleeping bag like a mad man.

"What's the matter?" Craig asked.

"Shit, shit, shit"

"What's the matter?" Craig said again.

" I just peed on the phone!" I whispered.

"What did you say?"

"I just peed on the Iridium phone." I screamed.

I jumped from the sleeping bag and pulled out the phone and batteries.

I wiped off the dripping phone as fast as possible. Opening it up, I tried to dry out every crack quickly. I tried to turn it on. A few lights came on but nothing happened. I turned it off quickly.

Oh my God, I thought. I've just short-circuited our expedition communications network with my pee.

Alan entered the tent. I was in a stupor, my mind racing. He asked me something, but I couldn't answer, my brain grasping for what to do next.

Then I heard him ask again, "What happened to the phone?"

Before I could respond, Craig said, "He peed on the phone"

Alan, with his dry sense of humor, said, "We'll keep it our little secret."

"Yeah, sure, whatever." My mind ripped through various options about what to do. Then I heard Alan laugh, open the tent and yell, "Guess what, everybody. The phone's buggered because Doug peed on it."

Needless to say, everyone quickly woke up.

Bill arrived in the cook tent first. He tried to soften my anxieties with gentle humor. However, in his eyes I could see pure terror. He knew the consequences of losing our primary communications system.

Paul came in without saying much. He grabbed his Leather-man knife and started taking the phone apart. It seemed hopeless to me. Thousands of dollars of the most sophisticated phone ever made and he thinks he can repair it? Get a life.

Then again, he'd done it before. On his 1986 trip they had navigated by sextant. As they neared the pole he found that they were getting mixed readings from one day to the next. He brought the sextant into his tent and took it apart with his Swiss Army knife. There, between the lenses, he found a crystal of ice. He wiped the ice away, cleaned the lenses and the sextant once again functioned perfectly.

He opened the back of the phone and wiped out the liquid. Okay, he wiped out my pee.

He turned the phone on. Nothing.

He took it apart again. Nothing.

He tried another battery. Nothing.

While Paul worked on the phone, Craig gave up trying to sleep and lit the stove.

Paul called for a pot. He placed a pot on the stove and a roll of toilet paper in the bottom, then the open phone on top of it, and covered the pot.

"We'll bake your pee," he told me with a smile.

I heard a few jokes about my aroma.

To be honest, the jokes were funny, but to me each was shot

to the gut. My feelings of joyful skiing and discovering my happy place vanished. Tornarsuk quickly took over my soul.

After half an hour of cooking, we tried the phone again. Miraculously, we got a signal. I dialed Kari's cell phone in Cincinnati. The phone

We baked the phone to dry out my....pee.

indicated a connection, but I couldn't hear anything. I tried again but still heard nothing.

"Kari, can you hear me? Are you there? I can't hear you."

Then my pager went off. The message: *I can hear you but you can't hear me.*

It was working! Sort of.

"The phone has been damaged," I told her. "It got wet."

Okay, so I didn't give her a full explanation. The phone got wet. That was the issue. There was no reason to go further.

"We need another phone," I said, knowing the odds were against our getting one. The phones were highly limited at the time. It had taken six months to get the phone in my hand.

Her page came in: *No problem. Will get another to Resolute ASAP.*

"Tell David we will contact via radio tonight as planned at 8:00 P.M.," I said.

Again we waited. Then my pager beeped: *Will tell David to be on the radio tonight.*

We'd made at least some progress. Paul grinned with satisfaction. Schurke Serendipity had struck again.

Suddenly my pager beeped again. This time it was David.

Planes grounded in Resolute. Bad weather. No resupply today. Commander Dave.

Celia came into the tent and tried to cheer me up by joking about how her clothes and the big white boots made her feel like an astronaut on the moon.

Alan talked about the relentless, relentless, relentless cold. How it never really left your consciousness.

I tried to participate in the conversation, but my mind was stuck thinking about my troubles. Because I'd been too lazy to get out of bed I'd destroyed my main purpose for the trip—to inspire parents and kids who were following us online.

I grew quiet, searching for a way out of the darkness that I was feeling.

At noon Craig served a breakfast of rice, grains, brown sugar, and powdered milk. I could barely taste it. The telephone consumed my thoughts as I sank into a deep funk. We had made such progress. We'd hooked the media with the Great Aspirations! Expedition story. Now without the phones, we were finished. A radio link could not be broadcast.

As I drifted into depression, I felt colder than ever. I pulled on my thick fleece pants for the first time when skiing. I cut some extra pads from my sleeping pad to add to my boots for additional warmth. In place of liner gloves I used a dry pair of liner socks on my hands.

Before taking off for the day I recorded my feelings in my yellow journal.

Cold. Fleece pants while traveling. Closed eyes and prayed.

I AM Ready to Give up—I need to find strength somewhere.

I want to go home. I just want to curl up and cry. Survival is a real issue at this point.

I can't snap my fingers and change this. It's at least two days before a plane can come in—this is about survival at this point. It doesn't help that everything smells like pee.

It was my third and worst attack by the Arctic Devil Tornarsuk. My first attack was in Edmonton and it was driven by a fear of the unknown. My second was during the whiteout and it was a very real physical pain and a fear for the future. This third attack was the worst yet. It ripped at my purpose on this expedition. I was clearly not the strongest or the wisest about exploring. But I contributed publicity to the team and gave the expedition a meaningful purpose.

As I wrote of my loss I did manage a bit of humor: *Feeling of being very alone out here. I feel like my purpose has been—pardon the pun—peed away.*

I strapped on my skis and started off into the wild. Fortunately, my funk did not hurt my ability to ski. I skied in the front with Paul. After about an hour we stopped to rest, and Paul noticed my funk.

"You have that woe-is-me look," he said.

"I feel like shit. I can't believe how stupid I was."

Paul's reaction was so bizarre to me, so unexpected, that I wrote it down verbatim in my journal. With the greatest calm and confidence he said, "Don't worry or sweat it. Something great will come out of this. It always does. Serendipity. It's all part of the process."

Paul is about living in the moment. Years later, Mike England, a friend on Prince Edward Island, would tell me two truths that explain Paul's view of the world:

1. Life is random
2. Everything always comes out as it should be.

Paul brushed past my self pity to the beauty of the Arctic scenery.

"I love the uniqueness of the Arctic," he said. "Every day is different."

We talked for a while about the admiral. About what he went through. About the relentlessness of his efforts. At a quick break to let the teams catch up, I looked in the back of my journal at some quotes from the admiral that I'd written before the trip—motivational quotes to give me a jolt of energy.

The true explorer does his work not for any hopes of reward or honor, but because the thing he has set for himself to do is a part of his being, and must be accomplished for the sake of the accomplishment. And he counts lightly hardships, risks, and obstacles, if only they do not bar him from his goal.

The admiral lost nine toes to frostbite. It's said that he would place tin cans in the toes of his boots to protect the stubs. Critics have said he was driven by fame and fortune. After traveling in that frozen wasteland, I don't think there is enough fame or money in the entire world to motivate me to spend twenty-three years in search of 90 North as he did.

Soon, more bad news arrived. On the pagers we learned that there had been a shooting at Columbine High School in Colorado. Thirteen students and faculty were killed and many more wounded.

The news added to my depression. We were on the ice promoting the Great Aspirations! principles, the kind of principles that spoke to the needs of young adults—a sense of belonging, accomplishment, fun, and leadership. And I'd peed on the phone!

As I grasped for understanding, I continued writing in my journal.

Why am I here? What drove me to do this? How can I simplify and focus on what really matters in life?

As I skied I thought about these words. What is my true purpose? Why am I on this earth? My business life had been more successful than I could ever have imagined. With that success had come the opportunity, and the responsibility, to focus my energies on the highest level of "self actualization," as Abraham Maslow would say.

For the last few years I'd focused energy on helping Dr. Russ Quaglia spread his teachings to families. This expedition was accelerating that awareness, and I was proud of that success. But I still didn't feel like it was my true purpose. There was something more for me to do on this earth.

As I skied my overactive mind explored a multitude of lives I could live. I could go back to school and become a teacher or professor. I could develop courses on innovation based on what I'd learned helping Nike, Walt Disney, and American Express invent ideas.

For the rest of the expedition, I thought about my purpose. I didn't expect to find the "answer," but by thinking deeply I believed I could find my purpose. The dreaming of alternate futures gave me an escape from the oppressive Arctic depression caused by destroying the phone.

As my dreaming ended, my mind returned to the situation at hand. Again the depression and cold engulfed me. The worst part of feeling cold on an Arctic expedition is the feeling that you can't escape it. There is no place to warm up. The cook tent created the illusion of warmth because it was warmer than the outdoors, but you only experience this illusion when your mind is in the right place. When your mind is in a funk, even the cook tent feels very, very cold.

When your mind goes, all you see is the ground in front of you. Your head tilts down to shelter your face from the cold wind or the glare of the sun. You look at the ice before your feet through the porthole formed by your hood. You become conscious of every energy expenditure—every lift of the sled, push of the sled, climb of a pressure ridge. Your skis become a burden.

Even though you don't fully see the surroundings, you feel like you're walking in one endless sea of white on white.

That afternoon I said a little a prayer. Not for the phone. For my spirit. Somehow I had to climb out of the funk or I would soon become a major liability to the expedition and myself.

At a rest stop, I learned that my teammates were praying too.

Celia told me, "One of my prayers this afternoon is to have the phone work again."

Alan added, "I talked to the angels, your phone will work tonight."

Soon the conversation turned back to the cold. I stayed quiet. I tried working through hundreds of possible scenarios. What if…what if…

As an entrepreneur I went into every business opportunity with two or more "back door scenarios," alternate possibilities for generating sales or profits if the first approach didn't work. However, in this case I had no options. And even when I did get an idea, my pessimistic mood immediately rejected it.

If Kari could get a phone—which was unlikely.

If she could get it to Resolute—which was impossible to reach.

If we could get a plane to fly up—which would cost forty thousand dollars.

Then I could go back to broadcasting our status to families around the world.

As we traveled through the afternoon, I worked and reworked the puzzle pieces. And with each failure to find a solution, I slipped deeper into depression.

I was skiing out front with Paul again. When we stopped to wait for the sleds to catch up, he reached into his pack and handed me a red balaclava hood that could be pulled up over my mouth and nose. His wasn't a microfleece light version like the one I'd bought in Edmonton. His was an industrial weight, go-to-the-pole version.

"This might help you," he said.

"You can't. You need it."

"I have an extra. You look like you need it."

I pulled down my hood, pulled off my thin and frozen light one and slipped Paul's over my head. I instantly felt warmer.

It was a priceless gift. A gift of relief from the cold. A gift of warmth.

As I put mine into my pack, I saw the bag of notes from Debbie and the kids. I opened two notes with a common theme.

My oldest daughter, Kristyn, wrote, "Please come back in 1 piece."

My other daughter, Tori, wrote, "To the pole and back again!"

The notes were like two slaps in my face. To my children, the return was more important than the going.

If I am going to return in "one piece" I needed to get my act together. As the sleds came into sight, I read Peary's words again:

> The true explorer does his work not for any hopes of reward or honor, but because the thing he has set for himself to do is a part of his being, and must be accomplished for the sake of the accomplishment. And he counts lightly hardships, risks and obstacles, if only they do not bar him from his goal.

I then wrote in my journal.

Now without phone connection.

I do it for me. I can do it. I can.

Paul's simple gift, the gift of my daughters' love, the admiral's words, and my writing of those words collectively turned my mind in a new direction.

They stopped the death spiral of Tornarsuk's negative energy.

Fresh hope in the form of a new purpose—at least for this trip—rose up within me.

Without the phone, and broadcasting for the charity as my personal reason for being on the expedition, I had to change **MY** aspirations. I had to become grounded in something more powerful than my external ego. I needed to do this trip for me. Not **ME** as in a selfish **ME**. Rather, **ME** as in the authentic Doug Hall who genuinely loves the outdoors. The Doug who loves to learn about and experience the adventure of life. The Doug who loves the adventure of discovering what is around the next bend.

Instead of being motivated by the unhealthy external ego, I needed to be driven by the healthy internal and authentic self. Until this point I had held back from throwing my soul into this trip. I was somewhat distant from the reality of the situation. I had fueled my existence on the ice through the promise of external rewards of fame from the media attention surrounding the Great Aspirations! charity.

With the possibility of media exposure stripped away, I needed a new purpose. I needed to be grounded in my true self, to become more fully present in this place. I needed to be here for the joy of the moment and the experience itself.

As I skied I focused my mind solely on the here and now. For the first time on this expedition I genuinely observed my surroundings.

I noticed a gentle mist in the air. I noticed ice formations. All around me the ice was carved in forms reminiscent of an ancient cathedral. The beauty of the mist, ice, and snow was beyond words.

Being out front with Paul, I could savor the silence, hearing only the swoosh of our skis. When we stopped to drink water, we heard pure silence. Not a dead silence, as in an ominous silence, but rather a pure, peaceful quiet.

There was a spiritual, Biblical essence to this place.

As I became aware of my surroundings, I became less aware of the cold. And even less aware of being tired.

For the first time it felt like I was seeing the Arctic as Peary and Schurke saw it.

Around 7:30 P.M. that evening, Paul stopped, pulled out a gun, and shot off a flare.

"Welcome to 89th Street," he announced. "We're at the 89th parallel. We're halfway to the pole. "

The idea of being halfway felt good. However, for the first time on this trip, I was disappointed that we were stopping for the night. I had enjoyed myself and couldn't wait to see what we'd find around the next bend.

It had been our shortest day of travel yet. We'd traveled just 11.4 miles. We weren't near a landing strip, but we had to connect with David by radio to learn the status of the resupply flight.

As we made camp, we found that getting a resupply was even more urgent. During the day's travel we'd lost another gallon of fuel when another tin sprung a leak.

At 8:00 P.M. we tried the radio. Paul climbed a nearby pressure ridge and had me hold the end of the antenna high in the air, tied to a ski pole. Connection was not assured as the signal is highly dependent on conditions in the ionosphere, which with the recent storms were probably turbulent.

After about half an hour of moving the antenna and calling out, we connected with David. The resupply plane was at Eureka, where the weather was good. But weather at the pole and at our location was not good. We have a cloud ceiling of about one thousand feet, and the North Pole was equally cloudy. By the time the pilot broke through the clouds over us and got a look at a potential landing strip, he wouldn't have time to get bearings, much less land the plane safely.

We agreed that David would send a message on the pagers

as soon as the planes took off. Then it would be our challenge to find a runway while the planes were in the air.

We tried again to fix the Iridium phone. We baked and baked. But unlike earlier that day, we couldn't even get a signal out. Again the jokes flew at my expense, but this time I laughed.

As we worked the phone without success, serendipity arrived again. Paul had an idea.

"I think Pen Haddow has an Iridium phone, maybe we can borrow his," Paul said.

I laughed. "Do you think we could rent it?"

"Let's call and find out."

Paul and I set up the radio again. I grabbed onto the end of the wire, as Paul got on the radio.

"Aspirations Expedition calling Pen Haddow. Aspirations Expedition calling Pen Haddow. Come in Pen." Paul said.

Nothing.

He tried again, "Aspirations Expedition calling Pen Haddow."

Suddenly the crackling of the radio was broken with a distinctively English voice.

"Haddow calling Aspirations. Is that you, Paul?"

"Affirmative, we're at 89 degrees."

"We're at the pole, conditions are no good for flying. Hope for pickup flight tomorrow."

"Affirmative. We were wondering if we could rent your Iridium phone."

There was a long pause. The radio clicked a couple times, as if Pen had started to talk and then stopped. Finally he came back.

"But I'm going out again on the thirtieth and need the phone back by then. I can't risk you not getting back to Resolute in time."

"Tell him we'll have another phone sent to Resolute for him," I said.

"Understand your needs," Paul said into the radio. "We

Paul called Pen Haddow.

will have another phone in Resolute for you to use in the event we do not return in time."

Another long pause.

Then Pen said, "You seem very confident. How are you going to get a phone to Resolute in a week? I have the only Iridium phone in the entire UK."

Paul paused, looked at me for an answer.

Without hesitation I said, "Kari. She'll make it happen."

Paul smiled and nodded. In the trip planning he'd experienced the miracle of Kari. She's one of those people who, when something seems impossible, becomes more motivated to make it happen.

"We have already alerted our base camp," Paul told Pen. "They advise that a phone will be in Resolute before you leave. We are certain of this."

As Paul tried to convince Pen, I got another idea. Paul had told me that Pen, like virtually all Arctic and Antarctic explorers, was regularly under funded. He was doing his current trip for a TV station to fund his real trip in a few weeks. Maybe some cash could turn the trick. And David was holding forty thousand dollars.

"Paul, tell him we'll give him ten thousand dollars to rent it. David has money."

Paul radioed, "For your trouble we're prepared to pay you ten thousand dollars in cash. Our base commander in Resolute has it with him."

Another long pause.

"I believe we can make this work," Pen said.

Paul looked down and smiled. I looked up to heaven and thanked God.

Schurke serendipity struck again. In the middle of nowhere we rented an Iridium phone!

Pen reported that his radio batteries and fuel were low and asked if we could relay messages to Eureka. "Need pickup as soon as possible," he said. "Guests are very cold and unable to move from tent."

Paul relayed the message to Resolute. They reported that they would check satellite pictures again at midnight and would fly as soon as conditions permitted.

Pen said, "We'll be here. Look for the red tent with yellow top."

When we got off the radio, Paul and I went back into the cook tent. Then, for the next hour we decoded what we had heard. The phone provided clear communication, but on the radio words came in fragments. Sometimes you'd miss half the words in a sentence, and it was hard to discern the tone of voice and emphasis of the speaker.

Paul wondered if Pen was in more serious trouble than he was letting on. The Malaysians must have freaked out in the cold. We might have to send a small team to dash to the pole to get him fuel if the weather didn't clear soon.

Pen was juggling the liability of caring for the Malaysians with the liability of calling in a plane that might not be able to land. If the guests got hurt he'd be liable. If the plane couldn't land, he'd be liable for paying forty thousand dollars. It was a very difficult situation.

Though I shared Paul's concern about Pen, the radio contact with Pen lifted my spirits. I felt better. From the depths of despair a miracle had occurred. You can call it serendipity, faith, or luck. They're all related. They all involve focusing on hopes for the future.

Pen's positive reaction to the offer of money is the answer to the first of the three Peary's Mysteries: *Why was he so quiet on his return to the ship?*

The simple answer is that like most explorers of the time, Peary was dirt poor, and he didn't want to repeat Roald Amundsen's mistake. In 1903, Amundsen was the first to cross the Northwest Passage. However, his story leaked to the mass media, violating his contract for exclusivity and forfeiting his best chance to pay off expedition debts.

Peary kept his story secret until he had first gotten news to the *New York Times*, which had loaned him four thousand dollars (ninety-six thousand in 2009 dollars). A letter found at the Berkshire Museum of Art and Science in Pittsfield, Massachusetts, confirms that the expedition didn't have the money to pay the crew upon its return to New York City. Specifically, the expedition was eighteen thousand dollars ($204,000) in debt.

This situation is confirmed in the books by his leadership team. Peary told them that he was staying quiet in case they met another ship that got back first and broke the story.

At dinner the debate on our rate of travel continued. Craig, Alan, and Paul wanted to move up the pace to more than ten miles a day. Corky agreed. The balance of the team, feeling beat up, was against increasing the pace.

Due to the different levels of skiing ability and physical condition of the team members, we kept spreading apart as we moved, causing a "Slinky" effect that increased each person's

THE PEARY ARCTIC CLUB.

"To Reach the Farthest Northern Point on the Western Hemisphere; to Promote and Maintain Explorations of the Polar Regions."

PRESIDENT, THOMAS H. HUBBARD.   VICE-PRESIDENT, ZENAS CRANE.

ORGANIZED, JANUARY, 1899.
INCORPORATED, APRIL, 1904.
INCORPORATORS:
MORRIS K. JESUP.
HENRY PARISH.
HENRY A. RAVEN.
JOHN H. FLAGLER.
ROBERT E. PEARY, C. E., U. S. N.
HERBERT L. BRIDGMAN, Sec'y and Treas,
"Standard Union" Building,
Brooklyn-New York.

New York, May 29, 1909.

Dear Mr. Crane;-

I regret that I am obliged to report that the funds of the Peary Arctic Club are exhausted, the appeal to the public in January having been practically fruitless. To carry the enterprise to completion, say next November, paying wages, and all other charges, will require, say $18,000, and upon the suggestion of Gen. Hubbard and Mr. Parish, I am writing to inquire whether you would be willing to join them in an equal division of this sum, of which a part might be repaid upon the return and sale of the "Roosevelt" though of that you must be the judge. I trust that you may be able to see your way to participate in the manner indicated, and so bring to a satisfactory and successful conclusion the work of a quarter of a century.

Yours very truly,

Secretary-Treasurer.

Zenas Crane, Esq.,
Vice-President of the Peary Arctic Club,
Dalton, Massachusetts.

P.S: - If immediate payment of $1,000 should be convenient, no further sum would be necessary before September. I also enclose draft of letter to Mrs. Jesup, which, as you observe, bears your name and therefore should, I think, have your approval.

Note found at the Berkshire Museum

sense of isolation and decreased their motivation. And ever since we saw the polar bear tracks, no one liked getting separated from the sleds.

Others argued that we should rest for a day and regroup. But with the full moon coming, the ice would break up even faster. If we didn't make miles now, we may miss our opportunity.

Craig broke the debate by reading a page he'd received: Go Team Ziggy. We're betting on you. Dan bus driver in Vegas. It was amazing the impact that the little guy in the comic strip was having with the people following our trip in the newspaper. Tom was also providing content for some of our nightly North Pole Telegrams on our Web site. Later I would learn about Tom giving voice to Ziggy's thoughts this way on the night of our debate about moving faster:

ZIGGY E-MAIL REPORT

Sometimes when I'm standing here shivering in minus 40 Farenheit temperatures, I wonder what in the world I'm doing here? (As far as handling the cold, I get frostbite just opening my refrigerator.)

Let's face it, when the going gets tough...I usually go eat chocolate chip cookie dough! I mean, I know that somewhere deep down inside me, there's a rugged Arctic explorer just screaming to get out. Unfortunately, he probably has trouble being heard through all these clothes!

I'm dressed in so many layers I know how the Michelin Tire guy feels. About three layers down, over my long johns, I'm wearing a Hawaiian shirt, just to keep me cheered up. I keep thinking warm thoughts–hot pizza, my fuzzy bunny slippers, and snuggling with my pets back home. It's kind of a Zen thing.

I admit, I get a little discouraged at times. All of us are cold, tired, and homesick. But it's then I remind myself of the big picture and remember why we're really here. We're doing this for a great cause, children and parents around the world. We're here to call attention to the Great Aspiration! charity – a program designed to get children and parents excited about life, inspired to follow their dreams, and to push their limits by going beyond where they are now.

I'll write again soon...ZIGGY.

Just before going to sleep I wrote in my journal about the day's events. My last words turned toward home: *I want to sit in the garden and grow roses and flowers and whisper into Deb's ear that I love you.*

As usual, I placed my liner gloves, hat, and socks inside my sleeping bag with me, using my body heat as a sort of organic dryer. Though the clothing never fully dried, the system worked amazingly well. When facing a challenge like reaching the North Pole, these little victories provide a little delight and a curious bit of hope.

Sadly, the radio contact was not recorded.

Chapter 12
Splish Splash

WEDNESDAY, APRIL 21, 1999
Distance to travel to the North Pole: 107 Miles
Temperature: -37° F

AROUND THREE IN THE MORNING I woke up freezing. I couldn't understand it. I'd followed my same routine, gone for a quick run, placed a water bottle with boiling water in the bag.

What had happened?

I quickly scanned my body and the sleeping bag. Everything seemed right. Then I rolled to the left and discovered that in my good feelings I had overstuffed my sleeping bag with wet socks, hats, and mittens. My body didn't have enough energy to dry off all the socks and gloves I put in the bag. Instead, they were "sucking away" my heat. I tossed the wet clothing out of the bag and instantly felt warmer. I pulled my hat down and went back to sleep.

At 7:00 A.M., the consequences of my actions became evident. Beside me lay a frozen sculpture of gloves, hats, and socks. I picked it up and knocked it against my backpack. A glove fell off, the fingers frozen in the shape of a demented monster. The balance of the mess was frozen solid.

Ugh.

I placed the entire mess inside my yellow bivy sack between my sleeping bag and sleeping pad. The area was still warm from my body heat, and I lay down on top of the mess to soften it, like a mama bird nesting on top of her eggs.

Craig asked what I was doing.

"Just a little problem with frozen gloves," I said.

I woke up with frozen gloves, but I was feeling good.

After about five minutes I got up and pulled them apart. Next was the ugly part. I pulled one pair of gloves and one pair of socks inside my sleeping bag with me. Within about five minutes they defrosted, and I could at least put them on. I'd learned the hard way that you have to pay attention to every detail. If you don't pay attention you pay the consequences. This morning it was my gloves. The day before I drank sloppily from my water bottle, the water sloshed on my gloves and they froze solid.

Paul was the first into the cook tent, "How are the boys doing?" he asked.

Craig and I, being among the youngest and smallest, were not only Tenderfeet, we were also the "kids" on the trip.

Paul reported that the weather wasn't good.

Craig reported, "We have fuel for today and tomorrow."

I piped in, "We don't have a landing strip."

For some reason it all seemed funny to us. We laughed. Not a nervous laugh. It was a fun laugh, as in, boy, won't it be exciting to see how we get out of this one.

"We're sixteen hundred miles north of Alaska," I said, "traveling on a moving sheet of ice, with little fuel left, with weather that looks like it'll storm any minute, and most amazing of all we volunteered to go on this trip. When do you think we should reevaluate our sanity?"

By 8:00 A.M. breakfast was ready, a hearty one of sausage and potatoes. If we're going to use the last fuel, no reason to hold back on the meat!

As is prone to happen when traveling with the benefit of Schurke serendipity, things started looking up. The weather started to clear, and then—*beep beep*—my pager went off.

> *One phone already enroute to Resolute. Second phone leaves today. Kari.*

Unbelievable. It had taken me six months to get one phone. Pen had the only phone in all of the UK. Somehow Kari had gotten two phones in twenty-four hours.

I gave Craig a high five. "Can you believe it?" I said.

"If I wasn't here I wouldn't. How did she do it?"

Before we could even start to guess—*beep beep*. The pager again.

> *Pickup flight still off. Bad weather at pole. Commander Dave.*

Time to break camp, pack sleds, and find a landing strip for the planes. To overcome the team's anxieties, Paul changed our means of travel. We would put more people on skis. Instead of two people on each of the four sleds, we'd have one per sled and seven people on skis. In this way everyone would be moving more than before, increasing warmth and travel speed. It also would reduce the weight of the sleds and help reduce the chances of dog burnout.

As mentioned earlier, on Arctic sleds you're not supposed to ride except on the smoothest of frozen leads. You're supposed to run beside or behind, helping push. But given the fatigue everyone felt, the rule often was broken.

The admiral's sled offered nothing to stand on. Our sleds have a small platform behind the back uprights, just enough room for one person—or two if you turn sideways. The sleds were also used by Paul in Ely for vacation dogsledding trips, where guests are usually not in the best condition. On previous North Pole trips, Paul didn't have platforms on the back of the sleds.

We adjusted bindings and got everyone set up to ski.

As the day started I was excited about the upcoming return of the phone, but I felt a deeper satisfaction about changing my purpose from the charity to being alive in the moment. I now was traveling for the sake of traveling—enjoying the scenery, skiing, and just being mindful.

It was odd to feel so good after feeling so bad. I was positively gleeful. Through the morning I sang to myself an eclectic list of songs, from Simon and Garfunkle's "Fifty-Ninth Street Bridge Song"—"Slow down you move too fast. You got to

I was feeling good, singing songs, and being in the moment.

make the morning last...Doot-in' doo-doo, feelin'groovy," to the great bagpipe tune "Amazing Grace"—"Amazing grace, how sweet the sound, that saved a wretch like me. I once was lost but now am found..."

I truly had been lost and found again. I'd been moving too fast.

As I sang my songs, the crowd around me didn't share my mood. It quickly became clear that a lot of my teammates hadn't done much cross-country skiing. And those who had experience felt the same frustrations I had gone through earlier.

As they struggled with the skis over the fractured trail of ice, fatigue built up as sweat froze to ice crystals on their eyebrows and beard stubble. Their pain and frustration were obvious.

By noon, everyone except for Craig, Paul, and I had taken off their backpack and tied it to the top of a sled, which bothered the sled drivers. The added load made the sleds top heavy and more likely to tip.

Around 3:30 P.M., Paul told me to ski back and tell everyone we would take an extended break at 4:00 and look for a landing strip.

The team grumbled through the break. Many of the skiers had ended up far behind the dogsleds.

Paul used the radio and tried to connect to Pen at the pole. He sat at the top of a fifteen-foot pressure ridge, his legs crossed. Despite the cold he had a look of complete calm.

He called and called for Pen as well as for the Eureka weather station. No answer. Either the atmosphere was disturbing communication, or they simply weren't at their radios.

After a break for snacks and water, Paul told the skiers to start off ahead of the dogs to try to keep the team together.

Around 5:00, we arrived at a lead that was about eight feet across. The ice was black and dark, indicating it was freshly frozen. Paul crossed first, his skis bouncing on the rubbery ice. Next, the skiers slid across with the dogsleds so the skiers on the other side could grab a lead line from the front of the dogs and run them across.

After a number of skiers crossed, it was my turn. By now the ice looked sloppy, water oozing up over the ice on the edges and covering it.

Paul said, "The ice is shot. Doug, go down farther."

I moved down to the right, maybe twenty feet, where the lead was narrower, about four feet across. But the south side was studded with blocks of ice, making it more difficult for the dogsleds.

The sun was shining from the left, the dogs were howling behind me, awaiting the run across the lead. I tossed my skis across to the other side, then with my poles in my hand, I took a couple steps back and then with all the energy I could muster leaped over the lead.

I made it easily. My right foot came down on the other side.

As I leaned forward to catch my balance, I was suddenly falling backward.

The edge of the lead I'd landed on had broken away.

Splash!

I dropped into the ocean like I was in a carnival dunk tank. It happened so fast, there was no time to leap, jump, or reach out.

Suddenly I was in to my neck and treading water in full winter gear, my backpack acting as a giant life preserver.

I fell in a microsecond, but once in the ocean time seemed to stand still.

My first thought surprised me. I instantly felt warm—warmer than I'd felt in days. I had stepped into a 61-degree heat wave. The air temperature was 30 below zero and the water temperature was about 31 degrees.

My second thought was to push my face down and my backpack up to keep it dry. If my down coat in my backpack got wet, I was a goner.

My third thought was that I'd read that when you fall in you have five minutes to get out before you go unconscious, nine minutes before you die. Being a bit of a mathematician, I then wondered if there was a plus or minus on the time to death. I mean, who measures this stuff? How do they really know?

I saw my teammates on the far side, their faces frozen in fear. They looked at me and at the ice cracking in front of them.

When the ice cracks on top of the Arctic Ocean, it splinters in many directions, like on the cartoons we watched as kids. When Elmer Fudd would shoot his gun into the ice, the ice would crack everywhere.

But now the person in peril wasn't Elmer. It was me.

Then I realized my teammates weren't standing still. They were going backward away from the edge.

"Wrong way," I screamed, spitting out salty water.

I swam to the northern side of the widening Arctic river, reached up, and pulled myself up. I got a handhold, and started lifting only to feel the sensation of falling, as the ice cracked again, sending me back into the water.

I swam over again, keeping my face down in the water and my backpack up as high as possible. I reached for a handhold and suddenly felt a ski pole. I grabbed on and was yanked upward.

As my head cleared the ice I saw that on the other end of the ski pole stood Corky Peterson—sixty-nine years of age.

He'd come to the edge, spread his legs wide to distribute his weight, and pulled me out of the water.

As I got out, I heard Paul yelling, "Get him in the snow; roll him in the snow."

I dropped and rolled as fast as possible, using the snow as a giant water-absorbing towel. Stop, drop, and roll. It's what you do if you fall into the Arctic Ocean, just as we were taught to do in grade school when the fireman came with his spotted dog to talk about fire safety.

Corky's photo of me taken just seconds after he pulled me out of the ocean.

When I stood, a stream of water ran down my back—*Yeoooowwww!*

I yelled to Corky, "Get a picture!"

He grabbed a camera and snapped a shot of me standing on the ice at 30 below. My legs and arms at this point were encased in ice as the water flash froze.

As my rush of adrenaline subsided, the cold flowed over me in waves. I jogged in place to get feeling back into my toes. I flexed my fingers to bring warmth back to them.

While I did my little dance on the ice, the rest of the team pushed the sleds across. At this point we had a choice. We could stop, put up a tent, and I could change into dry clothes, which is exactly what I wanted to do, or I could ski to increase my body temperature and push some of the water out of my clothes.

The chances of hypothermia are significantly lower if you ski. But it's difficult to find the mental energy to do it. You want to get into warm clothes and curl up near a fire, not grab ski poles and push off into the snow. I'd also added ten to twenty pounds to my weight from the water in my clothes.

Still, we needed to get that resupply, and there was no landing spot nearby. We had to keep moving. Paul asked how I felt, and I said, "I'm shook but fine. Lets go find a landing strip so I can rent the most expensive wireless phone on earth."

Paul laughed and led off, I followed with Craig just behind me. Craig was an incredible friend. When I'd slow down he pushed me on. "Come on, Doug, let's go, let's go." He kept up his chatter and encouragement.

"Hey, don't you say that to the dogs?" I yelled back.

"It works for them so why not you? Stop talking and get going."

As I skied, I checked the damage from my little wetting:

Toes: feeling squishy. Fortunately I was wearing the NEOs and the scuba boot liners when I went in. My toes were fine, but the socks outside the liners were squishy.

Legs: cold and clammy. When I skied fast they felt warm. When I stopped for a moment the cold whipped through the shell pants and accelerated the cooling effect of my frigid, wet long underwear.

Hands: the worst part. Really cold. Almost numb. I pulled my fingers inside my mittens into a fist. I tried skiing with my fingers wrapped into a fist with the straps from the poles just around my wrists. It didn't work well. I needed a stronger grip to provide balance. I alternated, bringing my fingers up to grab and in to get warm.

Torso: ice armor. The ice-crusted jacket weighed me down. As I started to move it softened into a damp mess. The faster I skied, the warmer I felt.

Gear: major shutdown of electronics. Leica camera and pager were dead. And, of course, the phone now was really, really wet!

Fortunately my GPS survived inside the pack in a plastic bag. The gear in the bottom of the pack was frozen, but my down jacket—the super warm one that I wore in camp—had been stuffed in last that morning and was at the top of the pack, very dry.

We skied for about an hour until we reached a series of pans of old ice that looked like a good place for a landing strip.

When we hit the spot for camp, Craig immediately pulled out the stoves to start boiling water. Others pitched a tent and put my sleeping bag in it.

I started to pull off my clothes but after that moment my memory is fuzzy. I remember taking my clothes off and suddenly switching from a constant, bone-cold shiver to feeling pretty good. Suddenly it didn't seem like such a big deal. But

With hot water bottles between my legs and under my arm pits, I slowly came back to the land of the living.

as hard as I tried to convince the others that I was fine, they kept acting like it was an emergency, especially Bill Martin.

"Put your feet on my stomach," he said.

"What?"

"We need to get heat into you. Now!"

"I'm fine, don't worry."

"I'm the doctor, you're the patient. Do as I say."

Bill grabbed my feet and held them against his bare stomach. I could barely feel any heat.

Then Craig whipped open the tent, his arms loaded with hot water bottles. Bill ordered me to get into the sleeping bag, and after I slid inside, he put one hot water bottle between my legs and one under each armpit.

They were hot. Really hot. I said something like, "Hey, I could burn something."

"Doesn't matter. Do it," Bill said.

I continued to say I felt fine, that they were worrying needlessly.

With the water bottles jammed up against me, Craig handed me some hot cocoa.

I could hear people talking outside the tent, Bill expressing concern to Paul about my condition. Lots of mumbling as I laid with burning bottles in my pits, feeling fine, feeling at peace, feeling comfortable.

Then, suddenly, I started to shiver. No, *shiver* is too small a word. My body shook and quaked, every body part shuddering involuntarily. My legs, arms, shoulders, and even chest trembled, a constant quivering that I couldn't control, like an earthquake tremoring through my body.

I called out, "Hey, hey, hey, Bill! I'm shivvvering prettttt-tyyyy baddddd."

"Great!" Bill called from outside the tent.

Great? I thought. It didn't feel all that great to me. After what seemed like two hours, but others later told me was fifteen minutes, the shaking slowly subsided. I started to feel cold but normal.

Later I learned that I had gone into hypothermia and back out again. When your body experiences cold, it shivers, which increases heat production by a factor of five. When your core body temperature falls below about 95 degrees, the brain decides to sacrifice the arms and legs for the vital organs. From 95 to 90 degrees it stops the shivering and saves energy to save your life but not your limbs. At this point experts advise that you are in an emergency situation and should be immediately taken to a hospital.

When your body reaches 86 degrees you lose consciousness but you're not yet dead. In general, cardiac arrest occurs when you hit about 82 degrees.

However, experts advise that even at 82 degrees you are not necessarily dead. The saying is "not dead until warm and dead." In fact, a thirteen-month-old girl was brought back to life after being outside for four hours. Her temperature was in the 60s, and her heart wasn't beating, but she was brought back to life and did not suffer brain damage. Doctors called it a miracle, their only explanation being that the cold must have slowed her metabolism enough to keep the brain alive.

After a short recovery, I got up and put on dry clothes and my big red down jacket. When I walked out of the tent I saw my wet clothes hanging from all the ski poles—socks, shirts, long underwear, all flapping in the breeze.

The clothes had been wrung dry and left out to "freeze dry." The wonder of today's gear is that the fabrics don't absorb water and can, therefore, be dried by super cooling. Once the water freezes, you beat the fabric and the ice falls off. You do it a couple times, and the clothing is nearly back to normal.

Feeling nearly normal myself, I headed to the cook tent to help Craig with dinner. As always, we started with a pound of butter and tossed in various frozen concoctions.

When I announced dinner, I tried to give it a little spin: "Lady and Gentlemen, tonight we have Amish Chicken with whole-grain rice with a hint of sun-dried tomatoes, French-style green beans, and our special spice—Craig's CEO Sun-dried Tomato Pesto.

Alan's response was typical: "Is it hot?"

"Piping hot," Craig said.

"That's all that matters."

As we ate I praised Corky, thanking him a dozen times for saving me.

Corky said he actually felt a little guilty.

Guilty?

"For the last four nights I've dreamed I was going to fall through the ice," Corky said. "Every night, the same dream. So when I saw you fall in, my first reaction was 'good, I'm glad it's not me.' Then I felt really bad. I couldn't live with myself feeling that way, so I had to help pull you out."

Mike said, "You leaped, and it broke away. You reached out as you fell in."

I didn't remember reaching out.

"When I looked up I saw you getting out like you were climbing out of the deep end of a swimming pool," Paul Phau said.

"You're only the fourth to go for a complete swim on my trips," Paul Schurke added. "On our '86 trip, Ann Bancroft went for a swim, and in '95 two guys fell in. They had to swim twenty feet to get out. They hold the distance record."

The more we talked about my "swim" my amazement grew. I had gone for a swim in the Arctic! I could have died! But it just didn't feel like a big deal.

I'd made a monumental shift in my attitude.

Paul left the Siberian Chalet cook tent and scouted the area for a landing strip. He called on the radio and confirmed with Pen that the plane was on its way. He advised Craig and me to get some sleep as we'd be needed in a few hours.

Before turning in I gathered our rolls of film and digital disks to put on the plane. David would then send the images to the PR group in New York. I paused for a moment to write David a note. I struggled to find the words to express my feelings. I wrote:

David,

This is clearly a much bigger deal than I realized. This is the real thing. It's far beyond what I expected. It's totally unreasonable, impossible, and ridiculous.

That said—I'm loving it. No matter what happens in the days ahead, I'm so glad I'm here.

I'm also really glad that you're on the end of our lifeline. Your faith, support, and commitment go far beyond what I deserve.

Hearing your voice each night, and even your tasteless, bad jokes, gives me incredible strength.

Your friend,
Doug

Paul woke us at two. The plane was due in about thirty minutes. He skied to the runway, which was about a quarter mile away, while Craig worked the radio to confirm the plane's arrival plan. Following Paul's ski tracks, I pushed the small sled that we were sending back along with some excess supplies.

When I reached the south end of the runway, I could hear the buzz of the plane but couldn't see it. Then—it was above us, its shiny gray belly promising a world beyond the one we'd come to inhabit for the past week. What a great sight! After days of white on white, it seemed like something from another planet. I can only imagine what it must have been like when the Inuit would see Peary's ship come into view.

To check the runway, the pilot dipped down about two hundred feet above the ground. As he passed over my head, he pulled up and made a big turn. Then he flew back above the runway again, pulled up, and turned in the opposite direction.

The plane was going away from me. The pilot apparently didn't like the landing strip for some reason and was looking for another.

Ugh. If he didn't find one he liked, he wouldn't land, which meant no phone, no resupply, no more hot Tang.

The pilot checked another flat pan about a mile to the east of us that ran parallel to the one we were on. He made one test pass then dipped down and skittered onto the ice. It was a relief to see the plane land except for the fact that I was a mile or more away and had to push the sled to his landing spot.

The ice was pretty smooth so I made good time, running perpendicular to the somewhat rectangular ice pans. Knowing the pilots would only stay on the ice for a maximum of thirty minutes to conserve fuel, I hurried to reach them. I pushed the sled up and over a two-foot pressure ridge where the pans had crashed together, and when I was about half way to the plane, I came upon a ribbon of black. A ribbon of black open water, about two feet across.

I looked left and right. The ribbon extended as far as I could see.

Memories of my swim and shivering earlier in the evening came flooding back. My legs started to shake.

I considered my options—go back the way I'd come and take the long way around to avoid the water, which would mean I'd probably miss the plane.

Or I could find the courage to go forward.

I thought for a moment about the consequences, said a little prayer, and focused more deeply than ever on the excitement of the adventure.

"Hey, chump." I said out loud to myself. "Time to be adventurous." I took a deep breath and then yelled, "Be bold, be brave" into the wind and pushed the sled with all my might. It skimmed across the water and barely reached the other side. Then I set off on a run and leaped across the water, clearing it by a foot.

I agreed to pay Pen Haddow ten thousand dollars to borrow his Iridium phone. He was happy.

Before reaching the plane I repeated this process three more times with two smaller and one larger open-water lead, each time yelling, "Be bold, be brave."

By the time I reached the plane, a party was going on. Pen was there with the two Malaysians who had won the TV contest and chosen to go to the North Pole. A film crew had come to film their experience, but when they landed on the ice a week before, the Malaysians froze—with fear. They wouldn't leave the tent. They had planned to stay for four days, but with the bad weather had ended up stuck for a week.

Craig and my teammates were also at the plane, having traveled a far shorter distance than I did. Someone had brought a dog and the visitors wanted to have their picture taken with it.

I headed straight for Pen to finalize our agreement.

"So there'll be a phone in Resolute?" he asked.

"One is already on the way and another leaves tomorrow," I assured him. "I could show you the page from my office confirming it, but I took a little swim and my pager's out."

"Been having problems, haven't you? What happened to your phone?"

Not wanting to go into details about the other liquid, I said, "So the deal is ten thousand cash for rental of the phone. If we don't get yours back before you leave, you can take one of the new ones sent to Resolute. Here's a note confirming our agreement. Give it to David Wecker, our base camp contact in Resolute."

"You'll also need to pay for any minutes you use," Pen said. "I've written down my address and the terms on this paper."

There was a bit of a pause, as Pen seemed to size me up. I tried my best to act like a real explorer. I stood a little taller and looked him straight in the eye.

"You're sure there will be a phone in Resolute?" he asked again.

"Absolutely," I said, my eyes focused and unwavering.

Slowly he reached into his pocket and pulled out the most precious piece of electronics I've ever received. In the leather case was his Iridium phone.

We shook hands just as the pilot called for everyone to load up again.

I yelled, "Yippee! Thank you, thank you, thank you."

Corky took this photo of the plane taking off.

Pen smiled and told me, "Remember what Churchill said: 'Never, ever, ever give up.'" Then he climbed into the plane.

I rushed back to the tent to call David. As Pen's phone wasn't preprogrammed, I had to manually dial the number for the South Camp Inn in Resolute. It was 3:00 A.M.

"Good morning, commander," I said.

"Great to hear from you again," he said. "What's that sound?"

"It's the plane taking off."

"That's wild. What's happened?"

As fast as possible I relayed the story of falling into the ocean and of the arrival of the plane.

"Slow down, I can't keep up," he said.

"Write faster. Type faster. I'm #$&@ cold."

David laughed. I saw no humor in it. I was huddled in a ball, my hands numb from dialing. Of course, my response only added energy to David's humor.

"Okay, got that," he said. "Type faster." He then added ever so slowly, "Doug...said...to...type...faster...he's...cold."

All I could do was laugh. And once I started laughing, I couldn't stop. It was welcome relief.

We joked a bit more, and I gave him some details for that night's North Pole Telegram. Then we signed off and I went to sleep. The phone was safely packed inside the leather case, inside the waterproof case. Far away from my sleeping bag.

This phone call, unfortunately, was not recorded.

Chapter 13
American Express Platinum Card

THURSDAY, APRIL 22, 1999
Distance to travel to the North Pole: 91 Miles
Temperature: -62° F

NOW THESE FELLAS HERE WERE OWNED BY A LITTLE OLD LADY WHO ONLY USED THEM TO TAKE HER TO HER WEEKLY BINGO GAME!

HONEST JOHN'S USED DOG SLEDS

Follow Ziggy LIVE on his Great Aspirations trip to the North Pole' at www.ASPIRATIONS.com!

I WOKE UP FEELING GREAT. I'd survived the emotional trauma of the phone and the terror of a swim in black water.

I went outside and beat the last of my clothes that had freeze-dried overnight, all the while singing, "Oh what a beautiful morning. Oh what a beautiful day."

As each person awoke, I offered a bright and cheery "good morning" and asked how each person was feeling.

"I don't know if 'good' is the right word for how I feel," said Celia.

Paul Phau was more philosophical: "The team has some significant physical ailments but nothing life threatening."

Alan was more blunt: "Do you really want to know?" By the look in his eyes I knew I didn't.

"You might stop singing this morning," Alan said.

Team morale obviously was low. The Arctic Devil Tornarsuk had taken hold of them.

Mike said, "Reaching the pole is not nearly as important to me as it was. A one-week trip would have been enough."

As the negativity grew, I could feel Tornarsuk trying to creep back into me. I turned away to make another cup of Brain Brew, focusing my energy on the magical aroma of the bean, which protected me from the downward spiral overtaking the cook tent.

Several people mumbled that David Golibersuch should have been sent out on the resupply plane. Others admitted they had thought seriously about getting on the plane themselves.

The bad moods worsened when they learned that the drink bag in the resupply didn't include Tang. There was lemonade mix, cocoa, and fruit punch, but no Tang. One after another they went to the drink bag and after reaching into it, they snarled, "No Tang?"

The admiral didn't enjoy the luxury of resupply. He had to take all of his supplies for the trip up and back, which explains why he was so compulsive about weight. Every pound of extra weight meant less food he could take on the trip. In his book *Secrets of Polar Travel* he documented how Shackleton could have reached the pole in 1909 instead of having to turn back ninety-seven miles from the pole because of lack of food. He could have made it if he'd not taken sleeping bags or tents. Shakelton's gear included four sleeping bags weighing a total of forty pounds when dry and two tents at three pounds each for a total of sixty pounds when dry. If instead he'd carried a hundred pounds of pemmican he'd have had twenty-five days of rations for his men, more than enough to cover the remaining ninety-seven miles to the pole and back.

Breakfast sparked more complaints from the team. It was my fault. Craig had trusted me to make the glop, and I'd tossed in the pound of butter, added water, rice, grains, and fruit flakes. I asked Craig what I did wrong.

"You didn't wait for the water to come to a full boil so it didn't hydrate right," he said

"I'm sorry," I said.

He shook his head. "Don't blame yourself," he said. "It tastes fine. They're all frustrated from skiing yesterday and having to wake up in the middle of the night."

David Golibersuch was the last to reach the cook tent. He looked bad. The arrival and departure of the plane had fueled his depression—Tornarsuk hung all about him. Because his boots had frozen solid, he wore only socks. Paul Schurke worked patiently on the boots while others grew more frustrated with David, but Paul ignored the negative forces and maintained his optimistic attitude, pushing the bottom of the boots while David pulled.

"You're getting them," Paul said encouragingly. "You're close. There you go." He wasn't fazed in the slightest by David's condition.

With the late-night wake-up to see the plane, everyone moved slowly. It was 11:30 A.M. before we hit the trail.

The day's temperature was the lowest yet, and the wind blew hard. My temperature gadget said eighteen miles per hour. Given the minus 20-degree temperature, we faced a temperature on our skin of minus 62.

"Have you ever been this cold?" I asked Alan.

"Never in my life," he said.

I was definitely cold, but I felt fine mentally.

To harness the dogs, we had to take off our outer mittens and work the metal snap rings on the collars with just thin liner gloves on our hands. The snaps had frozen. I knocked them with my knife to move them while trying to contain the restless dogs, which were jumping and thrashing around. The minute you moved one dog, the others howled in anticipation. They were ready to hit the trail and were also standing proud, letting the others know who was boss.

I found I had to anticipate the cold. If I left my hands out too long they became too numb to warm. I had to work in shifts, working a snap for a couple minutes, then pulling my hands inside my jacket and placing them under my armpits to thaw. It's a slow process, but in time it became second nature.

I unsnapped one of the dogs, and just as I was moving him to the sled, I heard a scream to my left: "Oh my God. The tent. Grab it."

One of our yellow tents bounced along the ice like a giant beach ball. They're self supporting, so when the gear was removed, off it flew in the eighteen-mile-an-hour winds.

I started to laugh but quickly stopped as it became clear that the tent was hopping away. A lost tent would make already tight sleeping conditions really, really tight.

It bounced along ten to twenty feet into the air. Paul and Craig chased it, scampering across the smooth ice that had been our airplane runway. About a mile from camp the tent caught on a chunk of ice. As the wind blew, a jagged piece of ice could tear the tent into pieces.

Finally Paul and Craig reached it, broke it down, and trekked the long walk back. By the time they returned, Paul was not in a good mood.

"We need to get our act together," he said. "I know you're feeling beaten up, but this is the real deal. This could have been a disaster. Wake up, people, and focus." Glaring at us, he looked every bit like a true explorer, dressed head to toe, as always, in black, which captured every possible bit of solar heat.

No one dared object to his admonition. No one grumbled. The dogs barked and howled and strained in their harnesses until Paul gave the signal to move out and, in that instant, the scene changed completely. The dogs fell silent, all of their energy focused on pulling the sleds.

Paul led the team on a winding trail back and forth, finding a way or making a way across the pressure ridges and open water all around us. We were traveling ten feet left or ten feet right for every foot forward toward the pole.

We faced one obstacle after the next, one open-water lead after another.

Paul Phau fell in water to the top of his boots.

A support on the back of one of the sleds broke.

Dog tie lines broke.

In the first hour and a half, we managed maybe half a mile traveling into the wicked windstorm. The wind blew from the left, burning into the left sides of our bodies. My left leg and left arm felt 20 degrees colder than the right side. I laughed at the idea that maybe I should walk backward part of the day so both sides would be equally frigid. The fact that I could find humor in the situation was a sign of a transition I had made.

The wind blew hard, carrying ice crystals that blasted our faces as we trudged along. The combination of the cold and the impossible travel weighed heavily on everyone. But having walked through the valley of death during the past few days, I saw things in a new light.

It was impossible. Of course it was impossible.

It was cold. Of course it was cold.

However, as Paul had said when I was in my deepest despair: "Don't worry or sweat it. Something great will come out of this. It always does. Serendipity. It's all part of the process."

We were traveling in a whiteout. Exactly like the one four days before. But today I was enjoying myself.

Paul stopped behind a pressure ridge to wait for the dog teams and skiers to catch up. I asked him about the team.

Bill and Celia bundled up at a rest break

"On every trip there are three distinct stages that every person goes through—shell shocked, maturing, and enjoying," he explained. "On this trip, a number of people haven't left shell shocked. They're surviving, not thriving."

I easily related to the stages.

Shell Shocked was a total panic. It was filled with fear of the unknown.

Maturing was a transition stage. I started to learn, adjust, and adapt to the new world. It was a continuous learning stage, making the adjustments in clothing to adapt to the cold.

Enjoyment was the stage I was now entering. It's about enjoying the moment. Living in the world. I still felt cold, but I adjusted my clothing without conscious thought, and the weather was simply something to deal with rather than something to fear.

Years later, when talking about the trip, I remembered this day differently from my teammates. I remembered vividly the whiteout on Sunday when I hurt my knee, but this second white-out didn't seem nearly so bad. Two of my teammates remembered them in reverse. They would say that this day was the worst of their lives.

In the afternoon, we faced a crisis. Someone behind us yelled, "Wait!" with an unmistakable urgency. Those of us in front stopped. Soon Randy's dogsled pulled up with David Golibersuch spread eagled across it in a hypothermic delirium.

David's arms and legs hung limp, his head slung to one side. Tornarsuk had taken his will to go on.

Paul helped him stand up and asked how he was feeling.

"I can't go on," David said, his face encrusted with ice.

"You can do it," Paul said. "I've seen you do it on Greenland trips. Pull yourself together."

"I can't," David said.

They went back and forth for a few minutes before David made a plea—one that was probably a first for Arctic explorers.

"Please let me use my American Express card," David yelled.

"No," Paul yelled back over the wind. "I'm not going to let you use your American Express card to get out of here."

David screamed, "Let me use it. Please. Please, let me use it."

The wind pounded us in the blinding whiteout. David looked totally defeated. His arms pleading, his face pleading, his entire body beaten.

Then Paul turned up the intensity. "Find the strength to move," he said. "If you don't, you'll die. We can't help you. Even if we called for a plane, it could be days. You'll be dead. Find the strength to move. You can and you will."

The D word got my attention. It also got David's. If Paul had planned it as a shock tactic, he played it well. When the iron man of the Arctic says you could die, you pay attention.

After Paul laid it on the line, we all stood quietly for a few minutes, all of us very conscious of the reality of the situation. We were on the edge of the planet in a frozen frontier walking on the ocean, on a shifting sheet of ice.

Help was not available. All we had was our inner spirits and our teammates.

❄

As we started moving again, Craig skied up beside me and said, "I'm guessing that was the first time in Arctic history that American Express Platinum played a role in an expedition."

I laughed, but was a little embarrassed because I was responsible for the bizarre conversation we'd just witnessed.

American Express is a client of my Eureka! Ranch and an expedition sponsor. They have a special service for Platinum and Centurion Card members in which they promise to evacuate you if you need emergency medical help, anywhere in the world. I had convinced my teammates to get Platinum cards.

My client had even joked, "If you get in big trouble and we evacuate you, it would make a great commercial."

Before the trip I asked Chris Stormann in my office to call American Express's Global Assist service to confirm that I would be eligible for medical help with my card. Here's a summary of the conversation:

Chris: I'm calling for my CEO, Doug Hall. He's going to the North Pole with Arctic explorer Paul Schurke and he's afraid if something goes wrong he'll need some help, and we want to know if he's covered. If you can come get him.

AMEX—[silence]…That is an area of the earth we've never dealt with before. It's never been done.

Chris: Okay, what does that mean—you can't help?

AMEX—[awkward silence]…We can do it, but it will take time.

Chris: Doug will have an Iridium satellite phone with him. Should I have him call this number?

AMEX—[very awkward silence] Yes, he can call this number. We have offices all around the world, but I don't think we have any at the North Pole. I have to see a map, one moment please.

(Holding)

AMEX—There's no problem. Have him call here. We actually had a case like this when someone was hiking in the mountains in Nepal. We had to get him out of there and get medical help. We can handle it. If an emergency occurs we'll find a way to get him out.

Chris: Great, that's what I need to know. He'll be happy to hear about this. I hope he won't have to call. Good-bye.

Through the rest of the day, team members took turns helping David physically and emotionally. We engaged his brain through continuous conversation. We built heat in his body by keeping him walking as fast as possible.

The wind was relentless. I kept up singing my songs and mentally traveling to various happy places.

I did dozens of tours of our Prince Edward Island farmhouse. I designed gardens, cooked gourmet meals, and watched the sunrise over and over again. I laughed as I reviewed memories of magic moments with my family and friends.

Our clothes, as I mentioned earlier, created a sense of isolation, which helped open the mind to freewheeling thoughts. Most of us wore several hats and a hood, which dulled the sound of wind and voices. We looked through a six-inch tunnel created by the wire frame in the lip of our hoods. It protected us from the wind but cut the field of vision.

The traveling was tough, picking our way through what looked like a hurricane-damage scene with blocks of ice rubble strewn everywhere.

Then we hit nirvana—a North Pole highway, a smooth frozen lead that would make our journey much easier. On the smooth ice we could ride the sleds. Team members scrambled onto the sleds, skiers grabbed towlines. It felt like water-skiing on a frozen river. We traveled four miles almost directly north, a welcome relief from the day of slogging.

Because my pager no longer worked after my swim in the ocean, messages were being forwarded to Craig's pager. During the day I received encouragement from members of my church. Information on my "baptismal swim" had been posted on the Web site, generating an increased sense of urgency. Church friends sent their prayers for God to give me strength and keep me safe. Before I left for the expedition, Roger Green, the minister at my church (St. Timothy's) had asked me to step forward during a service and asked the congregation to pray for my safety. At the time, the blessing seemed a little excessive. Over the last few days, I had been glad for it. I needed all the help I could get.

During the day I attached moleskin, a protective bandage, to my nose, which already had a black patch indicating dead skin. Ceila had been the first to notice the frostbite. I hoped the moleskin would prevent further damage and prayed the frostbite was limited to the top two layers of skin.

Frostbite occurs when water molecules in the skin cells freeze. In the early stages, affected areas take on a white, waxy appearance and feel numb and hard to the touch. More severe cases result in a bluish black color, which was the situation on my nose. Left untreated, frostbite can lead to gangrene and amputation.

As we skied, Craig and I discussed various options for tonight's menu. Given the team's low morale, he wanted to cook the dinner of dinners. With the added fuel from the resupply we could create a multi-pot meal.

We decided on a Mexican dinner.

When we hit camp, Craig and I started cooking as quickly as possible. We turned up the stoves extra high to make sure everything was ultra hot. Craig cooked the rice and beans, while I fried tortillas in butter with a sprinkling of brown sugar and cinnamon.

The team loved it. We made extra, and they ate every bit of it.

As we sat in the cook tent, Paul explained the urgency of the situation with David. "At the risk of sounding melodramatic, to stop in a windstorm is to die," he said. "The only thing you can do is warm yourself from the inside out."

David was the last to enter the cook tent. He had made tremendous progress after a few hours in a warm sleeping bag, with hot water bottles and a little soup. He wasn't "healthy" but he also wasn't as depressed and negative as he'd been during the day.

"I remember waking up hurting badly," he said. "I had frostbitten toes the first day, I twisted my ankle the

David Golibersuch came back to life on the phone.

second day, and I had frostbitten fingers the third day. Today I was feeling miserable. I remember feeling pretty cold. When I felt I lost it completely, I was mumbling, shivering out of control, shaking, and crying like a baby. I just couldn't pull myself back. Large parts of things that happened during the day I don't remember."

He paused but kept our attention. We were happy to see him back on his feet and eager to hear more about what he'd gone through.

"As well as being a great leader, Paul is quite a psychologist," he said. "I remember him yelling at me, asking me if I was going to be the least common denominator for the day. I remember him saying, 'you can't change your situation but the one thing you can choose for yourself is your attitude.'

"What pulled me back was the human touch, other people who cared a lot. I remember everyone on the team at some point in the day walking with me, talking about kids and hobbies. Another big factor was that thousands of people are pulling for us."

As David spoke, I understood very well what he was saying. I'd felt the same pull of negativity from Tornarsuk, just as most of us had felt it at some point. But I was also conscious of how good I felt. The coldest day had been, for me, the best day of the trip. I felt cold and tired, but it was a comfortable cold and tired.

That feeling continued through the phone call that night. I was calmer, clearer, lighter, and less urgent. I described the day's challenges in an almost philosophical tone. The call ended with more information on the continuing saga of NASA Mike. The issue today was that Mike didn't want to bring our extra food bag and fuel on his flight to the pole—even though that was the food we'd use to feed him!

I confirmed that I was paying ten thousand dollars to rent the phone, and that David should pay Pen from the cash I'd given him.

We also learned Elizabeth Arnold from National Public Radio (NPR) would be coming to the pole as part of a series called Radio Expeditions, a coproduction of NPR and the National Geographic Society. We reviewed the media list for the next few days. It looked great. At the pole we'd be talking to *CBS This Morning* and the Fox News Channel; and on ABC News.com we'd do a live chat at noon, considered "prime time" by Internet folks.

I slipped in a happy birthday to my mom, who turned seventy that day. I hoped she was on the phone and hoped she was making progress in her battle with cancer. After I said it, I was consumed with fear about her cancer. I pushed it from my mind, focusing on good memories. I couldn't allow myself to become consumed by fear for her health.

When we got off the phone, we joked about Elizabeth, wondering what sort of ditzy reporter would be joining us. Looking at our motley crew, I wondered what sort of report she'd make upon her arrival. With the reporter, the NASA team, the Malaysians, and Pen Haddow, the North Pole seemed like a very busy place.

www.Aspirations.com has
audio from this day's phone call

Chapter 14
Glorious Sunshine

FRIDAY, APRIL 23, 1999
Distance to travel to the North Pole: 75 Miles
Temperature: -21° F

I SURE HOPE MY MAP IS RIGHT, BECAUSE ONE OF US IS AT THE **WRONG** POLE!!

Follow Ziggy LIVE on his Great Aspirations trip to the North Pole at www.ASPIRATIONS.com!

WE AWOKE TO SUNSHINE and an Arctic heat wave of minus 21 degrees. Though the sun's rays had little impact on our physical warmth, our moods lifted dramatically.

That morning Paul did a series of interviews...8:10 A.M. with Minnesota News Network, 8:20 A.M. on Wisconsin Public Radio and a Minneapolis television station, and 8:50 A.M. with the *Minneapolis Star-Tribune.*

He compared this trip to his previous four. "It's new and different every time," he said. "The landscape is never the same. It changes every day."

I was amazed when he revealed his new perspective on the satellite pagers. "I was very skeptical, but they're worth their weight in gold," he said. "It was a wonderful feeling getting messages from loved ones."

Paul did interviews across the USA.

He also went on to describe the great weather we were having. "It's 20 below zero today, which is a blessing because it holds the ice."

After Paul's calls I was interviewed by the Associated Press and a couple newspapers. During both Paul's and my interviews, we were asked for our perspective on the Columbine shooting. We did the best we could to respond but didn't fully understand the situation and felt it inappropriate to take advantage of the tragedy to mention the Great Aspirations! principles.

Later I learned that we had a very relevant story to tell. Apparently, a key part of the motivation of the two shooters was a feeling of isolation from the rest of their classmates. According to Dr. Quaglia, the most important dimension to instill in children is a sense of belonging.

Paul remarked that we were close to the spot where his last journey to the pole ended. He said we'd need luck on our side to make it because the cycle of tides was against us. We were one week away from a full moon. The gravitational pull causes higher tides, creating more open water. We would see—and have to negotiate—more broken ice, more open leads, and more active pressure ridges collapsing into the ice and pushing upward.

During the Golden Years of Arctic Exploration from 1810 to 1910, Peary was arguably the most determined and scientific explorer. Fridtjof Nansen, a Norwegian, was probably the most imaginative and the luckiest. He was the first to successfully cross Greenland, which he accomplished by blending his Nordic wisdom of winter travel with that of the Inuit. He was the first to blend cross-country skiing with dogsledding. He invented new kinds of sleds, sleeping bags, and cooking equipment.

Nansen was intense when it came to motivation. As mentioned earlier, instead of starting from the west coast of Greenland, where there were plenty of people and retreat was easy, he started from the east cost and destroyed snow bridges as he went so that the only way to escape was to go forward, thereby eliminating wasted time thinking, "What if we turned back?"

Nansen replicated the same strategy of eliminating the possibility of retreat when he froze a ship into the ice near Russia and tried to drift to the pole. When it became clear that they were going to drift south of the pole, he set off with dogsleds and tried to reach the pole. When food supplies ran low, he headed to shore and miraculously was picked up by another expedition.

Nansen really loved the high Arctic. He wrote:

> What is the charm of the Arctic? Health, glorious health!
>
> Your muscles twitch with a desire for action. You eat like a horse, and sleep twelve or fourteen hours without a dream.
>
> Before you is the vast unknown: all around you is silence and solitude.

It's been said of Nansen that when his skill and genius didn't work, his luck saved him. Like Paul Schurke's serendipity, Nansen had great luck.

❄

Breakfast was a disaster for the second morning in a row. We got behind in our cooking and had folks looking over our shoulders as we cooked, putting empty cups down to have them filled.

It was a spin on the Mexican theme from the night before— eggs, taco meat, and mashed potatoes. In the rush of cooking we dumped in too much salt. The glop ended up mushy and not very hot. Though people complained again, they ate it quickly. They were eager to get going to the pole and out of this place.

After breakfast, Paul cleaned and redressed David's frost-bitten hands and feet, which were black and oozing. I've never had a strong stomach when it comes to medical stuff and had to turn away for fear of vomiting. Fortunately, I married a registered nurse who isn't fazed by anything medical.

Paul blended tender care for David's frozen appendages with some firm words.

"You've got to pull it together," he said. "If you don't, you'll jeopardize the entire expedition. I've seen you ski in Greenland. You can and must ski hard today and get out of this funk. I want you out in front of the teams, skiing hard."

David's frostbite was so severe he needed help eating, holding his water bottle, and twice the day before, teammates had to help him take a pee. Craig and I looked at each other as we cleaned up from breakfast, wondering if David would make it or not. We also wondered about ourselves. We felt good, but we'd both felt the pain and Arctic depression that had infected David.

After David left the cook tent, Paul sensed our anxiety. "Today should be filled with blissful boredom," he said. "That'll be good after yesterday."

We nodded—but not convincingly.

Sensing that we were both a little anxious about our own abilities and feeling down about breakfast, he continued, "I go through good and bad cycles like you guys do. Sometimes I wonder why am I here. In the valleys of the roller coaster I find myself mumbling. I go through cycles of feeling down too," Paul told us. "It's all part of it. But when the sun shines down on me out here, it's a heavenly radiance you normally don't feel. The circumstances and the conditions give God a chance to exercise His promises and His wrath in a bigger way on me than He normally does. I'm always enriched by that."

When Paul spoke, it was like listening to a riddle from Yoda.

Paul concluded with a challenge, speaking to Craig and me but also to himself. "I think the greatest danger in life is not to take the adventure. Too many of us arm ourselves with insurance policies. Too many of us are dying slowly, measuring out our lives in teaspoons, as the poet once said."

I madly scribbled down Paul's words in my journal. After he left, I read them. Once again it seemed like I was listening to Yoda from *Star Wars*. I didn't fully understand everything he said, but he made me feel less embarrassed about my past stupidity. He also motivated me to attack the trail ahead.

As we moved toward the pole, the conversations in the cook tent kept running through my head. It's clear that Arctic travel requires great physical stamina, but it requires even more mental strength, which must come from within. It can't be given to you. It can't be purchased in a store.

You must have an internal fire that keeps you going.

Responding to Paul's pep talk, David skied out front. He acted like a different person, and his renewed energy inspired all of us.

I laughed when I saw Celia wearing Rollerblade kneepads. She looked like she was ready for a roller derby. "I'm tired of being beaten up by the ice," she said. "Go ahead and laugh, but by the end of today you'll be begging me for them."

We all joked around while moving forward with a new sense of positive energy. As we trekked along, I worked up a sweat, feeling, for the first time, uncomfortably hot.

At a rest break Alan got a page from Tony Blair, the Prime Minister of Great Britain: "Alan, our warm wishes, thoughts, and prayers are with you. We wish you all well as your expedition progresses."

The British have a long history of Arctic exploration. The father of exploration is thought to be John Barrow, Second Secretary to the British Admiralty. He is credited with launching the most ambitious program of exploration in the history of the world in the early nineteenth century.

Barrow was a dreamer interested in filling the blank spaces on the maps of the world. He was also driven by a need to find a use for his naval forces after the conclusion of the Napoleonic wars. The Royal Navy underwent a massive disarmament, reducing its ranks from one hundred thirty thousand to twenty-three thousand men. It was easy to discharge the enlisted men, but officers had political leverage. After eliminating everyone he could, Barrow ended up with one officer for every four men. And an estimated 90 percent of the officers had nothing to do and were put on half pay.

Barrow decided to use the navy to explore central Africa and to find a northwest passage above Canada. Thus, England set off on a massive exploration effort. The officers quickly learned that, while the Arctic was very cold, the death rates among explorers were much lower than in Africa. Arctic assignments became very popular.

The Royal Navy's pride and ego worked against them in the Arctic. They believed that by using large ships and military discipline they could "tame the Arctic." They rejected Inuit methods. Instead of wearing furs, for example, they wore tight-fitting wool garments. Instead of using dogs to pull sleds, they used manpower.

The Norwegians—Fridtjog Nansen, Otto Sverdrup, and Roald Amundsen—learned from the Inuit and used their methods, as did Peary. At the South Pole, Amundsen, using dogs, beat Englishman Robert Falcon Scott—whose men hauled his sleds—by a month, and, most importantly, came back alive while Scott and his team died.

The competition between nations in exploring the poles provides the answer to the Second Peary Mystery: *Why did he take Henson instead of Bartlett on the final push?*

Critics have claimed that Peary took Henson instead of Bartlett because he had something to hide. They say that Bartlett, who was an expert at navigation, could have provided an independent witness. I believe that the honest answer to why Bartlett was not chosen was because he was an Englishman. He was from Newfoundland, making him at the time a citizen of Great Britain. The race to the pole was the "space race" of its time. Taking Bartlett would have been like NASA taking a Russian to the moon with the Apollo 11 team, just to validate the trip.

Peary was a flag-waving Navy officer. I believe that Bartlett understood Peary's rationale, which is why they remained very good friends throughout Peary's life. In fact, the Peary papers at the National Archive include notes with jokes sent from Bartlett to Peary just before he died.

In the whiteout, we trudged along with our heads down to avoid the wind and flying ice crystals. We now could walk normally and see the beauty around us. The landscape offered a variety of shapes and textures and more shades and hues of white than seemed possible. Parts of the ice field looked like a highway hit by an earthquake, with hundred-ton blocks of ice fractured and scattered everywhere. Other parts offered a soft, sculptured quality—old pressure ridges carved and molded by the wind. And everything glistened in the glare of sunlight.

In the afternoon we passed a section that looked like a graveyard of icebergs—tall, towering chunks of ice. I had an intense urge to stop every five feet to take pictures of the beauty, and I did take quite a few. I gradually had become more aware of the sensory aspects of the Arctic—the crunch of the wind-blown snow crust, the swooshing and panting of the dogs, the brilliant shades of blue and white.

Corky's simple gear worked fine. And his moustache grew icicles quickly.

As we moved along, I felt comfortable in the Arctic world and even felt fine in my clothes and with my gear, which until that day I had fussed with constantly. Given the amount of thought I put into buying it, I had assumed I wouldn't give it much thought after we arrived. My gear system was as advanced as I could make it. Corky, on the other hand, relied on basic stuff. He wore wool pants he'd simply pulled from his closet, using bread bags with elastics as vapor liners for his feet and a $19.95 wind suit from Kmart as a wind layer.

My high-tech boots cost more than everything Corky brought with him. As I became more comfortable during the trip, I realized that warmth is more a matter of mind-set than gear. Corky felt as warm as I did. He was also more thoughtful in how he managed his emotional- and physical-energy reserves.

Late in the afternoon we entered an area where the snow had formed four-foot drifts. We had no choice but to push through.

Alan drove the first sled, which quickly became a snow-plow. Craig and I took off our skis and each grabbed a side of the front of the sled and pulled as Alan pushed. We sank to our waists in the deep snow, kicking and pushing, trying to catch traction.

As we pulled, the dogs strained even harder. They're driven by the examples humans set. After about an hour we hit hard snow again. My heart pumped madly, and I was covered in sweat. I pulled on my skis and set off ahead to give the dogs something to chase. On the hard surface we made good time. By the time we made camp, we had covered twenty-one miles, our longest day yet. We'd now traveled almost 150 miles with just over fifty more to go.

That night Craig decided to go all out for dinner again. In one pot he cooked noodles, dried tomatoes, and vegetables. In the other pot, I cooked chicken in a pool of butter with Ziggy's Zesty Southwest Grill Spices.

Everyone enjoyed it, and spirits ran high as we sat together and ate. Everyone shared the pages they'd received. We had messages from Alaska, South Africa, Europe, and Mexico.

Paul shared stories about other crazed attempts at reaching the pole. He told us about the Japanese guy who tried to ride a motorcycle from Resolute. For food he brought jelly beans in his handlebars. And of the French team that tried to use a horse to go around Ellesmere. They had to cut holes in the floor of the plane for the horse's legs. And of the film crew that brought a planeload of thousands of plastic penguins to make the Arctic look like the Antarctic for a film.

Paul also told a story a reporter from *New York Times Magazine* shared with him about Peter Freuchen, a Danish explorer who in 1923 hid from a storm in a snow cave that was not much bigger than a coffin. The next morning the walls of the cave were so icy, and the snow so heavy, that he couldn't dig his way out. After hours of frustration, he got an idea. "I had often seen dog dung in the sled track," he wrote, "and had noticed that it would freeze as solid as a rock. Would not the cold have the same effect on human discharge? Repulsive as the thought was, I decided to try the experiment. I moved my bowels and from the excrement I managed to fashion a chisel-like instrument which I left to freeze." Peter used the chisel to successfully escape!

Paul's story was met with repulsive groans, and renewed comments on my peeing on the phone.

For the first time we talked about what we'd do at the pole. We talked about what it would feel like, the photos we would take, the things we would do when we reached it.

Craig remained cautious about such discussion. "I think it's still too early to get 'up' for the pole," he said. "One day at a time. We never know what tomorrow could bring."

The admiral shared Craig's view.

> On this last expedition (1908-09) I did not permit myself to dream about the future, to hope, or to fear. On the 1905-06 expedition I had done too much dreaming; this time I knew better. Too often in the past I had found myself face to face with impassable barriers. Whenever I caught myself building air castles, I would either attack some work requiring intense application of the mind, or would go to sleep—it was hard sometimes to fight back the dreams, especially in my solitary walks on the ice.

For the first time, I was annoyed by the responsibility of making our nightly phone call. It had been great fun at first to report the essence of the day. It had been a welcome distraction. With my mind running at slow speed, due to the cold, it would take me a couple hours each afternoon to develop a story line for that night's North Pole Telegram.

Today, I hadn't spent the afternoon thinking. It had been, as Paul predicted, a day of "blissful boredom." I'd stayed fully present in the moment, enjoying the unique sensations of the high Arctic. With no story planned, I had to improvise, which I knew would frustrate David, but he'd figure out something to write. It was okay for us to have a "light news day."

Just before I dialed, Paul gave me an idea for a joke to pull on David. I went for it.

"David, we're at Camp Golden Ring, a very famous site in exploration history," I said. "Very famous among explorers, inside 89° 30'."

"Why is it so famous?" David asked.

"The Golden Ring is the little spinner on a globe that you can turn to show time zones," I told him.

He bought it. And later I learned that around the world the story was told in newspapers about the famous "golden ring."

The bulk of the phone call focused on the logistics for the arrival of NASA Mike and the return of gear and the team from the pole to Resolute. NASA Mike still insisted that he couldn't bring the bag I'd left behind. I insisted that I needed the bag.

"You have to get the bag on the plane or else I'm dead," I told David. "It has all the sponsors' flags in it for the photo shoot."

I knew I could fake the photos in Resolute, if necessary, because frankly it all looked the same, but after all I'd been through, it would bother me forever to look at photos not taken at the top of the earth.

David reviewed all the details on NASA Mike. I relayed them to Paul.

"NASA Mike wants to bring sixteen hundred pounds of our stuff back, nine dogs plus some of our people to take care of the dogs," I said. "He wants to book five people into our Arctic Bed and Breakfast. They slept on the ice last night and apparently they're grossly under-equipped for the trip."

"We'll take care of them," Paul said. "We'll give them a tour. We'll have sleeping bags, dinner, the works."

Then, as often happened, the phone disconnected a number of times. When we reestablished a good connection, I made requests of David in Resolute, Jon Paul in New York City, and Kari in Cincinnati.

"Anyone know how to get a Swedish flag?" I asked.

"I know how to make a Venetian blind," David said.

"Be serious. Randy is looking for a Swedish flag for a picture at the pole."

"We'll see what we can do," David said.

"Okay, next, can you find the Russian ice station? Like in the movie *Ice Station Zebra*. Paul heard a helicopter overnight and thinks they're close. We'd like to go visit."

"I'll call the Kremlin," David replied.

"I'll work it from here," Kari said more helpfully.

While the conversation continued, people around me in the cook tent talked about the folks coming to the pole. The ever-helpful Craig mentioned that they didn't know what they were getting into.

"You better tell them," he told me.

I told David, adding that NASA Mike and the NPR lady should know it could be three or four days before they can leave. It sounded to us like they thought they were taking a bus ride to Central Park. "Talk to Pen Haddow about what it's like to get off the pole." I said.

"I'll talk to them," David said, "though Mike's not the best listener."

We reviewed the media coverage and learned that because of the Columbine situation, we were rapidly losing our media opportunities. Jon Paul said they were trying to pitch our Great Aspirations! Program as a tool for helping with the issue, but it was difficult to get anyone to listen.

When I got off the phone, Paul was hard at work at the stove. He'd tossed in a chunk of the lard that is usually fed to the dogs and some popcorn.

'Nothing like something dry and crunchy when you're at Camp Golden Ring," he said with a smile.

He was right. I'd never had better popcorn in my life. Then again, I'd never had pure lard on popcorn either. Fortunately, the calories were invisible at Camp Golden Ring.

The conversation went on and on, with everyone in a good mood. They eventually headed off to sleep, leaving Craig, Paul, Alan, and me in the cook tent.

I asked Paul the ultimate question once again: "This is your fifth trip. Why do you do it?"

"It's like hitting yourself with a hammer—because it feels so good when you stop."

Alan, Craig, and I shook our heads in disbelief, but we also sort of understood what he was saying.

Alan brought out his Walkman tape player and a pair of miniature speakers. To the music of U2, Thin Lizzy, Van Morrison, and other Irish rockers, we talked and laughed. Suddenly there was a deep rumble of ice moving. A pressure ridge was either collapsing or forming nearby. The high tides were coming.

Unlike on previous days, we had a good laugh about the rumble. We're not scared of the Arctic. We're ready to go to the top of the earth.

This attitude of not stopping, not giving up, was a defining quality of the admiral. His motto was a quote from the Roman philosopher Seneca, *Inveniam viam aut faciam*, a Latin statement meaning "I shall find a way or make one." It embodied the essence of how he led his life. The motto was so much a part of him that when Admiral Peary High School was created in Rockville, Maryland, it was the centerpiece of the school song that Sari Hines, Class of 1963, wrote in his honor.

Thy motto, Peary High School, "We Will Find or Make a Way,"

As a Flag unfurled in a snowy world inspires our hearts today

"I will find a way or make one," our motto e'er will be.

In grateful praise our voices raise, Peary High to thee!

In life's great strife and turmoil, When with troubles we are tried,

The things that we have learned from thee, Will ever be our guide

"I will find a way or make one," our motto e'er will be.

In grateful praise our voices raise, Peary High to thee!

And as the North Star glowing is a beacon in the night,

We'll e'er be true to the navy blue and the snowy Arctic white

"I will find a way or make one," our motto e'er will be.

In grateful praise our voices raise, Peary High to thee!

*www.Aspirations.com has
audio from this day's phone call*

Chapter 15
Craig Meets Tornarsuk Again

SATURDAY, APRIL 24, 1999
Distance to travel to the North Pole: 53 Miles
Temperature: -46° F

*T*HE ARCTIC ROLLER COASTER CONTINUED. Good days followed by bad days. Two days before, we trekked through brutal cold and snow. Then we enjoyed a balmy day with no wind. Now the wind had come back.

Craig got up first. When he came back from his morning constitutional he said, "I'm wearing my fleece pants today. It's really cold."

Paul Schurke arrived in the cook tent early and offered to make breakfast. He said he wanted to help us out, but I wondered if his offer stemmed from our previous two breakfasts, which had been admittedly bad. I didn't mind the help, but Craig was upset about Paul running his kitchen.

It was the first meal Craig didn't cook. He'd been incredibly diligent and took great pride in his cooking.

Paul is not a gourmet. He rummaged through the food bags and tossed stuff into the pot of boiling water. He plopped in two chunks of butter, then a half bag or so of rice pudding mix, then some chunks of caramel candy, a half bag of brown sugar, and finally a bag of peanuts.

The look on Craig's face was priceless. I had to look away, so he wouldn't see me laughing. I couldn't bear to tell him, but Paul's concoction actually tasted pretty good. Then again with the amount of sugar and fat in it, how could he go wrong? Other than more discussion about reaching the pole, everyone mentioned how great breakfast tasted.

I was moving slowly, my muscles and joints sore from skiing but was pleased when Craig and I decided to ski together

After loading the sleds, we set off, hoping to make up time.

to give each other some companionship on the journey.

With the ice flow continuing southward, we lost nearly two miles in the previous twelve hours so we needed to make up some time and distance. We loaded the sleds and headed off. The skiers started out first, following Paul. The sleds brought up the rear.

Having helped load the sleds, Craig and I were the last to leave, struggling to put on our skis as the group eased across the white landscape. The sleds sped away on the smooth surface and soon Craig and I realized we were very much alone.

We quickly made our way in the tracks of the dogsleds, thoughts of polar bears dancing in our heads. I found myself looking left to right, thinking I saw something moving, worrying that I wouldn't even notice a white bear approaching in the snow and ice.

The sleds, meanwhile, continued to rush ahead of us, and on them we'd put the two guns, which Craig and I surely couldn't reach before the bears attacked. What kind of vacation was this?

Apparently thinking similar thoughts, Craig picked up the pace. But the pace of the team remained equally fast, and we

The view from far behind is very, very lonely.

didn't gain much ground on them. The dogs had lots of energy and the trail was relatively smooth, so the sleds hummed over the ice. Craig and I pushed to near full throttle, and my hands started to freeze. My body, sensing sudden energy needs, sent blood from my fingers and toes to protect the most vital organs. My logical brain said, "Stop and warm up your toes and fingers." My emotional brain said, "Ski faster, you could get eaten by a polar bear."

After about twenty minutes, I noticed a transformation. My fingers and toes felt warm. I learned later that my body entered an aerobic state and with my heart pumping faster, my brain said, "No problem with the core, send blood to the fingers."

Our bodies have a central command center that is part of the most primitive part of the brain that seeks mainly to preserve itself. When confronting stress or extreme cold, it first preserves the brain and core trunk of the body. When the command center perceives that the risk has passed, it opens up blood flow to the extremities. I realized that much of the cold I felt when skiing or working the sleds was simply because I didn't get my heart pumping hard enough.

We caught up with the dog teams when they ran into a wall of pressure ridges. The team's pace slowed considerably. One

This was the reality as sleds crashed.

mile took two hours. The wind whipped up nearly to a white-out, obscuring the trail and sapping our energy.

But Paul pushed us forward. He wanted to cover fifteen to twenty miles that day so we could reach the pole on Monday.

After being the caboose early in the morning, I moved to the front with Paul in the afternoon. Craig skied alongside Alan's sled.

We hit a series of two- and three-foot pressure ridges, forcing the dog teams to stop and start and stop again, which created large gaps between skiers and sleds and even between the sleds. Once again we fell into "slinky mode," stretching out and pulling back.

Going over the ridges, the sleds tipped and skiers fell. I took a few tumbles, but with my new mind-set, I laughed instead of cursed.

Paul Schurke kept looking back at the train of people with a steady glare, his mood growing darker and darker. I tried to joke with him but got no response. He was in another place.

Just after 1:30 P.M. he watched as one of the large sleds toppled while the team jumped off rather than run with it down a pressure ridge—a move that was good for their safety but tough on the sleds. It was on a similar fall that the fuel canisters broke.

Getting the sleds safely over the pressure ridges required continuous heavy lifting.

Paul stood and waited until the teams were all within hearing distance, and then he lit into us. Standing just five feet from him, I caught the full force of his blast. He scolded us like naughty children. I don't recall his exact words, but they were along the lines of, "Damn it, I'm tired of the handholding, and I'm not going to do it any more. When are you going to learn? You can't ride the sleds. The dogs are going to burn out. You have to hang on over the ridges. No excuses. Get your act together. Dog burnout means the end of the trip. Get off the sleds *now*."

No one said a word. No one seemed to breathe. We heard only the whistle of wind and the clank of the dogs rustling in their harnesses. It was one of those moments when you feel totally exposed to the world. Paul turned and headed north, leaving us to sort out what to do.

We silently moved forward, following Paul, each of us thinking about what we were doing and, even more, thinking of what we were not doing and what needed to be done.

My thoughts floated wildly. I felt angry that some of my teammates were not in the aerobic condition they needed to be in. Then I felt guilty about my anger. I was clearly no shining star. Three times I had seen the edge of my soul and had done battle with the Arctic spirit of Tornarsuk. I had ridden huge emotional waves like everyone else.

We all struggled as the demands of the trip tore us down to our most basic levels. Celia would say later, "I won't say that I was brought to my knees, but it would have been hard to slip a piece of paper between them and the floor."

I shifted back to skiing beside one of the big sleds, giving Paul some distance. When the sled came to a ridge, I kicked off my skis and grabbed the side of the sled to play Arctic Cowboy while Craig grabbed the other side. A sled never had so much tender loving care.

After the trip, Paul said he regretted losing his temper. In an interview with David Wecker, he said, "On a trip like this, each phase involves maturing as a team. There's the initial confusion, then they reach a point where they can function. And there's a final phase, where they soak in the scenery and savor a landscape different from any they'll ever see again.

"In that maturing phase, there were two days when far too many people stumbled back into the shell-shocked zone. Sleds were tumbling one over the other, adding immensely to my workload. So there I am, screaming at Doug Hall, 'Damn it, I'm tired of the handholding, and I'm not going to do it any more.' Doug happened to be front and center when I said it, although it was aimed at the whole group.

"But the response was appropriate, and everyone got it together. And after I'd said what I said, I felt an initial angst. These poor people had paid big money for an experience. But they all nodded and responded respectfully. The fact that they could do a group kick-in-the-butt reflected to me the caliber of the team at that point."

He identified one feature in particular that made this team different from others he has led: "There was a handful of folks who were about as prepared as a neophyte can be, then a significant circle who'd blown off the seriousness of training of the past year. Never before on such a trip have I had such extremes of people who were as plugged in as one could be and others who weren't."

Here again, he referred to the sleds.

"I'm sure people were riding the sleds. From the beginning, they knew they'd be expected to put in ten to fifteen miles a day on their own power on the sea ice. As I recall, every time I turned around, at least three mushers were riding on the sleds. When you do that, the payload goes from a thousand pounds to two thousand. Clearly the group had never been faced with dog burnout."

As we headed north, I heard a lot of grumbling about David Golibersuch, who had taken a bad turn again.

Mike, Doug, and Craig. Craig's frustration was clearly visible.

"Good God, Dave, get moving," I heard someone yell. I turned to see David plodding along at a very slow pace.

At around 3:30 P.M. we took our first break of the day and morale had sunk low.

"This is my worst day yet," Craig said. "How are you feeling?"

In truth, I was feeling okay, but seeing the pain in Craig's face, I said, "Let's see. Both feet have blisters, my nose is frostbitten and black, and my digestive system is swimming in fat and sugar. I'm great!"

Craig didn't smile, which wasn't like him at all. I decided to keep an eye on him.

The group remained pretty quiet during the break and for the rest of the afternoon. Everyone just focused on putting one foot in front of the other. Paul's rant still echoed in everyone's mind. Some became more intense, pushing harder. Others shook their heads in disgust, becoming more and more furious with Paul.

About an hour later the sun came out and the wind died down, bringing new energy to the team. Our pace quickened. If the conditions of the morning had continued, our chances of making the pole would have started to evaporate, as they did on Paul's last attempt.

When the sun shines, the landscape becomes a dazzling, shimmering, awe-inspiring show of ice and snow and crystal blue sky.

Back home, when the snow first falls, it's white and pristine. As the days go by, it gets dirty and ugly. Here, the snow is always pure white. There is no dirt, no sign of man's touch anywhere—only beautiful (and, at times, blinding) whiteness.

As I trudged along I came upon a stretch of old sea ice with vibrant greens and almost Caribbean blues. A short time later, in the center of a flat pan of ice, about a mile across stood four thirty-foot ice monoliths, standing straight up like the rocks of Stonehenge. Later we came to a collection of standing snow sculptures looking like they were crafted by an artist on pedestals of ice. It reminded me of the sculpture garden at the Louvre in Paris.

When we reached the piece of ice that would be our home for the evening, everyone quickly went to work turning it into our campsite. I dug a hole in the snow for the cook tent, Corky assembled the top frame, and Craig worked the stove to get some water going.

Suddenly, he stood up and started walking down the trail. His movement was sudden and strange. Something was wrong.

"What's the matter?" I said as I chased after him. He picked up his pace.

"I lost the pager, I have to go get it," Craig said.

"You can't, it could be miles."

"I have to. I have to find the pager."

When I caught up to him, I looked in his eyes. They had a faraway glaze, as if he were under a spell. Tornarsuk had invaded his spirit.

As I walked alongside him, I pleaded and pleaded but he kept walking. Finally, I tackled him, shouting, "You can't find it. It's gone. It's lost. We'll use someone else's."

He looked at me and slowly came to his senses. "I guess so," he said.

We walked back to camp, me playing the role of court jester trying to make him laugh. Throughout dinner I kept an eye on him.

Collectively we'd made 166 miles. Thirty-four more miles to the pole. I asked for suggestions for what to name our camp and getting none declared it "Camp Happy Days," hoping to lift the prevailing mood through positive thinking.

Determined to take back his kitchen from Paul, Craig made a two-course meal. For the appetizers, he served butter-fried tortillas with pepperoni slices and Swiss cheese. The main course was

Craig was feeling good as king of the North Pole Bistro again.

couscous with chicken, veggies, and Parmesan cheese.

When everyone praised the meal, Craig was back as king of the North Pole Bistro, a role that restored his state of mind.

At dinner, the discussion focused on making it to the pole, which seemed like a sure thing now.

"I could crawl thirty-four miles if I had to," Alan said.

I asked the eternal question—why are we doing this? Why are we really doing this?

"As is said, if you have to ask why then you'll not understand my answer," Corky replied.

Paul Schurke spoke of adventures in a different way: "As a culture we're so far up Maslow's pyramid, our basic needs in everyday life are so fulfilled, we're just here for enlightenment and self-realization."

"When I get home, life's challenges will seem a lot smaller," Corky said.

Others offered their opinions. None quite satisfied me.

Our nightly phone call was relatively routine. We were particularly concerned about the NPR reporter, Elizabeth Arnold. "Does she really understand what she's getting into?" I asked. "If she gets up here she might not get out for a while."

"She says she understands," David said.

When Paul got on the phone, David put Elizabeth on the phone.

"It's a full-blown winter camping scene up here," Paul said. "You can deal with that?"

"As long as you have a good tent I'll be fine," she replied.

When we got off the phone we were not convinced. How could anyone be prepared for relentless cold? And, if she didn't move a lot, she'd get really, really cold. The only time you're really warm is when skiing.

Our concern had nothing to do with her being a woman. In fact, as a woman she has a genetic advantage in that women physically have more … how can I say this delicately? I'll quote Will Steger, coleader with Paul of the 1986 trip, who described a woman on that expedition named Ann Bancroft.

> Among the eight of us, Ann had the best body type for cold weather: short, medium-framed, with a high metabolism, and—thanks to female physiology—an extra layer of body fat. This is not to say she didn't suffer from the cold, but I sensed that she had greater resistance to it than did those of us with leaner bodies.

That night as I prepared for bed I discovered that I had miscounted the batteries for the phone. I found two extras!

It was like finding gold. I wondered for a moment who I should call. It didn't take long to decide.

After a few rings, Debbie answered.

As we talked I was swept by a feeling of closeness and

My high-school sweetheart, my wife, my best friend on earth

connection, the thousands of miles between us melting away. I was struck by her absolute confidence that we would succeed.

I was also struck by the pride I could hear in her voice. She was as excited about the trip as I was. We shared a magic moment on the ice, one I still recall vividly today.

After hanging up the phone I prepared for bed by taking a short run to raise my body temperature. I also ate a chunk of a Rookie Pemmican bar I found in my pocket. I'd found that eating something just before going to bed fueled my body. As my metabolism converted the food into nutrients, it gave off heat and warmed me.

As I drifted into sleep, I wondered how much of Craig's funk that day was caused by losing his purpose as cook when Paul made breakfast, just as I had surrendered to depression when I lost my purpose by losing the phone. Craig's sense of purposelessness no doubt intensified when he lost the pager we were sharing.

www.Aspirations.com has
audio from this day's phone call

Chapter 16
The Arctic Devil Is Only Sleeping

SUNDAY, APRIL 25, 1999
Distance to travel to the North Pole: 34 Miles
Temperature: -21° F

Follow Ziggy LIVE on his Great Aspirations trip to the North Pole at www.ASPIRATIONS.com!

*P*AUL WAS FIRST IN THE COOK TENT ON SUNDAY. As I made my Brain Brew coffee, he asked if I had any extra.

"I planned to go decaf on the trip but today seems like a day for coffee," he said.

I knew his theory about caffeine throwing off the metabolism and was surprised by the request, but I set up the brewer and made him a cup of Brain Brew along with Craig. As we waited for the others to wake up, Paul explained how this trip was different from previous ones.

"On past trips everyone wanted to ski, so we rotated people from skis to sleds," he said. "On this one, everyone wants to be on the sleds. I should have forced the rotation. It's a little late for learning how to ski in the Arctic."

Paul split up snacks and lunch food.

Working the sleds was both harder and easier. It was easier on your body if you rode the sled, harder when you went up and over the pressure ridges.

Skiing uses significantly more aerobic energy on a continuing basis but it is a steady effort that leaves you feeling warm and healthy. But, if you have poor form, skiing is a nightmare. Having gone through the ugly and the good as a skier, I offered to help some of the team to become more efficient skiers.

Craig was determined to make a great breakfast. Following Paul's lead he went sweet. It was rice pudding with dried apples and strawberries along with a healthy dash of honey and cinnamon.

It was delicious!

After breakfast Paul laid out a tarp in front of the cook tent and asked everyone to bring their snacks and lunch foods.

"On a trip like this, group gear is individual gear, and individual gear is group gear," he said. He clustered the lunch foods into piles and asked everyone to pick one for lunch for the next two days. We were short on rations—not dangerously short, just short on the good stuff, the peanuts and chocolate and other indulgent stuff. The dense, chewy Rookie Pemmican bars were in far greater supply.

Paul also asked for my ski poles. He needed adjustable poles to repair one of the sleds that had broken a support yesterday when crashing a pressure ridge.

I gave them up reluctantly, remembering the moment I'd gotten them. It was just after a training trip the previous February in Jackson, New Hampshire. On my way to the airport I'd stopped at an outdoor outfitter in Conway, New Hampshire. I was looking for a spare tip for the bottom of the poles.

I couldn't find spare tips in the aisle so I asked the clerk at the sales desk, who responded with, "Sorry, if they're not on the shelves, we don't have them."

I wasn't convinced. I gambled: "I didn't see any. That's too bad. I'm going with Schurke to the pole, and I really need some."

"Paul Schurke?" the clerk asked.

"Right. Of Wintergreen Lodge in Ely, Minnesota."

I'd said the magic words. Instantly I went from an outdoor "pretender" to the real thing. In five minutes I had two replacement tips from "out back" with no charge. I also had to spend twenty minutes reviewing the trip—the dates, the plan—with six of the sales clerks who were called over to hear the story.

The sales clerk was an enthusiast, a zealot for the outdoors. To connect with someone who was doing a real trip gave him hope that one day he'd be on his way to places at the ends of the earth.

Paul took the poles, snapped off the tips and handles, and threaded them into the broken backstays on the sled. Voila! It was ready to go.

This kind of improvising is common. When gloves got wet, people used socks as mittens.

My feet were significantly warmer wearing the wet suit booties. Many of my teammates had originally made fun of my decision, but before long every empty plastic food bag became a vapor barrier to help keep their feet warmer.

It's a matter of resourcefulness. When you run out of toilet paper, a snowball works perfectly, though the chill can be extreme.

Our pockets filled with lunch, we set off on our journey.

At the start of the day it looked like it would be an easy one. Then it got ugly. After about a half mile of skiing, we suffered a crisis.

Bill Martin had to stop due to severe pain in his back. The day before, while descending a pressure ridge, his foot wedged between blocks of ice and momentum jerked his body forward. The initial diagnosis was that he might have ruptured a disc or at least torn ligaments in his back.

He'd tried to ski to loosen it up, but the pain was too great. He begged us to leave him behind. He'd taken pain killers, but the pain overwhelmed him. Hurt worse than his back was his pride.

"I'm sorry, Paul, it just hurts too much," Bill said.

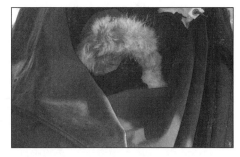

I felt sorry for him. Bill had encouraged me, nudged me forward, and believed in me when it made no sense to believe in me. Not to say that I deserved believing in now.

The sled became an ambulance as Bill was tied down inside it.

At least he hadn't lost his sense of humor. As we wondered what to do, Bill said, "Save yourselves, you crazy bastards. Just leave me a gun with one bullet in it."

"What can we do?" I asked.

"We'll create an ambulance," Paul said without breaking

stride. He went right to work, untying one of the sleds and pulling out sleeping bags. We helped Bill slide into a sleeping bag and tied the lines over him.

The real question was would the dogs be able to handle his weight. They seemed to sense the urgency of the cause and pulled with a new vitality as we set off again.

Going up the pressure ridges was not too bad for Bill, but going down was a nightmare. I can't imagine the feeling of bouncing along inside a sled. At a big ridge, just after lunch, I heard Randy calling out, "Hike, hike, let's go dogs."

Then he screamed, "Oh shit, get off, get off." The team working the sled dove to the sides, the sled sprang loose and crashed down the pressure ridge—with Bill inside it!

He survived the slide down the ridge and told us the screams terrified him more than the ride. Every movement hurt his back, but the sled provided a protective cocoon, buffering

Arctic skiing required a blend of skill and free spiritedness.

him. We pledged to be more careful with his sled.

I spent most of the day helping people with Arctic cross-country skiing. They were making it harder than it needed to be. The key to cross-country skiing for long distances is balancing the energy expenditure between your arms and legs. The arms provide a push in coordination with the kick of the feet. Done right, you end up balancing your use of energy. Done wrong, skiing becomes drudgery. The skis become weights, adding more strain, and the arms end up being used simply to keep balance, the legs bearing the entire burden of movement.

When you're skiing on a shifting surface of ice rubble, the

challenges grow even bigger. I encouraged them to change their form, promising that they'd go farther with much less effort.

I showed Celia how to use her poles to reduce the load on her legs by planting her poles at a diagonal angle and pushing off with them instead of simply picking them up and down vertically to maintain balance. This method uses more energy, but provides much more thrust and a more balanced fatigue between arms and legs.

To speed up our progress, Paul switched the teams, putting Craig on the big red sled to give Alan a break from the pushing and pulling. He also took Mike off the tow sled so Craig controlled two sleds by himself. I skied back to help Craig, who had a great time juggling the two sleds.

Around 4:00 P.M. we came to a valley of pressure ridges that ran at an angle to our trail. Up ahead lay a freshly frozen lead. I was skiing in front of Craig's dogs, and Paul called out for me to swing the dogs to the right to get a better angle for the

I fell for Paul's trick and got run over. (Photo by Paul Schurke.)

sled. I grabbed the lead dogs and, standing to the left of them, pushed them to the right, away from Paul. He yelled for me to take them farther to the right.

Suddenly I heard a whistle to my left, and the dogs instantly turned and charged left toward Paul, running me over in the process.

"What the …?" I screamed.

I looked up to see Paul coming toward me with his camera in hand. He'd tricked me into a rookie mistake. I should have been on the other side of the dogs to get them in position.

Nothing was hurt except for my pride. It was the kind of prank that breaks up a long day, a trick you can laugh at when you are feeling of sound mind.

Around 6:00 P.M., our normal stopping time, Paul said he wanted to reach the fifteen-mile point before we stopped. At 8:00 P.M. I made a quick call into the phone bridge to say that we'd be calling in at 11:00 P.M. Around 10:00 P.M. we made

A good tired

it to fifteen miles from the pole. We declared it "Camp Countdown." We'd traveled our second-longest stretch—nineteen miles, which convinced me more than ever that Peary's claim of an average of twenty-five miles a day was very reasonable.

We went to work on camp. I was tired, but it was a healthy tired that comes from working your body hard. Craig said he felt the same way, having enjoyed working the two sleds. We started making dinner right away, which, given the limited food selection, was an eclectic mixture of potato pancakes, vegetables, and beans.

About 11:00 P.M. I dialed into the phone bridge. I gave a quick report on our twelve-hour day of traveling, our location, and Bill's condition. During the morning and late afternoon, I had spent hours thinking about our North Pole Telegram.

I told David, "Today's report was inspired by my son Brad. Before I left, we talked about what the chance was that I'd see Santa. He said, 'I don't think you'll see him because he's only out at Christmas. He stays in his magical ice cave the rest of the year. But, if you see any short people with pointy ears, they're called elves, and I think you might see them.'"

I went on to tell David I would give him a collection of random thoughts from the day, much of it probably over-the-top sentimental, but that was how I was feeling.

"Go ahead," he said. "I'm used to you being long-winded. I'll make it work."

"If all goes according to plan, tonight will be the night before the North Pole, which sort of feels like the night before Christmas." I went on to say that Brad's question about seeing Santa had been on my mind. As we skied, the sun was shining straight into my face, and the ice sparkled and glistened into a rainbow of colors. A couple of times I thought I saw faces. It could have been the sun playing tricks on my eyes, or it could have been Santa playing tricks on me.

By evening I reached two conclusions:

1. There is no Santa Claus.

2. Santa Claus is very real.

Yes, both are true. The seeming contradiction lies in the person. To the Scrooges of the world, the spirit of Santa does not and cannot exist, but within the child and adult who believes, hopes, and dreams, Santa lives eternally.

Santa exists when we're willing to give up our current reality and believe. Santa is about having faith in our dreams, our family, and in our friends—and about them having faith in us. It's what ties us all together.

It's sort of like the faith we've had on this journey. We

believed that when Dave Golibersuch had his difficult day, he would be renewed and, indeed, he came back the next day to lead our pack. The faith that Bill's back would recover. And the faith that, tomorrow night, we would all stand together at the North Pole, grateful for this gift.

Santa is about many things. He's about charity, love, and, most important, faith. Though I haven't seen Santa with my eyes, I've felt his spirit. I've felt it in the faith that our family and friends have in us. I've felt it in the faith that's developed among the members of the team.

I've felt it in the moments of serendipity—moments that turned disasters into miracles: Paul recovering his backpack, recovering my ability to ski following the ugly day of the first whiteout, finding an Iridium phone in the Arctic. Each of these events was magical. I can't say that Santa had something to do with them, but I also can't be sure he didn't.

When I finished my sentimental speech, I asked David to put some great food in the pickup plane—donuts, a steak or two, and a few other hedonistic treats.

David said, "What about Blubber Crisps?"

"Not really what I had in mind."

"Hey, there aren't many options here in Resolute."

Again there were issues with NASA Mike. He didn't want to carry our stuff, and he didn't want to bring Elizabeth Arnold.

We made it clear: If he didn't do what we asked, he'd have to find another bed and breakfast at the pole—and we hadn't seen any vacancy signs along the way.

Then we reviewed the plans. Two planes would arrive on Tuesday afternoon with the NASA group. The planes would take back half of our group, leaving behind a few dogs and sleds along with sleeping and cooking equipment to host the NASA team.

After the call, the team forgot about pain and frustration and focused on reaching the pole. Corky said it would fulfill a sixty-year dream: "I remember like it was yesterday, sitting in school in the third grade, looking at the globe and wondering how it would feel to stand at the pole."

"For me it started when I was eight," Alan said. He'd received Action Man as a gift. Action Man was an action figure that was popular in the UK during the late 60s and early 70s, sort of like G.I. Joe. Alan's particular Action Man was outfitted with a polar parka with fur-trimmed hood, a team of three plastic husky sleddogs, and a plastic sled. That toy, along with the stories of Robert Scott and the writings of Jack London and Robert Service, inspired his dream of standing at the North Pole.

Others on the team had run out of energy. The battles of skiing had taken their toll. Instead of being driven by the love of the goal, they were motivated by anger and frustration. They were driven forward only by a desire to escape this frigid hell.

It seems like the secret to success in the Arctic is to believe. If you believe you can, you do. If you believe you can't, then you don't. And the blessing of serendipity only happens to those who believe.

www.Aspirations.com has
audio from this day's phone call

Chapter 17
A Thing to Discover

Monday, April 26, 1999
Distance to travel to the North Pole: 15 Miles
Temperature: -21° F

Follow Ziggy LIVE on his Great Aspirations trip to the North Pole at www.ASPIRATIONS.com!

*A*s I woke up, my thoughts were not of the pole. My mind was on food—specifically the food bag David would send with steak, fresh fruit, maybe even donuts!

That morning, I did a phone interview with the *Nashua Telegraph*, the newspaper in the area where I grew up. When asked about the Arctic world, I said, "It's breathtaking. It looks like the surface of the moon in white. It has an eerie kind of beauty, white on white." I went on to explain that I was absolutely in awe of what Peary accomplished in 1909.

Celia was one of the first in the cook tent.

"How you doing?" I asked.

"Not good. I have blisters on blisters," she said.

"How's Bill?"

"Not good. He thinks he might have ruptured a disk."

Paul, too, was feeling pain. He'd broken a tooth on a frozen PowerBar. These supposedly high-tech food sources are horrible at below-zero temperatures. My crispy M&M's and bite-size Snickers bars had been perfect snack food. When I'd ended up with a couple PowerBars from the communal food sorting, I'd warmed them up before eating by placing them in pockets sewn into my long underwear top for warming the phone batteries. It took about thirty minutes to turn a frozen PowerBar into a soft taffy bar.

As I stood in the tent, the hiss of the stove broke the silence. Craig turned the stove on high to heat the water as quickly as possible. The steam warmed us, melting the crust of frost that still coated the inside of the tent. My eyes watered a little from the gas given off by the stove, but the warmth felt so good I didn't mind. When someone enters or exits the tent, steam billows out while those of us inside feel the bracing cold immediately.

The stoves had been a continuous hassle throughout the trip. Even that morning Craig had to work for thirty minutes to light it. We'd complained to Paul about the stoves, but he didn't see a problem. Craig's approach to lighting the stoves, admittedly, was gentler than Paul's. Craig pumped the stove and warmed the gas manifold with his lighter. Eventually, when it got warm enough, the gas vaporized and the stove lit. Paul simply poured gas over the burner and lit it, sending a whoosh of gas and three- to six-foot flames into the air. The tent miraculously never caught fire, and the stove was ready in minutes.

Bill entered the tent with a stiff, gentle walk, obviously in severe pain. I cleared a spot for him to sit, but he said he'd rather stand.

When I asked how he felt he said, "It's tough. I'm usually the one taking care of others. God is teaching me some humility."

"What's it like riding inside a sled?" I asked.

"Terrifying," he said. "It feels like I'm inside a coffin."

I can't imagine it. His willingness to do it proved the level of pain he was feeling.

But he retained his sense of humor. As he shuffled around the cook tent he said, "Just call me Grandpa Bill. Hey, would you be greatly offended if I pee in your tent?"

I wasn't sure if he was serious or how I should respond.

"I'm kidding, but last night was the lowest moment of my life. I was afraid to hydrate because I'd have to go to the bathroom, and after your pee experience in your sleeping bag I figured we didn't need another."

Despite his absolute agony, Bill remained my mentor.

"Your playful spirit is a real treasure," he told me. "You're a man who hasn't lost the little boy inside. Keep laughing and playing. So few people have a playful spirit"

I felt guilty as he talked to me. I was having fun, but it was clear that he wasn't. I was amazed by his compassion.

Breakfast was a hodgepodge as Craig cleared out the pantry—apple-strawberry flakes, mixed nuts and grains, spaetzle, and brown sugar with milk. It actually tasted pretty good.

David Golibersuch arrived late. I helped him get his food and change his socks. The liner socks were soaked in blood, and his left big toe had swelled to twice its natural size and was an ugly combination of green and black.

As I helped him put on his boots, he said, "You get today's Matthew Henson award for helping." I was just thankful that I was helping with socks and not with going to the bathroom as others had.

As we finished breakfast, the team displayed various emotions. Some showed a new energy for what, in theory, was the last day of traveling. Others prepared for the next phase of what they had come to see as a death march.

We'd traveled for just fifteen minutes when Paul stopped, kicked off his skis, and climbed a twenty-foot ice ridge. He scanned the horizon

Paul looked north and saw three black lines along the horizon.

for a long time, a seriousness in his body language.

I looked north to see what concerned him. A bear? An ocean of open water? A crashed plane?

I wanted to call to him, but his demeanor made me pause. I turned my attention to the sky. I recognized something I had read about in the admiral's books—three parallel black lines, which meant there was water ahead. The lines were a reflection in the sky of black water.

Paul climbed down. "She's not going to make it easy today," he told us.

The admiral warned that it would not be easy to achieve the pole.

> In the Arctic the chances are always against the explorer. The inscrutable guardians of the secret appear to have a well-nigh inexhaustible reserve of

Digging down the sides of the lead

trump cards to play against the intruder who insists
upon dropping into the game. The life is a dog's life,
but the work is a man's work.

In twenty minutes we saw a massive lead, a flowing river
forty feet across, with walls on either side about six feet tall.
We turned west, searching for a place to cross. After about a
mile, we came to a sharp bend in the lead. Chunks of floating
ice had been caught in the bend. The canyon walls were still
sheer cliffs.

"Time to make a ramp," Paul said. "Start digging."

Using our skis as shovels, we toppled the side of the ridge
into the water on the floating ice. Paul walked across with
a couple of others and dug down the far side. Now we had
a bit of a ramp down to the floating ice bridge and up the
other side.

I walked across to help run the dogs. My job was to grab
a rope and run as fast as possible to pull the dogs forward,
keeping them on line as they went down, across, and up the
other side. In the middle, the ice flow shook side to side as I
crossed.

I got set on the far side for the dog teams holding a line. On the signal, I ran as fast as possible, pulling the dogs, keeping them moving, as first Randy and then Craig guided the dog teams across the lead.

Paul told me to pick the trail for the team to follow, to be, in effect, the lead dog.

"How do I know the direction?" I asked.

"Watch your shadow. At noon your shadow points directly north. Right now it's ten o'clock so your shadow is 30 degrees to the left of North. At two o'clock it's 30 degrees to the right."

For the first five minutes I was excited to be out front. Excitement quickly turned to terror. I faced decisions every few minutes—left or right? What's the best path for the dogs? What's the best path for the sleds?

The glare of sun reflecting off the ice hurt my eyes, a feeling I'd not experienced until I was put out front. Prior to leading the team, my eyes moved up and down, here and there, but mostly I focused on following Paul's tracks. I stopped and pulled out my sunglasses. Paul had said that on every trip he suffered a level of snow blindness, and now I understood why. I had not been wearing sunglasses because my breath created frost on them.

As we moved along, I had to decide between taking a path that was shorter but included pressure ridges or a longer one that was easier to travel.

Corky skied up front with me, which provided a certain amount of comfort. When we came to a field of fractured ice, I tested it with my poles and slowly walked out to check the strength of the ice. I signaled to Corky to follow. We skied about thirty feet across when suddenly we heard a rumble from our right. The ice was moving. The rumbling grew louder and louder until a fifteen-foot pressure ridge collapsed into the ice with a roar.

I picked up the pace but worried about the trail behind me. The others had seen it and moved farther to the left, away from the freshly broken ice.

Running between ice ridges

The tensions of leading were intense. I thought about Paul leading for days on end. The mental strain of looking, checking, and guessing had to weigh on him.

I continued to look at my watch and shadow. I also kept looking back over our trail, trying to judge how straight I was guiding the team. After an hour or so Paul skied to the front and took the lead again. I eagerly gave up the job.

Not long afterward we hit a huge lead that must have been 150 feet across. The ice was marshy, and open water yawned on either side of us as we approached. It was cold enough that a thin skin of rubbery ice had formed, but it was pulling apart near the middle of the gap. I held my breath as I skied across, my skis bobbing up and down on the flexible surface.

Everyone made it across, and we

Craig's feet took a small dip as the sled sank into the water.

continued on the path Paul chose for us. Not long after, we headed into a narrow canyon of ice, sliding along a frozen lead just wide enough to run the sleds through.

At the end of the canyon, we moved onto a flat plain of rubbery ice, which ended in a crack too wide to jump. We bridged the gap with a large sled and one by one we climbed over the sled to the far side. As we climbed onto the sled, water gushed out of the lead onto the edges of the ice.

"Take it slow," Paul said. "It'll take far less time than if we have to dry you off."

We crossed some ten major leads in about nine hours of travel, covering just eleven miles. We had four miles to go. While we stopped to rest, people talked about feeling beaten up. The anxiety of crossing the open water created an emotional fatigue that was just as real as the physical effort.

Craig and I felt good, and we both wanted to have a strong finish.

"You ready to ski hard?" he asked with a friendly challenge.

"If you can handle it," I said.

Working over a small lead (see video of this at www.aspirations.com)

We let Paul get ahead of us and then we set off on a race. Craig took an early lead, as his lighter body allowed his skis to float over the drifts while my heavier weight thrust deeper into the snow.

The course was Arctic wild. One moment we flew across crusty moguls carved by the wind, the next we slogged over deep drifts, the next we stepped our way over ice boulders strewn like a child's spilled marbles.

Reaching down into a part of my body that just a few months before I had not known existed, I tapped into an inner strength. I willed my middle-aged body to ski, ski, ski like the wind.

With a burst of energy, I cut Craig off on a corner and took the lead. As I passed I screamed the phrase my trainer Dick Steurerwald had taught me: "Hoka Hey." And for the first time in my life I actually felt the meaning of the phrase that traditional Lakota warriors would yell as they charged into battle.

Roughly translated it means "what a great day to die." Not die as in I hope to be dead, but rather, as in "what a great day," so glorious and magnificent that if I'm taken from this earth at this moment I'm ready to go or, as the American beer commercial said, "It doesn't get any better than this."

It was a most excellent racetrack. The path Paul laid out weaved back and forth, around blocks, giving excitement to the race that would end on a flat pan of ice.

The sun was lighting the scene from our left, showering the ice with a yellow glow.

I gasped for air as we raced. After ninety minutes or so, Paul called for us to stop and wait for the team to catch up. We were exactly one mile from the pole.

He shot a flare that went off with a bang. Unfortunately, it terrified the dogs. They reacted like most dogs do in the presence of fireworks—they immediately did a 180, heading south for all they were worth. Randy and Alan soon wrestled them to a stop.

Paul asked for Corky to come to the front to lead us into the pole with Paul guiding him with his GPS.

Craig and I moved from the front to the back, where David Golibersuch had gone into another funk. His skis scraped along, but his heart wasn't in it. Craig and I skied on either side of David, trying to encourage him, to excite him about reaching the pole.

Paul's flare indicated we were one mile from the pole.

As we traveled the last mile, the dog teams and skiers sped up. David slowed down.

"I can't do it," he told us. "Carry me"

Craig played the good cop, exhorting him forward.

"You can do it," Craig said. "You've made it this far. Think how great it will feel when we're there"

I played the bad cop: "There is no way I'm carrying you. Move your sorry butt."

"Just a little farther," Craig said. "Almost there."

"I can't, I can't go on," David said, focusing more on Craig than on me.

"You'll make it there if you have to crawl," I screamed. "Move it." I was getting very cold as the ski race generated sweat, which now, at our shuffling pace, froze quickly.

The team continued to pull away from the three of us. Soon we heard whoops and screams as the team reached the pole.

Craig and Alan celebrated reaching 90 North.

Next we heard a bang, as Paul shot off another flare, this time in celebration.

In the distance I heard Paul yell out, "Corky, welcome to the top of the world."

I looked at my watch—it was 8:27 P.M.

I smacked David in the butt with my ski pole. "Come on, let's move it."

I don't know if it was the sound of the celebration or the whack on the butt, but David picked up his speed.

As we reached the team, the celebration was in full bloom. Some people cried, and there were hugs all around.

Tears flowed down Bill's face as he lay in the sled. I reached down and hugged him. Without his support I never would have made it.

A couple minutes after arriving at the pole, Alan showed me a page from my brother Bruce.

Doug, hope you guys are almost there! Savor every moment. You guys deserve it! Congratulations to all and get home safely. Boy will that burger taste good. Tell Santa I've been good. Bruce

How appropriate, I thought. I got my first set of cross-country skis with him. We'd earned the money to pay for them shoveling driveways in our Nashua, New Hampshire, neighborhood.

As I took notes on the celebration I was surprised by my feelings. I felt excited but at the same time disappointed. It looked no different from anywhere else we'd been. I'd known from the start that it would look the same, that there wouldn't be a striped barber pole or a permanent marker to mark the spot. But it just didn't seem right. Standing there felt the same as any other place, the day the same as any other since we arrived.

I understood how the admiral felt after he reached the pole. As he wrote in his journal:

> The pole at last! The prize of three centuries, my dream and goal for twenty years, mine at last! I cannot bring myself to realize it. It all seems so simple and commonplace. As Bartlett said when turning back, when speaking of his being in these exclusive regions, which no mortal has ever penetrated before: "It is just like every other day!"

I turned on my GPS to record the location. I'd been unable to enter 90 North as the destination. The best I could do was enter 89.999. When I called the manufacturer and asked why I couldn't enter it, they said, "We don't program it for 90 North because no one goes there."

The way to get the Garmin GPS to read 90 North was to be there.

Like a beachcomber searching with a metal detector, I moved it back and forth, trying to get as close as I possibly could to the actual spot around which the earth rotated.

The GPS read 89.92, then 89.95, then it read 90 North!

I hit "save." Eureka! This was *the* spot. I probably should call the Garmin Company that made the GPS and tell them that it is possible to get a reading of 90 North. All you have to do is go there.

I had my picture taken with Craig. It's one of my favorite images from the trip. It had been very important to him that he thrive on the trip—and he had. My goal had been more modest—survival. With the help of all, I'd done even more than that.

Craig and I had been a good team. When I lost it, he helped me pull together. When he lost it, I helped him.

We'd struggled with cook stoves and the team's oscillating feelings toward the food. We'd had some great laughs and a genuine experience.

I wanted to know what others felt. So I pulled out my yellow book and played the role of journalist. I asked "How do you feel?"

Corky: "I'm speechless."

The two tenderfeet on the Aspirations! Expedition

Alan: "I'm choked up, ask me in a couple minutes."

Randy: "I've been blessed. And I am on top of the world."

Bill, lying strapped to the sled, let his tears flow.

Then Alan said, "I feel privileged. Through willpower, strength, and fortitude we made it. I feel like the world is spinning beneath my feet."

Back to Corky: "Old farts retire, take up golf and fishing, and are soon dead. I'm sixty-nine years old, and I skied the last sixty-nine miles. I'm so thankful to Paul for having me lead in. I didn't want to be a stunt on this trip."

Myself, I felt happy to be standing on top of the earth.

However, to be honest, it was also disappointing. The trip would soon be over, just as I was starting to get the hang of traveling in this frigid desert.

The pole is an imaginary spot on top of a shifting sheet of ice. It exists only in a mathematical sense. It's as much a state of mind as a location.

I remembered how A.A. Milne described Pooh's search for the North Pole in his classic children's book *Winnie-the-Pooh*:

"What is the North Pole?" Pooh asked.

"It's just a thing you discover," said Christopher Robin.

Having found my way to the pole, I felt proud. Now it was time to go home.

With the ice moving south at four miles per day, we headed across the top two miles toward Siberia to find a landing strip for the NASA plane. If all went well, we'd drift back to the pole the next day.

At about 9:30 P.M., I skied up front to tell Paul that we needed to stop so I could call in to the phone bridge because people would be waiting to hear if we made it.

It was brutally cold; the stop at the pole chilled everyone.

Paul untied a sled, pulled out some sleeping bags, and had

me climb in to dial the call. I tried to make the call as fast as possible, as I could hear lots of grumbling from my teammates.

Tired and hungry, they were not happy to be stopping for the call.

The phone kept disconnecting, which delayed the process. Finally I connected and told David, "At 8:27 P.M., with Corky Peterson in the lead, Paul yelled out, 'Corky, welcome to the top of the earth.'"

David said, "Good"

Good? Good? After all I'd been through, the best he could say was "good"? I had hoped for a bit more excitement.

As the grumbling outside the sled grew louder, I gave David some quick information and told him I'd call him back later. I climbed out of the sled, we retied the sled, and headed to home sweet home on the ice.

We quickly whipped up dinner—chicken, wild rice soup, and noodles. It was hot and tasty. After the emotional day, folks were ready to eat and hit the sack. There was a feeling among us of total exhaustion: physical, mental, emotional, and spiritual. I called David to get details on press coverage and fill in more details on our arrival.

I made a particular point to celebrate Corky. I was genuinely impressed by him. At one point the day before I'd come up beside him to coach and encourage him. Corky's response was a classic: "I'm going at full speed. It's all I got. But I can do it forever."

"Full speed is all any of us has," I said.

That morning he told me, "I'd like to challenge all those folks out there, just like we're trying to do with parents and kids, to take action on their dreams and aspirations, whatever they may be."

I hope that when I'm Corky's age my attitude and aspirations are as strong as his.

The balance of the phone call covered logistics.

"The planes left Resolute today at 1:00 P.M. with the NASA

team," David said. "The weather is good in Eureka. You should expect them tomorrow afternoon."

We reviewed the interviews for the next few days. The Colorado shooting had pretty much wiped out our major network coverage with ABC, CBS, and FOX. We were primarily going to have local newspaper and radio stories.

"What's the data on the Web site?" I asked, "I need to know the numbers when I talk to the media over the next few days."

"We have 29,065,000 hits on the Web site," Kari said. "Twenty million saw newspaper articles, two million have heard you on the radio, ten million on television, and some seventy-five million a day read Ziggy. The amazing thing is that we're getting fifteen hundred hits a day from Europe, eight hundred from Malaysia—which must be because of the Pen Haddow trip, and fifty a day from Australia."

After the call I learned that we were going to have lots of vacancies. Only Paul, Craig, Corky, and I opted to stay after the NASA planes left the next day. Everyone else wanted out as fast as possible.

Craig and I looked at each other. There had been moments during the trip when we both wanted out, but this wasn't one of them. Rather than escaping, we didn't want the good feeling to end.

Sitting at the top of the earth, I thought of Admiral Peary and his small team that reached this spot. Craig and I talked about what it must have been like, how it was the same and how it was different, how much easier it was for us using today's high-tech clothing, tents, and sleeping systems instead of igloos and furs.

I launched into an explanation of the evidence that Peary had made it to the North Pole, detailing the science of the mystery that fascinated me but that very obviously bored Craig, as it bores most people.

At the risk of boring you, the reader, let me say that the answer to the last of the three Peary mysteries—*Did Peary Make It To The Pole?*—is *yes*. If you're bored by scientific minutia feel free to skip the rest of this chapter.

To those with a passion for scientific mysteries, here's the long answer:

In the admiral's time, there was no such thing as GPS. Explorer navigation by sextant involved measuring the sun's altitude above the horizon at a specific time, then doing a series of computations and a set of navigational charts.

Given that the pole itself sits on a shifting sheet of ice, it's difficult to "prove" that you have actually arrived.

No, correct that—it was *impossible* to prove you were at the North Pole. In fact, when the Norwegian explorer Nansen was asked why he believed the admiral, he said, "You have his word for it. The character of the explorer is always the best evidence of claims."

Throughout time, all you could do was take the explorer's word for his achievement. In fact, to those who claim that the admiral didn't provide proof, I would say neither did the others who claimed "farthest norths." These include—

Henry Hudson	1607	81° 30'
W. E. Parry	1826	82° 45'
A.H. Markham	1876	83° 20'
Fridtjof Nansen	1896	86° 14'
Duke of Abruzzi	1901	86° 34'
Robert Byrd	1926	90° Fly to pole
Amundsen	1926	90° Fly over

In 1990, for the first time, hard evidence concerning whether Peary had reached the pole was discovered and brought to the debate. Using new data and methods of analysis, The Navigation Foundation (www.navigationfoundation.org) concluded that Peary had indeed been to the North Pole.

Beyond detailing that the methods used by Peary to navigate were identical to those used by Roald Amundsen to reach the South Pole, the report provided two pieces of factual data that would have made Peary the Engineer proud.

Ocean Depth Measurements: The foundation confirmed that Peary's soundings of the depth of the ocean placed him very close to where he said he was. This was based on new data released by the Defense Mapping Agency based on bottom depths measured by U.S. submarines patrolling under the Arctic ice. Most importantly, they show conclusively that British author Wally Herbert is incorrect in his conclusion that Peary was twenty miles west of where he thought he was.

Photo Analysis: William Hyzer, an expert in optical instrumentation, photogrammetry, forensic engineering, electrical contact physics, and illumination engineering developed a method to quantify the location of the photos that Peary took at the North Pole. Hyzer has graciously permitted me to quote from his article in the March 1990 edition of *Photomethods.*

The sun's elevation (vertical angle above the horizon) and azimuth (horizontal angle along the horizon from due North) are known quantities for any given year, day, and instant of time at any given geographical location. Time or location can be determined if one or the other is known along with the sun's elevation or azimuth angles. Azimuth angles often are revealed by the shadows recorded in photographic images.

Among the many photographic negatives exposed during Peary's 1909 expedition, presumably made in the immediate vicinity of the pole, several had visible shadows.

For eighty years, Peary's claim to the pole has been argued pro and con. To some he is a hero; to others, a fake and a fraud. Only the shadows know for sure. At long last they revealed their secret through close-range photogrammetric analysis. Measurements of the sun's angles in the Peary photographs by the Navigation Foundation place the explorer no more than fifteen miles away from the North Pole—which, for all practical purposes, is where he always claimed to be.

Since this first analysis of photo shadows, two additional photos have been identified that were originally considered of no value because they were overexposed as a result of the camera being pointed toward the sun. However, when deliberately "underexposed" the sun and the horizon are clearly visible. Again I quote from *PhotoMethods*.

The factual evidence indicated, beyond a reasonable doubt, that Peary made it to the pole.

William Hyzer analyzed these and other Peary photos and is elated over the discovery: "Finding these images is like being handed a micrometer to measure the diameter of a hair when the best you had before was a ruler with a magnifier," he states. Hyzer computed the sun's angle as 6 degrees and 45 minutes. The sun's elevation at the North Pole at the time these images were reportedly made on April 9, 1909 was 6 degrees 42 minutes. Considering that 1 degree of arc corresponds to 1 nautical mile, the lines of position computed from these photos are additional proof that Peary truly reached his goal. (Net he was about 3.5 land-based miles from the North Pole. This is well within the area of eight to ten miles that he crossed as he went back and forth in each direction from the point of the photo.)

Bottom line: The scientific, factual evidence indicates far beyond a reasonable doubt that on April 6, 1909, Admiral Robert E. Peary, Matthew Henson, Ootah, Egigingwah, Seegloo, and Ooqueah were the first to reach the North Pole.

If you'd like additional, scientific analyses of Peary's trip, I suggest the book *Robert Peary and Matthew Henson at the North Pole*, by William E. Molett, published by Elkhorn Press.

www.Aspirations.com has audio from this day's phone call

Chapter 18
Camp Admiral Peary

TUESDAY, APRIL 27, 1999
Distance to travel to the North Pole: 0 Miles
Temperature: Who cares!

W E SLEPT TILL 8:00 A.M. THE NEXT MORNING. Craig got up to light the stoves. After our days of drifting south, on the last night the Arctic Ocean changed direction. We awoke a half mile farther from the pole! Go figure.

We made a breakfast of fruit flakes, mixed nuts, rice, brown sugar, cinnamon, and milk. As we ate the glop, we hoped that Commander Dave had really outdone himself in the resupply food bag.

We made a lot of phone calls to the media—Paul, Corky, Bill, Celia, Mike, and Alan. What was most impressive was the number of e-mails that came into pagers from around the world as folks read about our arrival on the Web site.

Alan brought me a page from an assistant to the Queen of England: "The Queen, who is aware of your safe arrival from your Web site, has asked me to convey her congratulations."

It was exciting to learn that Queen Elizabeth was watching. However, the next page was much more meaningful to me: *"Yippee. Yea. Way to go. Awesome. You're cool. Love Deb, Kristyn, Tori, Brad."*

We expected the NASA group to arrive around 2:00 P.M..

Around 10:00 A.M. the radio crackled and we heard that the pilots were ahead of schedule and would be with us in twenty-five minutes.

Oh no!

Paul and Craig pushed and tugged the sleds to smooth the sea ice. We filled black trash bags with snow and used them to mark the runway.

Then we heard the drone of two planes on the horizon. They made a low pass across the strip some thirty feet over the ice.

Everyone waited as the pilot assessed the situation. If he felt the runway was inappropriate, he could reject it as they had done with the resupply flight days before. In that case, we would hike to a new strip. Or, if nothing was close, he'd turn back and go home. We'd be out of luck.

The planes made a huge banking turn, and came around again. This time they landed, the skiis on the plane bouncing on the hard-packed ice. The planes then taxied to within thirty feet of our camp. Door-to-door service!

The NASA team and Elizabeth Arnold climbed out of the plane. They had a curious look about them—a freshness that came from sleeping in a bed, eating regular food, and taking a shower. To our eyes, they looked almost artificial. I felt like a wild ape looking at a human for the first time. The most interesting part of these creatures was their eyes. They were very big. Huge, in fact. Eyes filled with absolute terror.

I knew that look. I'd worn it a couple weeks before.

I scrambled to find the bag that had our "North Pole stuff." I distributed the banners and stuff to teammates for photos, and then I asked everyone to gather for a knighting ceremony.

Yes—knighting. Some years earlier I had purchased at a London auction the title and rights as Lord of the Manor of Threshfield, England. Threshfield is an ancient village in North Yorkshire.

Battling for the title at an auction with pen and checkbook was more humane than the way the title would have been passed for hundreds of years—through physical battles.

As the Lord of Threshfield, I have the right and duty to name knights. I also must have them ready to defend the Queen if she calls for them.

To be fair, being a Knight of Threshfield is not nearly as prestigious as HM Queen Elizabeth's Knights of Bath. However, a knighthood is a knighthood.

As part of the promotion of the pole expedition, I had promised knighthood to the sponsors and my teammates. I'd taken some flack from *Outside Magazine*, which claimed it was ridiculous, and of course it was.

I gathered the team for the appropriate ceremony. I explained their duties so there would be no surprises if the Queen asked them to defend her. A ski pole served as my sword as each was sworn in as a knight and an appropriate medal placed around his or her neck. The medal read,

Knights of Threshfield
"You are hereby anointed
Knight of the Lord of
Threshfield. Sworn to
nurture and defend the
five virtues among
children of all ages,
those being Aspirations,
Belonging, Excitement,
Accomplishment, and
Leadership."

To be honest, most of my team members were somewhat skeptical. The only one who really bought into it was Alan, who was from Ireland and could see the humor in poking a little fun at the British aristocracy. He wore his medal with pride.

The pilots indicated it was time to load up. A bed for Bill was created from some seats. One team of dogs was loaded, along with a sled.

Before the planes left, we gathered for a group photo. As we got together, I remembered our sponsors and scrambled in the sled bag to find a North Pole banner. I handed it to Craig.

The North Pole doesn't look like the North Pole without a flag so I found the American flag and handed it to Corky. Then I searched through the prop bag that had come up and found the stuffed Ziggy and Fuzz. With great pride I knelt in front with Craig. (It made sense that the tenderfeet would be on the ground in front.) I smiled knowing that this definitely was the first time two cartoon characters had been part of an expedition.

As the team broke from the group photo, we hugged each other. Then they climbed on the planes and took off. Our NASA guests stood in shock for a few moments as the sound of the planes faded and silence fell across the landscape. Everything became very quiet.

The Aspirations Expedition team with Ziggy and Fuzz

The NASA team soon got busy setting up gear for the first Web cast from the pole. Elizabeth Arnold from NPR seemed nice enough. In between soliciting sound bites, interviews, and perspectives, she asked if it was possible to borrow our phone to call into NPR's *Morning Edition.*

In the middle of the afternoon Paul suggested a two-mile trip back to the North Pole. He called out "Line for the North Pole Tour forms to the right."

We set up the NASA team with four dog teams on two empty sleds. I offered Elizabeth the short skis, which were best for beginners. She opted for the long ones, and we were off.

Actually, Elizabeth was off like a rocket. I chased. Up and over moguls, around ice blocks, she clearly was not a rookie. As we waited for the dogs to catch up, I asked, "Where did you learn to ski?"

"I'm from Alaska originally," she said.

I laughed. She certainly was no prima donna reporter. I would learn later that she had been "discovered" by the national network during her coverage of the Exxon Valdez oil tanker spill in 1989 that dumped 10.8 million gallons of oil.

We had a blast skiing. With a temperature of a "balmy" minus 5 degrees, it felt great. And without a backpack to wear or a camp to set up at night, it was incredibly fun.

On our way to the pole, we stopped to talk to a team from the Spanish Army that had skied up from the other side. It had taken them sixty days to reach the pole. They had pulled their gear in sleds weighing a couple of hundred pounds each and had received two resupplies. I couldn't even imagine it.

They were very ready to go home. A Russian helicopter would pick them up that night around midnight. I asked them what they were going to do when they got back. In broken English, Francisco, the leader, said, "I am going to drink …" he paused to find the right word … "professionally."

"Professionally?" I asked.

"Very professionally." He pantomimed drinking from a huge goblet. "Very professionally."

I offered him a Great Aspirations! Expedition patch. Politely, he took it. Then I reached into my pocket and handed him a couple Snickers candy bars. His eyes lit up.

After saying good-bye we skied on to the pole itself. There was no sign of our having been there the evening before; 90 North had drifted.

Paul stuck a ski pole into the snow where the GPS registered 90 North. Then the foolishness began.

Paul brought out a stethoscope and oil can to "oil the earth's axel."

I pulled out my yo-yo to do "Around the World" around the world.

I ran around the ski pole counter clockwise—going around and around to make myself, in theory, thirty-nine years old again.

I carved a heart in the snow in honor of my wife.

I had my photo taken with Craig, Paul, and Corky. That photo is my second favorite photo from the trip. Here is the grizzled veteran and the three who had no business being there: Corky who was too old; Craig, who was too inexperienced; and me; who was too out of shape *and* inexperienced.

We headed back for camp, and at around 8:30, I realized we were going to be late for our 9:00 phone call. I picked up the

Corky, Paul, Doug and Craig at the pole

pace and raced like the day before with Craig. "Hoka Hey," I yelled as I skied to the camp.

As I crossed over a pressure ridge, I could see the camp a half mile away. Flying above the black cook tent was the American Flag, backlit by the sun. The flag had flown over the U.S. Capitol in Washington; my congressman, Rob Portman, had gotten it for us. Seeing the backlit flag flapping gently in the breeze gave me a lot of pride in what the team had done. In a small way I understood the way members of the military and NASA space missions feel.

As I skied toward it, my mind made random connections between the flag and life. I thought of my ancestor Lyman Hall, who signed the Declaration of Independence, pledging his life, fortune, and sacred honor for freedom from Great Britain. He nearly lost his life as the British accused him of high treason, burned his home, and chased his family.

I also thought of my most famous forefather on my mother's side, Jacob Holder, who fought with honor on the British side. He'd been held as a prisoner of war following the defeat of Cornwallis in Yorktown. After the war his property

The Stars and Stripes flying at the pole once again

in Pennsylvania was confiscated with no compensation. He was given a grant of land in New Brunswick, Canada.

I felt pride in both.

Both had been willing to push themselves to the limit. Their lives stood for something. What is right and what is wrong is never clear. What matters most is that your life has a purpose. That you're willing to get up, get out, and do something to make a difference in the world.

Admiral Peary was as flag-waving an American as there has ever been. After the coded message was sent to the *New York Times* he sent a telegram that said quite simply: Stars and stripes nailed to the pole.

I dialed into the phone bridge. Kari was the correspondent tonight as David was en route to the pole as part of the pickup team. I reported the day's events and read the inscription inside the time capsule we'd bury the next day.

> *We, the members of the North Pole Aspirations! Expedition '99 Team, thank God we have arrived at the top of the world in good health and spirits. To our families, friends, and our valiant team of Canadian Inuit dogs, we extend our eternal gratitude for their help in making this dream come true.*
>
> *On the brink of a new millennium, we stand here at the North Pole, a crossroads of time and place, because you believed in us and we believed in ourselves. We set out on this expedition with the mission of helping parents inspire their children. Now more than ever, we understand the importance and the power of believing in achieving.*
>
> *To our fellow parents around the world we proclaim it's time to believe that every child has something special and unique within them. It's time to believe that the smallest things we do, and don't do, make a difference in their lives and that these small differences become significant over time.*

It's time to believe wonderful surprises are waiting to happen. All of the hopes and dreams we have for our children are within our grasp. All we have to do is reach out and believe in them.

Thank you and God bless,

Paul Schurke	*Celia Martin*	*Randy Swanson*
Bill Martin	*Alan Humphries*	*David Golibersuch*
Doug Hall	*Craig Kurz*	*Paul Pfau*
Corwin Peterson	*Michael Warren*	

Inside the time capsule is a CD containing the dreams from hundreds of children, the Great Aspirations! Parent Workshop audio program, along with photos from Admiral Peary and Matthew Henson's gravesite. It also contains a pine bough from the tree near the admiral's gravesite. When Peary went on his trips, his daughter gave him a small pillow with pine needles so he'd remember Eagle Island.

The phone bridge was opened up so that I could speak to my parents as well. My mom and dad listened from Florida each night despite my mother undergoing aggressive treatment for cancer.

"Dad, I can hear you." I said,

"Hello, I didn't know I could speak," Dad said.

"You can tonight. Hi, Mom," I said.

"You reached your goal, honey. All of you. Very proud of you," Mom said. Then she asked a question that only a mom would ask: "Aren't you hungry?"

I explained that I was doing well and that maybe she could go on a trip like this someday.

"Not me," she said. "Not Mum. I'm going to Hawaii."

I started to ask her how she was doing with her battle with cancer, but I stopped myself. It wasn't that I didn't want to know; it was just that I still had a long journey back to land, and I needed to maintain my focus.

I enjoyed champagne at the top of the earth with Craig.

After the call it was time for a celebration dinner and party. David's goodie bag was a little disappointing. There was no steak or donuts. There was reindeer, musk ox, and caribou jerky. Apparently shopping in Resolute is a little sparse.

We did, however, have tons of the food we'd left in Resolute, and with Craig's cooking artistry we soon had a feast: pasta with tomato sauce, veggies, sundried tomatoes, and Italian spices.

We also had the most precious commodity of all—fuel. Seven gallons of fuel. So we had *heat*. We ran both stoves full bore.

We also had champagne, a special bottle carved with the expedition logo on it. I placed it inside my jacket to warm it up. Having been outside for some time, the alcohol would be at the same temperature as the air, around minus 20. Drinking it could cause frostbite.

"This is the first time I've ever had champagne warmed before drinking," Elizabeth said.

We ate, drank, and told stories.

Our visitors were gripped by the stories, amazed at the journey we'd traveled.

Craig and I went to sleep about 2:30 in the morning. I went to sleep feeling great. Like Ziggy says: Achieving your goals is like being on top of the world.

www.Aspirations.com has
audio from this day's phone call

Chapter 19
Going Home

*T*HE NEXT MORNING WE DID LOTS OF INTERVIEWS along with more photos. Late in the day two planes arrived carrying Craig's parents, Rick Sweitzer, David Wecker, and Bob Setzer, a friend of Corky's.

While we loaded up the planes, Rick set up a table with a white tablecloth, champagne, and treats.

Craig's parents had appropriately brought along a Honey-Baked Ham. Having lived hand to mouth for weeks, we simply grabbed slabs of ham and stuffed full slices into our mouths. To her credit, Craig's mom didn't even wince at our poor table manners. We consumed literally pounds of ham in minutes.

Celebrating with lots of good food—and champagne

The pilot advised that we had just twenty minutes to celebrate because he was concerned about the bad weather. As the tourists celebrated, Craig and I got back to the task at hand. We loaded the dogs onto our plane along with the sled.

As we finished loading, Craig pointed to the crowd. "Is that something?"

It was a picture of contrasts. Paul and Corky stood with the tourists, looking like grizzled Arctic veterans. Paul's hat hung sideways off his head. Both wore rumpled clothes that had clearly seen better days. And yet they held champagne glasses and ate appetizers from a platter on a formal white tablecloth, as if at a fancy dinner party.

A feast of HoneyBaked ham at the pole

I reached up and gave Craig a high five. We walked over for one last drink of champagne and a couple more handfuls of food. The moment could have lasted forever.

Soon the pilot called for us to load up. All the tourists went in one plane along with the NASA folks. In the other plane sat the dogs, Paul, Craig, Corky, and me.

As the plane took off, I looked at my watch, 6:28 P.M. I looked back one last time at this magic place. I wrote in my journal, "We're on our way home. But it won't be the same. I've experienced Santa." I also surprised myself as I wrote, "I'll be back."

What a long strange trip it had been. I started out terrified, and now I wished to come back. There is something about the Great North that is very, very addictive.

The view from the air was shocking. We saw open water everywhere. We talked about the fact that it won't be long before a trip like ours won't be possible due to global warming.

Since then I've seen various "experts" report: 1) Each year we lose Arctic ice equal to the size of Lake Superior, 2) In the past thirty-five years the Greenland Ice Cap has declined by the size of New York, Georgia, and Texas combined, and 3) it's predicted that in the next ten years the sea level will increase from four inches to three feet because of Arctic ice melt.

We talked about how our experience had differed from that of our teammates. While the others got off the ice sooner, they had missed the opportunity to celebrate. They missed the sense of belonging that the four of us had developed as we played host to the NASA folks. They missed the sense of accomplishment that we felt from looking in the eyes of the NASA folks, who looked like we had on the first night out. They missed the excitement of the on-ice celebration—both the party the night before and the party when the planes arrived. They missed the sense of leadership we felt taking the NASA folks on their late-afternoon trip.

In some ways, they'd missed the most magical part of the trip.

We talked of our feelings.

Corky said, "This trip is one of my life's defining moments. For the rest of my life I'll thank you, Paul, for letting me lead the way into the pole."

Fonseca 1977 was our drink for the long flight home.

"I came into this trip with high expectations," Craig said. "I've learned a level of mental toughness that I didn't expect. The relentless cold took a lot of energy to beat down."

"I believe this is a magical place," Paul said. "I really enjoyed the theater of light and beauty. I also enjoyed spending time in introspection while traveling."

Before we all settled in for a nap, I pulled out of my bag a bottle of Fonseca 1977 Vintage Port. David had brought it up with him. It was my answer to the question, "If you're at the end of the earth and you can have but one bottle, what would it be?"

My new favorite for my next adventure is eighteen-year-old Highland Park Scotch Whisky.

Fonseca is my favorite brand of port. The vintage was the year that Debbie and I graduated from high school. I opened the bottle and poured it into our mugs that had not been washed in weeks. We toasted Paul for his leadership, our teammates for their commitment, our families and friends for their support.

The port was a total *wow*! Smooth, silky, and magnificent.

Greatest Bottle Update: Since this expedition, Fonseca 77 has become my second choice. Today, my first choice would be eighteen-year-old Highland Park Scotch Whisky. It has been named the best spirit in the world, a selection I heartily endorse. I am so impressed with it that I recently presented the distillery manager with a sealed vial of North Pole water. You can see it at their distillery on the Island of Orkney, north of Scotland.

We all took a nap for a while, and when we awoke we learned bad news from the pilots, who had been in contact with Resolute via radio—Bill's back pain involved possible spinal cord injuries. Bill and Celia had been evacuated by emergency air ambulance directly to Florida. David Golibersuch might lose at least one toe, and Paul Phau suffered from severe frostbite. They both might need to be evacuated.

I prayed for the guys, hoping they'd be okay.

We learned later that Bill suffered a tear in his left hamstring muscle and pulled ligaments in his back. He healed without surgery. He continues to lead expeditions to mountains around the world.

David Golibersuch was not as lucky. He ended up losing a piece of his toe to frostbite. He turned the experience into a positive one, becoming a rather prolific speaker, giving hundreds of presentations on what he learned from the trip.

Reflecting on the experience, he said, "The trip was tough for me. I was really

I felt much better than I looked.

looking forward to it and had trained really hard. I had a couple of bad breaks early on, and it quickly went from fun to a matter of survival. It has inspired me to become a different person. I've always been a pretty independent person, but this trip has showed me that it's okay to reach out for help from others."

Alan retained his sense of humor. He said, "I'm going to get a tattoo to remind me of this moment. It's going to say, "don't do any more stupid cold trips."

We landed in Resolute at 2:05 A.M.. We staked the dogs behind a building at the airport and then went to Aziz's South Camp Inn.

I called Debbie to say I was safely off the ice. Then I hit the kitchen at the inn, where they served us a hearty soup and fresh bread.

At 4:30 a.m. I hit the shower, peeling off layers of grime. As my body warmed in the steamy water, I realized I was covered with over a dozen bruises. I had a cut on my hand, blisters on my feet, and bruises I had not noticed on the ice. In the Arctic, cold provides a frame of reference. Little aches vanish as survival against the cold takes precedence.

When I got out of the shower, feeling like a new person, I looked in the mirror at my unshaven face and frostbitten nose. The shower had softened the dead skin, and with a quick pull I peeled it off.

I was starting to look like the person who had left. But I was not the same. I had felt and seen a new level of extreme that few get to glimpse.

Craig said he felt the same way.

"I'll never be able to look at the world the same way again," he told me. "We've pushed borders of extreme pain and endurance. The frustrations of everyday life just will not compare."

"We take a lot for granted," I said. "Take these sheets—the pattern of red roses and green vines. They're amazing. They're probably the cheapest sheets in the world, but at this moment, they're finer than the ones I slept on at the Ritz in Paris."

As I fell asleep, I felt an incredible peace come over my entire body—a deep peace and calm. Whatever the future brought, I was ready for it.

The admiral came back from the pole to a world of chaos. The Peary-Cook scandal consumed him. He spent the rest of his years battling for his honor. He died of pernicious anemia on February 20, 1920, at the age of sixty-three.

His wife, Josephine, stated the truth of his death when she wrote.

> No one will ever know how the attack on my husband's veracity affected him, who had never had his word doubted in any thing at any time in his life. He could not believe it. And the personal grilling which he was obliged to undergo at the hands of Congress, while his scientific observations were examined and worked out, although it resulted in his complete vin-dication, hurt him more than all the hardships he endured in his years of research in the Arctic regions and did more toward the breaking down of his iron constitution than anything experi-enced in his explorations.

Josephine Peary

I arrived in Cincinnati on Sunday at 3:52 P.M.. The family met me at the airport with a stuffed polar bear that had a little medal on its chest that said I Believe.

I came back with a bigger view of the world. I can see with more breadth and depth than before and learned that nothing is ever as bad as it seems. I learned that great things do happen if you believe. The focus of believing goes by many names—God, Santa Claus, or simply serendipity. In all cases it's a mat-ter of believing in the inherent good of the world.

Needless to say, the trip continues to resonate in my mind ten years later. The experience, the people I met and places I saw, inspired me to write this book and to create a stage show.

That's where we started—at the first performance at Victoria Playhouse on Prince Edward Island. And it seems a fitting place to end:

Doug moves stage right as the lights dim. A church lectern appears. The effect is of a church. Doug speaks directly to the audience. Images of Doug's mom very slowly appear and disappear on the black screen as he speaks.

Forty-eight hours after arriving home in Cincinnati, Debbie and I were on a plane to Florida to see my mom. Her cancer was worse than she had let me know.

Forty-nine days after I left the pole, my mom died.

At her memorial service I spoke a few words. Coming so close after my Arctic adventure, they capture my feelings of both the North Pole adventure and my mom.

Friends and family, we're gathered here at the Church of the Good Shepherd to celebrate the life and living spirit of my mom, Jean Hall. It's appropriate that this church, which served as the backdrop to our youth, should also be our pulpit today for declaring our thanksgiving for Mom's living spirit. If this building served as the stage, Mom was the director, producer, and playwright. As only a mother can, she fueled our hopes, dreams, and great aspirations.

My mother's grandmother, Wilamina Keith, emigrated from Scotland to Canada. She came to North America bringing an optimistic attitude, an attitude that was passed along to my mother's mother, then to my mother.

My mother knew what we could do, she knew what we should do. My mother knew, long before my brother and I knew, that we both would earn the rank of Eagle Scout. She knew long before my brother and sister and I knew, that we would thrive as adults. Our successes were preordained. Her spirit commanded it.

My mother was born in Canada and loved it dearly. In particular she loved the green fields, red sand, and blue bays of Prince Edward Island where as a family we spent so many summers. Just a few miles from my parents' cottage is the farmhouse that was Lucy

Maud Montgomery's inspiration for the Anne of Green Gables books.

As a girl, my mom found much to admire in Anne's character, in her spunk and zest for living life to the fullest. Like my mom, Anne was a girl who acted on her dreams, who pursued her aspirations vigorously.

Recently, as I reread *Anne of Green Gables*, I found a passage that brought me comfort and reminded me of how my mother regarded the great circle of life. The passage follows the passing of Anne's adopted father, Matthew Cuthbert.

To paraphrase the words of Lucy Maud Montgomery, "Mom's encouraging us to have our interest in life return to us...she likes to hear us laugh...and she likes to know we find plea-

sure in the pleasant things around us.... She is just away now and she likes to know it just the same."

Mom was never one to be sad for long. She would take great, great time in planning, but when an event was finished, it was finished. It was time to move forward.

I believe she is looking down today encouraging us to take action—to take action on our dreams.

It's time for all of us to do the same. Mom is gone from this life, but she lives in eternal life. Mom, we know you're in good hands now. And we thank God

for giving us the gift of your life and spirit to inspire us and to hold dear.

Mom, in honor of you, we shall go forth and take action with our lives. And always remember that you live and will continue to live in us as long as we live our lives to our fullest potential. Mom. I love you. We all do.

(Doug moves center stage, stepping down into the audience. A spotlight on him. The balance of the stage is black.)

Friends, there it is—the simple answer to why.

The simple answer to why *I* went to the North Pole: It's the same reason the painter paints, the teacher teaches, and the preacher preaches. It was my destiny.

To paraphrase Admiral Peary, the North Pole was something that deep inside me I knew was something I *should* do, I knew was something that I *must* do.

Deep inside all of us is a little voice that, if we listen closely, tells us what we *should* do, what we *must* do.

Ladies and gentlemen, it's time to believe.

It's time to believe in that little voice.

It's time to believe in our children.

It's time to believe in one another.

It's time to believe that everything we do and don't do makes a meaningful difference in the world.

Most importantly, it's time to believe in our dreams. It's time to seek out and pursue our North Pole— whatever or wherever it may be.

Benjamin Franklin said many things that mean a lot to me. But one thing in particular sticks out. It's how I lead my life. In fact, it's so important to me that when I'm laid to rest in Springbrook, Prince Edward Island, at Saint Thomas church, it will be carved on my tombstone. As Franklin said over two hundred years ago…

"Up Sluggard and Waste Not Life—in the grave will be sleeping enough."

Like Dorothy and friends in *The Wizard of Oz*, you have the heart, the courage, and the brains that you need. In fact, you've always had them.

The time for believing in your dreams is **NOW**.

The time for making a difference is **TODAY**.

The person who can make the greatest difference is **YOU**.

So what are you waiting for? **GET UP! GET OUT! AND GET GOING!**

Epilogue

North Pole Tenderfoot **Theater Review**: Despite my rookie status as an actor and playwright, Charles Mandel, the *Guardian* reviewer was very kind.

Never mind that it was one of the hottest nights of the year on P.E.I.

Inside the Victoria Playhouse, things were plenty cool Tuesday night as Doug Hall recounted the rigors of his northern journey in the world premeier of North Pole Tenderfoot.

The one-man show is a carefully structured monologue containing dramatic peaks and valleys and plenty of self-deprecating humour. In that way, it is very reminiscent of actor Spalding Gray's work and indeed has much the same rhythm as Swimming to Cambodia, *Gray's best-known monologue.*

Hall is a self-confessed theatrical tenderfoot as well, and at times it showed. He was visibly nervous, often stumbling over lines or not quite hitting video cues (which play a large role in the show). And a couple of times he fumbled with props. Those problems constitute nothing more than opening night jitters, however, and it is likely Hall will overcome them.

These are but minor quibbles, though. North Pole Tenderfoot *is surprising and, as intended, inspirational. At a time when it seems as if every inch of the globe has been explored, Hall renews our sense of adventure. Hall's terrific anecdotes from the top of the world create a gripping and memorable story.*

The show, as Hall would say, is "cool!"

The expedition reached millions of children and parents around the world. In addition, we raised about $500,000 in cash and over $500,000 in services. However, as a result of my hours of thinking deeply about my life's purpose, I decided that my purpose was not the Great Aspirations! charity. I concluded that my real purpose was to bring wisdom and hope to small businesses, entrepreneurs, and inventors.

Over time, I closed the Great Aspirations! charity, and distributed the money to the University of Maine and to the College of Piping and Celtic Performing Arts, to support scholarships for island youth. The director, Scott MacAuley, was an enthusiastic supporter of using the Great Aspirations! principles to guide the pipe band program. As a result of Scott's leadership, the youth band went on to beat adults and take the North American championship and to place fourth at the world championship.

The www.Aspirations.com Web site has been recently rebuilt, however, and it will continue to be supported by my company.

The life purpose that I found as a result of the expedition continues to grow stronger. It started with a new book for small business owners called *Jump Start Your Business Brain* (named one of the one hundred best business books of all time by CEO READ). This book was followed by Brain Brew Radio, a show for entrepreneurs that I co-hosted with David Wecker and that was distributed by Public Radio International. (It can still be heard at www.BrainBrewRadio.com.)

This show led to a series of TV specials for the Canadian Broadcasting Network where they gave me the nickname "The Business Robin Hood" for giving my big-company wisdom to small-business dreamers. The series resulted in other TV appearances, including as a judge on the first season of ABC TV's *American Inventor*.

An alliance with the U.S. Department of Commerce's National Institute of Standards and technology's Manufacturing Extension Partnership network has enabled me to exponentially expand my ability to "bring meaningful hope" to entrepreneurial dreamers. As of this writing, the MEP Eureka! coaches that we've taught have helped small businesses generate hundreds of millions in net extra sales.

Support from the governments of the United States, Canada, and the United Kingdom has enabled my Merwyn Research company to create the Planet Eureka! International Innovation Network, which helps improve communications and connections between innovators and businesses worldwide. (www .PlanetEureka.com).

Lastly, I've connected with a visionary team at the University of Maine to help them create a new field of study that's branded as Innovation Engineering. It's offered as an undergraduate minor and graduate school certificate and is focused on teaching students how to create, communicate, and commercialize meaningful ideas, no matter what their degree, career, or passion.

North Pole Tenderfoot
Discussion Guide

The purpose of this discussion guide is to "connect the dots" between the story and your life. The questions are designed to be used individually or in a group discussion.

Why would you or would you not go to the North Pole? If time and cost were not an issue, would you go to the pole? Why would you go? Why would you not go?

Courage Connections: Doug found courage to defeat Tornarsuk because of "courage connections" from Paul, Admiral Peary, and the notes from his kids. Who inspires courage in you?

Mindfulness: When Doug achieved awareness, he became fully aware of the beauty of the Arctic. Contrast this view with how one of the other team members described the scenery: "There was a boring sameness to it. After several days, I thought every snowdrift, every lead, every pressure ridge, looked about the same." Do you "see" the beauty that is around you each day, every day, every moment? How could you increase your awareness?

Serendipity: Paul Schurke said, "Don't worry or sweat it. Something great will come out of this. It always does. Serendipity. It's all part of the process." What does serendipity mean to you? And what can you do to increase your chances of having a "fortunate accident." When you move forward in awareness, serendipity is more likely to occur. The more we are perpetual learners, the greater our chances of having wonderful discoveries.

We Know What We Need To Do: We know from an early age what we should do. However, it's in the doing that we get ourselves in trouble. What have you always wanted to do? What is your true dream? What does the little voice inside you say that you *should* do? What does it say that you *must* do?

Motivation: Admiral Peary said, "The true explorer does his work not for any hopes of reward or honor, but because the thing he has set for himself to do is a part of his being and must be accomplished for the sake of the accomplishment. And he counts lightly hardships, risks, and obstacles, if only they do not bar him from his goal." What motivates you?

Vision: Do you focus on the future or the past? If we're not careful, we end up holding onto old images of ourselves because they're familiar and comfortable. A focus on the past holds us back, as if we're simultaneously stepping on the gas and the brake. Instead, challenge yourself. How would you like to be different in ten years? Having defined your vision of the future, what do you need to do tomorrow to turn your vision into reality.

Belonging: The single most important predictor of healthy aspirations is a sense of belonging. Think about you and your life. What do you "belong to?" To whom are you important?

Get Up! Get Out! Get Going!: The very last word in this book goes to Paul Schurke, leader of the Aspirations Expedition, taken from an interview with Paul by David Wecker in Resolute after we returned from the North Pole.

> For Paul, the allure of such a trip is in watching Arctic greenhorns break through the initial shock and develop as a functioning team.
>
> "Here, you're operating with people who've been dropped off on the dark side of Pluto. If they all survived in reasonably good health, it's a success. They all get an A for coming off the ice with parts and pieces intact.
>
> "What I find compelling about adventuring and expeditions is that you're living life in fast forward. You are obliged around the clock to operate at capacity—emotionally, physically, spiritually, and mentally.

"The transformations are absolutely profound. If we all gathered next year and did the same thing over again, we'd have a better time. But the sense of personal transformation would be significantly diminished."

Paul is particularly drawn by the intensity of the experience, which he has found only on adventures like the Aspirations Expedition.

"The world of winter has been a gift to me. It's a natural human instinct to narrow your realm of experience to a comfort margin. Any time you have to expand that window, it's both an opportunity and a threat to one's comfort and general equilibrium.

"But in the winter in particular, that window goes from something this small to something this big. When you're thirsty, you're really, really thirsty. When you're hungry, you're really, really hungry.

"And on the other side, when you're feeling good, when you've pulled off a successful day in horrendous conditions and you have the camaraderie of friends around you, it's wonderful. The extremes of that emotional roller coaster result in a vitality you just can't experience in any other setting."

So, I say once again, "What are you waiting for?"

GET UP! GET OUT! GET GOING!

Please Send E-Mails

Thank you for taking the time to read my story. I would *LOVE* to learn what you think of *North Pole Tenderfoot*. Please send your comments, suggestions, and reactions to:

DougHall@DougHall.com
(513) 271-9911
Eureka! Ranch International
3849 Edwards Road
Newtown, Ohio 45244 USA

North Pole Tenderfoot – The Play

If you would like to book the play as a full two-act program or as a one-hour motivational lecture for your organization, contact me or the Eureka! Ranch at the phone number above.

Other Stuff

www.Aspirations.com is loaded with tons of free stuff. On the Web site you'll find:

- **Parent Workshop**: This is a sixty-minute parent workshop that provides ideas for inspiring your children, grandchildren, and yourself. You can download it as an audio file or in script form.

- On this Web site you'll also find audio from the nightly phone calls from the Arctic, plus video and color photos from the Arctic.

www.DougHall.com features information on my various books and lectures.

www.EurekaRanch.com contains information on my companies.

www.BrainBrewRadio.com is a twenty-four-hour Internet radio station for inventors, innovators, and entrepreneurs.

www.PlanetEureka.com helps innovators communicate with and connect to business requests.

The Four Core Great Aspirations! Parenting Principles

Everyone has hopes, dreams, and aspirations. This program is about GREAT Aspirations! It's about having the courage to realize your fullest, greatest potential. It's about having the courage to do something great with your life, your family, your work, your community, and the world.

Advanced statistical analysis of over two-hundred-fifty-thousand child-motivation data points identified four core principles that when in place help children and adults have the foundation necessary to have Great Aspirations! In short form they are:

> **Belonging:** Belonging is about having a sense of community and a feeling of connection. It's created when kids know that they are really heard, feel that what they do matters, and believe that how they feel is recognized.

> **Excitement:** Excitement is about the joy of living. It's about fun, curiosity, creativity, and all the wonders of life. Parents are the most important spark for igniting enduring, meaningful excitement in children's lives.

> **Accomplishment:** Accomplishment is about believing "I can" rather than "I can't." It's fueled by a feeling of optimism, overt goal setting, and healthy risk taking.

> **Leadership:** Leadership is about children with the courage to take charge of their own lives. It's fostered through responsible decision making, trust, and children taking on the responsibility of leading others through teaching, or mentoring.

Belonging

Belonging is about having a sense of community and a feeling of connection. It's about kids who know that they are really heard, feel that what they do matters, and believe that how they feel is recognized.

Belonging is fostered by:

- **A Sense Of Community**—It's important for children to feel that they are a part of a greater mission. That there are other people on whom they can depend—and other people who depend on them. Children with a strong sense of community feel more confident and secure. First and foremost, community begins with family. However, let's not forget the other communities that can nurture belonging: school, church, sports teams, neighborhood friends.

- **Connections**—Connections are the glue that hold together a community. Without them, a sense of belonging withers. And there's no better way to create connections than through meaningful conversation. Children need to have meaningful contact with other human beings. Core to this is spending time in fully conscious conversation with your children each day.

- **Celebrating each child's individuality**—To feel a strong sense of belonging, children need to feel proud of their individuality. We need to celebrate children for being themselves. To not only allow, but also applaud, their unique strengths and interests. That means supporting all aspects of their personality—from learning styles, to haircuts, to friends, to interests.

Three quick ideas for inspiring **Belonging**

1. **Oh, What a Great Day!:** At the 99 percent confidence level, research indicates that children who sit down together as a family for dinner, at home or at even a fast-food restaurant,

have significantly higher feelings of belonging. To enhance the experience, go around the dinner table, wherever you are, and have each family member report something good that happened to them that day—something they're thankful for, something that made them happy. Kids of all ages love it. It gives them the chance to be on center stage—to have everyone listen to them and only them. What a feeling of connectedness!

2. **Let The Games Begin:** Research shows that families that play board games together have a significantly greater sense of belonging. Turn off the television, pop some popcorn or make some brownies and play cards, board games, or what ever is appropriate for your family.

3. **Be Friendly To Their Friends:** Kids with a significantly greater sense of belonging say their parents encourage them to invite friends over more often. Even more importantly, they agree that their parents respect and talk to their friends when they do come over. If you want to know what's going on in your children's lives, talk with their friends. They're a great gateway to your children's lives.

Excitement

Excitement is about the joy of living. It's about fun, curiosity, creativity, and all the wonders of life. Parents are the most important spark for igniting enduring, meaningful excitement in children's lives.

Excitement is fostered by:

- **Curiosity and Creativity**—Creativity is about stimulating your kids' minds. Stimulus for the mind is made up of sounds, tastes, textures, scents, or any combination thereof that provokes a response in the brain. Taking your mind somewhere other than where it is right now. It is about living a life of growth. Curiosity is about asking "why," and creativity is about asking "why not."

- **Joy**—Joy is what builds memories. It comes from fun, from enthusiasm, from just plain being a part of a child's life. Joy is a universal rite of living. Children with joy rarely feel tired or bored. They're quick to laugh, genuinely happy, and full of boundless enthusiasm. It doesn't cost a lot of money to provide a joyful environment at home—just a little time and imagination.

- **Be A** Hero **Parent**—There are a lot of ways to have fun as a kid, but none is more meaningful or has a deeper impact than spending time with Mom and / or Dad. The data indicates that kids with the most joy are the ones who spend time with Mom and with Dad. They also feel that their parents are more fun than most other parents. It's fun for kids to play with friends. But it's FUN with a capital F to spend real time with parents.

Three ideas for inspiring **Excitement**

1. **Don't Act Your Age:** To quote the song by our friends Scott Johnson and Rob Babcock: "The problem with grown ups is they act like their age. The older they get the less likely they'll play. So serious, so busy, so this and so that. They haven't a time for a ball and a bat. But I've got a plan that'll make some enraged. It's a big adult sign that says Don't Act Your Age."

2. **Instigate Involvement in Extracurricular Activities:** The data is clear: children with the greatest feelings of excitement are involved in numerous outside activities. It takes time, discipline, and sometimes money on the part of parents to get children involved in anything from scouts, sports teams, music lessons, church groups to dance or karate lessons. Beyond these children's classics, invite children to get involved in your hobbies. Include them in your interests, be they photography, golf, cooking, restoring an old car or boat, growing a flower garden, or furniture refinishing.

3. Develop a Discovery Habit: Research indicates children with a greater sense of excitement ask significantly more questions in school and are—by nature—much more curious. Open yourself up to curiosity and discovery. Keep your eyes open to opportunities to learn. Try everything from science museums, to the local zoo, to surfing the Web for the answer to a question that that comes to you or your children. Open your mind to discovery and your kids will too.

Accomplishment

Accomplishment is about believing "I can" rather than "I can't." Accomplishments are fueled by a feeling of optimism, overt goal setting, and healthy risk taking.

Accomplishment Attitude is fostered by:

- **Optimism:** Building a positive mental attitude is critical. Research shows that children set their expectations at an early age. There is a nearly perfect correlation between a child's level of achievement in grade three and grade eleven. It is critical that step-by-step, day-by-day we build positive mental attitudes within our children.

- **Goal Setting:** The research is clear that kids with an attitude of accomplishment have parents who set high standards for them. (Note, the key words are the last ones: *for them.*) Kids need goals that are set appropriately for their personal growth. Set goals too low and no sense of accomplishment is developed. Set goals too high and kids give up in frustration.

- **Healthy Risk Taking**—Kids with a sense of accomplishment are healthy risk takers as exhibited in their spirit of adventure. They are open to trying new things, to learning and to being adventurous. Healthy risk taking comes from learning how to dust yourself off after a failure, standing up, and trying again.

Three ideas for inspiring **Accomplishment**

1. **Win don't Whine**: The data is clear. Kids with an attitude of accomplishment believe that "they will be the best at what they do someday." These are kids on fire with positive thinking. Watch yourself in your language. When something bad happens, do you blame others? Do you whine and whine and whine? Or do you take responsibility, look at the bright side, learn a lesson, and take positive action?

2. **Overtly Articulate Goals:** At a 99 percent confidence level, research indicates that children with an attitude of accomplishment set high goals and expectations for themselves in school. To help your kids become great goal setters, model the power of goals as a family. Have each family member publicly declare a goal to accomplish in the next month. Keeping time short helps build momentum. Track progress in some manner. Moms and dads aren't exempt. Parents should declare their self-improvement goals, be they to lose weight, run in a 5K race, stop smoking, or learn how to use the family computer.

3. **Go For It:** Research indicates children with an attitude of accomplishment love to learn new things and find out how they work. As adults we have a tendency to get into ruts. Reading the same magazines. Eating the same foods. Going to movies that are sequels. This week, open yourself up to new adventures. Declare your desire to try something really new and go for it as an individual, or—even better—as a family. Try bowling, a cookout at the park, a local community theater, or a Saturday morning hike.

Leadership

Leadership is about children with the courage to take charge of their own lives. Leadership is fostered through responsible decision making, trust, and children taking on the responsibility of leading others through teaching, and mentoring.

Leadership is fostered by:

- **Taking Responsibility For Decisions**—Accepting the consequences of your actions is critical to nurturing leadership skills. All kids, even the youngest, have the ability to make responsible decisions. To think before they act. To be aware of the effect their actions will have on others. But they can't learn good decision-making skills, the kind that mark a true leader, unless you give them the opportunity to make decisions and then feel the pain and joy that result. As parents we must be careful to not over-protect our kids from failure.

- **Courage**—Children with courage have enough self-confidence and self-esteem to lead their own lives and to lead others. When kids have true courage, they know that even if things turn out badly, their sense of self worth and their support structure will still stand by them. A key way they gain courage is through the confidence and trust that parents place in them. Recognize that trust cannot be given. Rather it must be built, step by step in hundreds and thousands of small events.

- **Mentoring:** Kids with leadership have the courage to be mentors to others. They have enough faith in themselves and their abilities to be able to teach others what they know. When children mentor other children, both sides gain from the experience.

Three quick ideas for inspiring **Leadership**:

1. **Kids Rule**: Research shows that kids with leadership skills have parents who encourage them to make choices and involve them in family decisions. So give up some parental control and let kids rule in significant portions of their lives. While you watch from the shadows if necessary, let kids make decisions, and, where appropriate, suffer consequences of their actions. It can start with little things like letting them decide how late they're staying up on a Friday night before a Saturday morning soccer game. It can grow to giving them some money to independently purchase, cook, and serve a family dinner.

2. **Public Service**: Data shows that children with leadership skills help other people even if they're not asked. Responsible leadership is about caring for others who may be less fortunate. It's about caring for those you lead. It's about caring about the consequences of your actions. Encourage your kids to lead public service efforts, from picking up trash at the playground to helping with the lawn of the senior citizen on the corner to volunteering time at the local homeless shelter or other public service cause.

3. **Plants or Pets:** Mother nature provides lots of opportunities to learn responsibility. Try giving your kids the long-term responsibility that comes from growing flowers, vegetables, or raising a puppy or kitten. Growing plants and training pets are powerful as they provide direct feedback of the consequences of children's actions.

About the Author

DOUG HALL IS FOUNDER AND CEO of Eureka! Ranch International, Merwyn Research, and Planet Eureka! Innovation Marketplace. All three organizations help companies use innovation to accelerate profitable growth.

Doug began his entrepreneurial career at the age of twelve producing and marketing a line of magic and juggling kits. After earning a degree in chemical engineering he spent ten years at Procter & Gamble where he rose to the rank of Master Marketing Inventor and shipped a record nine new business initiatives in twelve months.

Doug is the author of four business books including *Jump Start Your Business Brain*, named one of the one hundred best business books of all time by business book expert Jack Covert. Media appearances include: co-host of Brain Brew Radio on Public Radio International, Truth Teller Judge on ABC TV's *American Inventor*, plus feature stories on NBC, CNBC, CNN, CBS, NPR, and CBC.

Doug serves on a number of boards and has been recognized with honorary doctorates from the University of Maine and the University of Prince Edward Island, Canada.

Dateline NBC described Doug as *"an eccentric entrepreneur who just might have what we've all been looking for...the happy secret to success."* Ellen Guidera, Walt Disney Company Vice President said of Doug, *"When Doug meets Disney, creativity ne'er wanes; our team explodes when he 'Jump Starts Our Brains!'"*

Doug and his high school sweetheart, Debbie, have three grown children. They split their time between Cincinnati, Ohio, and Springbrook, Prince Edward Island, Canada, enjoying bagpipe music, Scotch whisky, Malpeque oysters, kayaking, and cross-country skiing.

In 1999, Doug turned an expedition to the North Pole into a fundraising effort for Great Aspirations!, a nonprofit organization he founded to help parents inspire their children. The story of that adventure became this book, *North Pole Tenderfoot*.

To reach Doug by e-mail	DougHall@DougHall.com
Doug's Blog	www.DougHall.com
Eureka! Ranch	www.EurekaRanch.com
Planet Eureka!	www.PlanetEureka.com
Merwyn Research	www.Merwyn.com

www.Aspirations.com